BRIDGING THE GREAT DIVIDE

BRIDGING THE GREAT DIVIDE

MUSINGS OF A POST-LIBERAL, POST-CONSERVATIVE EVANGELICAL CATHOLIC

ROBERT BARRON

A SHEED & WARD BOOK

ROWMAN & LITTLEFIELD PUBLISHERS, INC.
Lanham • Boulder • New York • Toronto • Oxford

Several of these essays appeared in publications or as lectures and have been edited and reprinted by permission. "The Virtue of Bi-Polar Extremism" first appeared as "The Danger of Moderation" in *Church* (Winter 1996); "The Trouble with a Beige Catholicism" as "Beyond Beige Catholicism" in *Church* (Summer 2000); "Paths and Practices: Recovering an Embodied Christianity" as "Just Do It: How Practice Makes Catholic" in *U.S. Catholic* (October 2000); "Lex Orandi, Lex Vivendi: The Liturgy as a Source for the Moral Life" as a lecture at Tulane University Judeo-Christian Studies Center (2003); "The Liturgical Act and the Church of the Twenty-First Century" in *Antiphon* (7:3, 2002); "The Trouble with Beige Churches" as "Beyond Beige Churches: Modernity and Liturgical Architecture" in *Antiphon* (6:3, 2001); "God as Artist" in *Angelicum* 80 (2003); "'I'm Waiting; I'm Waiting': An Advent Meditation" in *U.S. Catholic* (December 2003); "Three Paths of Holiness" in *U.S. Catholic* (October 1998); "The Grandfather and the Voice from the Whirlwind" in *Chicago Studies* (Spring 2004); "A Sermon for Children of the Seventies" in *U.S. Catholic* (February 2000); "Thomas Merton's Metaphysics of Peace" in *Josephinum Journal of Theology* (Summer/Fall 2003); "'Comes a Warrior': A Christmas Meditation" in *The Sign of Peace* (Christmas 2002); "Priest as Bearer of the Mystery" in *Church* (Summer 1994); "Priest as Doctor of the Soul" in *Church* (Winter 1995); "Mystagogues, World Transformers, and Interpreters of Tongues" in *Seminary Journal* (October 1999); "Evangelizing the American Culture" in *Second Spring: An International Journal of Faith and Culture* (issue 3, Autumn 2002).

A SHEED & WARD BOOK

ROWMAN & LITTLEFIELD PUBLISHERS, INC.

Published in the United States of America
by Rowman & Littlefield Publishers, Inc.
A wholly owned subsidiary of The Rowman & Littlefield Publishing Group, Inc.
4501 Forbes Boulevard, Suite 200, Lanham, Maryland 20706
www.rowmanlittlefield.com

PO Box 317
Oxford
OX2 9RU, UK

British Library Cataloguing in Publication Information Available

Library of Congress Cataloging-in-Publication Data

Barron, Robert E., 1959–
  Bridging the great divide : musings of a post-liberal, post-conservative evangelical Catholic / Robert Barron.
    p. cm.
  Includes bibliographical references and index.
  ISBN 0-7425-3205-4 (hardcover : alk. paper) — ISBN 0-7425-3206-2 (pbk. : alk. paper)
  1. Evangelistic work—Catholic Church. 2. Spirituality—Catholic Church. 3. Catholic Church—Liturgy. I. Title.
BX2347.4.B37 2004
282'.09'05—dc22

2004008460

Printed in the United States of America

♾ ™ The paper used in this publication meets the minimum requirements of American National Standard for Information Sciences—Permanence of Paper for Printed Library Materials, ANSI/NISO Z39.48-1992.

To my students, past and present, at Mundelein Seminary

CONTENTS

Contents

Cultivators of a Flourishing
Garden of Life

BEFORE LEAVING FOR THE CONCLAVE THAT WOULD ELECT HIM
Pope, Angelo Giuseppe Cardinal Roncalli, commented apropos the top
leadership of the church, "we are not here to guard a museum, but to cultivate a flourishing garden of life." This statement of the man who would
become Pope John XXIII can be construed simplistically as a call for an
open-minded liberalism over and against a musty conservatism, but a
more careful reading reveals greater subtlety and nuance. I am convinced
that Roncalli's observation—which did indeed name the spirit that informed the council he called—functioned as a prophetic summons to a
richly imagined Catholicism, both progressive and conservative, both
stubbornly alive and stubbornly traditional. Like a two-edged sword, the
Pope's adage, even today, cuts against cramped and uncritical ideologies
on both ends of the ecclesial spectrum—and therefore, to shift to a more
pacific image, it simultaneously builds a bridge between what must be
conserved and what can be reconfigured.

  Let us begin with the more obvious interpretation of Roncalli's exhor-
tation. It clearly targets a form of conservatism that envisions the doctrines
and practices of the Church as museum pieces, precious *objets d'art* which
cannot be touched lest they be marred. In his opening address to the fathers
of the Second Vatican Council, John XXIII railed against "prophets of
doom and gloom" who saw any change in the Church as a betrayal of the

heritage, and in the same speech, he distinguished between the enduring substance of the faith and the ever changing forms in which that substance is expressed. He saw what, a century before, John Henry Newman had seen, namely, that the dogmas of the Church do not exist on the printed page but rather in the play of lively minds. This means that they are continually turned over, searched out, judged, discussed, amplified, considered, and reconsidered—all in a dynamic, intersubjective conversation. For Newman, this process of development is not obfuscating but clarifying; without it, ideas have neither depth nor breadth nor range. This is why he tended to chose organic rather than aesthetic images to express the nature of doctrine: the unfolding of Catholic thought is like a mighty river, which becomes more powerful, interesting, and rich as it flows; or it is like an ancient tree that sends its roots deep into the ground and gives rise to new branches and leaves season after season. The most oft-cited line of Newman's *An Essay on the Development of Doctrine* is situated in this context: "In a higher world it may be otherwise; but here below, to live is to change, and to be perfect is to have changed often." So indeed, Pope John's Newman-like image of the "flourishing garden of life" effectively holds off a stuffy traditionalism.

At the same time, it implicitly criticizes a freewheeling, unstructured, and uncritical liberalism. As any devotee of the art will testify, the successful cultivation of a garden involves an enormous amount of hard work and attention: cutting, pruning, digging, weeding, fertilizing, and so forth. More to it, a gardener must understand the nature of the plants with which he is dealing; he must become a student of their growth patterns and life cycles; he is required to know what makes them flourish and languish; he must be cognizant of the sorts of plants with which they are compatible and incompatible, and of the environmental factors— from insects to rain, cold, and humidity—that affect his blooms. So the garden of Catholic life and thought must be carefully tended. Newman knew the paradoxical truth that development of doctrine and the presence of an infallible teaching office are not mutually exclusive but mutually implicative. It is precisely because dogma unfolds over time that it must be monitored by someone who can distinguish adequately between legitimate evolution and corruption. To stay with one of Newman's own images, the ancient tree of the Catholic faith sometimes sends off errant

branches, whose very lifelessness can compromise the growth of the organism, and these, accordingly, must be pruned. Or it can take into itself
harmful influences from the environment around it—poisons in the air
or soil—which have to be eliminated. Thus the Arian branch of the
Christian tree—strong and vibrant for so long a period of time—had to
be, it was eventually determined, cut off lest the whole organism be ad-
versely affected; and the various forms of Gnosticism—toxic from the
earliest days of the Church up to the present—must be, it is judged, kept
out of the root system of the plant. Who has done this determining,
judging, pruning, and protecting over the ages but the canny gardeners of
Christ's church.

Another apt metaphor, along Newmanian lines, is that of the game.
A game of, say, basketball is open-ended, freewheeling, creative, continually flowing in unpredictable ways. No team has ever taken the basketball
up the court in precisely the same way, because every dribbler is different,
every offensive configuration unique, every defense peculiarly arranged.
This limitless variety is what makes the game fun to watch and even more
fun to play. So the Catholic conversation is ever new, surprising, efferves-
cent. St. John passed the Paschal Mystery on to Polycarp, who tossed it
to Irenaeus, who conveyed it to Origen, who sent it to Augustine, who
handed it to Aquinas, who discussed it with Bonaventure, who whispered
it to Meister Eckhart, who conveyed it to John of the Cross and Teresa of
Avila, who passed it to Newman, who carried it to de Lubac, Balthasar,
and Rahner, who bequeathed it to us. And each time that the mystery
was passed (handed on, *traditio*), it was given a unique spin. No one of
those figures ever spoke the mystery in precisely the same way as his or
her predecessor; each one carried it in a particular fashion. And we will
play the game in accord with our own predilections and in response to
the demands of our own time. Christianity is a flow, and it would be
counterproductive, finally pointless, to try to stop it.

At the same time, anyone who has ever seriously participated in a
game knows that indispensable conditions for successful play are structure, order, rules, and mutually agreed-upon limitations. Basketball
would be no fun whatsoever if one were permitted to dribble outside the
boundaries of the court, to manhandle one's opponent, or to carry the

ball under one's arm. The challenge and beauty of the game depend, to a large degree, on the maintaining of its structured integrity. So the play of the Catholic conversation unfolds according to rather stringent rules and disciplined by a whole set of binding assumptions, principles, convictions, dogmas, and creeds. Without these, it would lose its identity, devolving into idle chatter, the unfocused and finally unproductive exchange of religious opinions. Furthermore, everyone knows that the very worst enforcers of the rules of a basketball game would be the players themselves, and not simply because they would be biased in favor of their respective teams. They would poorly officiate because, involved in the movement and excitement of the competition, they would lack the requisite dispassionate objectivity. Though everyone dutifully boos when the officials take the court, any serious student or player of the game knows that the enforcers of the rules are necessary to ensure the enjoyment of the play. In a similar way, the practitioners of the structured conversation of Catholicism—teachers, preachers, professors—would tend to be the worst keepers of the boundaries and for largely the same reason. What they need is an attentive but relatively disengaged participant whose outsider status would allow for the requisite objectivity in the judgment of the rules. This authority, whose voice adjudicates disputes and whose activity both interrupts the play and causes it to resume, is the magisterium of bishops and Pope. Though there is a natural tension between the teachers and the judges, the former know that the latter make possible much of the fun of the conversation.

I rehearse these images because I am convinced that they help to clarify an ecclesial situation that became sadly muddled in the years following Pope John's council. I came of age in the late sixties and seventies of the last century, in the immediate aftermath of Vatican II. What I witnessed during that period was a terrible war of attrition between two extreme camps (with, admittedly, numerous shades in between): progressives overly in love with the culture and pushing myriad reforming agendas and conservatives desperately trying to recover the form of Catholicism that predated the council. Some of these liberals were so enamored of growth, play, and free development that they allowed John XXIII's flourishing garden to become overgrown and untamed; while some of these traditionalists were so attached to an outmoded cultural expression of the Church's life that they effectively killed off the plants in the garden, pressing their dead leaves between the pages of a book. The point, as I have been arguing, is to cultivate the living thing which is the Catholic form of life—and this means that one must eschew, embrace, and transcend both extremes. It is only when one goes beyond an attitude of indifference to the structure and indifference to development that one is ready to be a good gardener.

This is why I identify the essays in this book as post-liberal and post-conservative. They represent the attempt of a theologian come of age after the council to push past a set of unfruitful ideological divides. But lest I succumb to what Richard John Neuhaus has legitimately criticized as a bland and finally contentless "beyondism," I also identify them as evangelical. The lifeblood of the Church, the vital principle of the flourishing garden, the sap within the tree of the tradition, the energy that animates and disciplines the game of the Catholic conversation is none other than Jesus Christ crucified and risen from the dead. Jesus, killed for our transgressions and raised for our justification, is the kerygma, the Good News, the evangel, and it is he who shines from the pages of the Gospel, in the sermons of Augustine, through the arguments of Aquinas, in the bright colors of the Sistine ceiling, in the mysticism of Eckhart, throughout the ministry of Mother Teresa, and the witness of Edith Stein. My hope is that the articles that are included in this collection—written on a variety of subjects over the course of twelve years—are indeed evangelical, radiant with something of that same glow. If they are (and only if they are), they can perhaps serve to bridge some of the divisions that have marred the body of Christ.

I would like to add just a word concerning the choice and arrangement of the articles in this collection. In the first section, "Building a Bridge across the Great Divide," I have gathered three pieces that express, in different ways, my impatience with the dysfunctional and obfuscating categories of liberal and conservative. To find a way forward, I rely on G. K. Chesterton's "bi-polar extremism" and Stanley Hauerwas's keen sense of an embodied and practiced Christianity. Next, I turn to a consideration of the liturgy, not only because it is often a lightning rod for disagreement in the Church, but also, and principally, because the liturgy, as the central, defining action of the body of Christ, is the place where what unites us should be most fully on display. The "source and summit of the Christian life" (*Sacrosanctum Concilium*), the Eucharist is the matrix for all that we are and do as followers of Jesus. A key figure for me in these essays is Romano Guardini, one of the chief architects of the twentieth-century liturgical movement, as well as one of the main critics of what happened to the liturgy after the council.

The most technical and theologically speculative essays are gathered in the next section, "At the Feet of the Masters." I am convinced that the great divide will not be bridged without some hard intellectual work. The theologians whose efforts stand behind the conciliar documents—Rahner, de Lubac, Congar, Balthasar, Schillebeeckx—were deeply serious people, and their writings reflect a subtle engagement with the great tradition. One of my suspicions is that a good deal of the postconciliar confusion followed from the fact that those who were charged with the practical implementation of the council (especially in this country) lacked the requisite intellectual formation to interpret the documents correctly. So I am going to lead my readers through some dense thickets in the work of James Joyce, Karol Wojtyla, Jacques Maritain, and especially that thinker whom the Catholic Church reverences as its *doctor communis*, common doctor, namely Thomas Aquinas. What I have found particularly attractive in Aquinas is his notion of the noncompetitive and therefore empowering transcendence of God. In a number of the articles in this third section, I ring the changes on this master idea.

The essays gathered in the fourth section, "Preaching the Message," represent a shift to a more homiletic and pastoral tone. With the mainstream of the great tradition from Origen to Newman, I am persuaded that theology and spirituality are fundamentally one. The more we know about God, the more our lives change. In these articles and sermons, I try to show some practical implications of Christian doctrine. In section five, "The Way of Nonviolence," I have brought together articles that center around the theme of war and peace. One of the most important ethical implications of the doctrine of creation is that all people are connected to one another through the God who continually brings them into being. We are all ontological siblings. This means that to live in nonviolence, even when faced with the worst provocations of one's enemies, is to live in line with what Hauerwas has called "the grain of the universe." An important inspiration here is Thomas Merton, who clearly saw the connection between a traditional Catholic metaphysics and a radical stance of nonviolence. Finally, in the sixth section, "Priesthood and Ministry," I include a number of essays on Church structure and practice. A key player here is the philosopher Friedrich Nietzsche, whose thinking, unfortunately, haunts our discussions of the relationship between priests and laity. For Nietzsche, the basic truth of things is power and the struggle for power; whereas for the Gospel, just the opposite is the case. The all-powerful God is the one who is able to empty himself totally out of love and to enter noncompetitively into relation with what is other. Until we rid ourselves of Nietzschean assumptions, we will make no progress in establishing the right balance between the ordained and the nonordained.

As I suggested, these articles were written over the course of many years and for various audiences and purposes. Read them all; read some; pick and choose according to your interest. My only hope is that in them you sense something of the Spirit of Jesus Christ, the one whose cross breaks down all the walls of enmity that divide us.

There are many people who have, over the years, taken the time to read and comment upon these essays. I would like to express my sincere gratitude to Fr. Stephen Grunow, Fr. Lawrence Hennessey, Fr. Raymond Webb, Mr. Michael Leach, Prof. Carol Zaleski, Mr. Thomas Levergood, Fr. David Burrell, C.S.C., Fr. Michael Baxter, C.S.C., Ms. Karen Sue Smith, Ms. Kathleen O'Connell-Cahill, Msgr. M. Francis Mannion, Dr. Daniel Van Slyke, Dr. Denis McNamara, Fr. Paul Murray, O.P., Dr. Michael Dauphinais, Dr. Matthew Levering, Fr. Andrew Greeley, Br. Patrick Hart, O.C.S.O., and Prof. Stanley Hauerwas. Their approbations and recommendations proved most helpful to me. I would also like very specially to acknowledge Mr. Jeremy Langford, who proved to be a fine, careful, and encouraging editor.

Easter 2004

Part I

BUILDING A BRIDGE ACROSS THE GREAT DIVIDE

Chapter One

THE VIRTUE OF
BI-POLAR EXTREMISM

T HERE ARE EXTREMISTS IN THE CHURCH TODAY, AND THERE ARE moderates—and all of them are wreaking havoc. They are causing such distress precisely because they are ignoring, each in a particular way, the strangeness that lies at the heart of Christianity. It is my contention that the chief problem we face in the Church is not lack of loyalty to Rome, not insufficient concern for the poor, not ignorance of women's concerns, not liturgical abuse, not theological imprecision, not resurgent triumphalism— though each of these is, I think, cause for worry. No, the chief difficulty we face is a lack of imagination, the inability to hold opposites in tension, the failure to be, boldly and unapologetically, bi-polar extremists.

I recently heard an address given by the most popular Catholic evangelist in this country. A central motif of her speech was that liberals within the Church are persecuting loyal orthodox Catholics, much as the pagans of the first centuries persecuted the fledgling Christian community. Accordingly, the speaker insinuated, the forces of liberalism must be opposed, resisted even to the point of death. Several times, during her address, she invited Catholics who disagree with her vision of things simply to leave the Church. Peppering her talk with lively stories and piquant rhetoric, she frequently elicited from the crowd laughter and calls of approval. About a year ago, in my hometown, a meeting of one of the better-known progressive groups in the Church was held. At the outset of their closing liturgy, several nonordained persons gathered around the altar and donned stoles of priesthood. Then, in unison, they dropped their stoles to the ground, symbolizing their renunciation of the hierarchical orders of the Church. In time, all the congregants at the liturgy put on stoles expressing the priesthood of all believers. This rather striking series of gestures drew much attention in the Catholic— and indeed secular—media and captured the imaginations of liberals both inside and outside of the Church.

The conservative speaker and the progressive liturgists have much in common. Both are passionate, focused, and capable of arousing an inspired following; both see clear battle lines drawn and both are deeply suspicious of the opposing camp. There is tremendous strength and energy precisely in the extremism of their positions, precisely in their unwavering and almost overstated confidence. It is also easy to see the dangerous one-sidedness that they have in common, the tendency to emphasize one dimension of the truth at the expense of the others. It is also not difficult to see the divisiveness, indeed the violence, to which such positions can give rise.

Now some in the Church, perhaps priding themselves on their intelligence and prudence, reject the extremism of the left and the right and opt for an elegant "middle" position, one that takes elements from both sides and blends them into a sort of compromise. Such moderates praise aspects of conservatism and liberalism, while retaining their right to dissent from other dimensions of the two positions that they find objectionable. They are careful, balanced, and often given to use the expression, "on the one hand . . . and on the other hand." And because of their moderation they are, more often than not, deadly dull, utterly unable to fire the imaginations or rouse the enthusiasm of great numbers of their fellow believers.

Thus it appears as though we have reached a fruitless and frustrating impasse. We can, it seems, opt either for popular but dangerous extremism or for prudent but uninspiring moderation. If we choose the former, the Church appears headed for a divisive and explosive future, and if we choose the latter, we seem destined to become more and more irrelevant, going out "not with a bang but with a whimper."

What I would like to propose—with the help of G. K. Chesterton—is a way out of this dilemma. Recently, I was perusing one of Chesterton's most popular books, *Orthodoxy*, and my attention was drawn to chapter 6, "The Paradoxes of Christianity." In this section of the book, Chesterton recalls his puzzlement when he read the critiques of Christianity that came from so many different quarters. On the one hand, Christianity—especially Catholicism—was criticized for being too worldly, too caught up in wealth, property, pomp, and ceremony. Where, for instance, was the spirit of the carpenter of Nazareth in the expensive theatrical display of the Vatican? On the other hand, Christianity was reviled for its excessive spiritualism, its indifference to the concrete concerns of the world, its tendency to pine after the "things of heaven." Similarly, some critics complained that Christianity, with its stress on sin, penitence, and punishment, was excessively pessimistic, while others held that, given its emphasis on the love of God, the intervention of the saints, and the promise of eternal life, it was ridiculously optimistic. Finally, certain enemies of the faith maintained, probably with Joan of Arc and the Crusades in mind, that Christianity was bloodthirsty and warlike, while others held, probably with Francis in mind, that it was too pacific and nonviolent. What puzzled Chesterton, of course, was not that the Church had its critics, but that its critics were so varied, so at odds with one another, so mutually exclusive. Whatever this Christianity was, he concluded, it must be something strangely shaped indeed to inspire such a wildly divergent army of enemies.

Then it occurred to him that perhaps it was not Christianity that was misshapen, but rather its critics. Perhaps it was they who, from their various eccentric points of view, saw the rightly shaped Christianity as distorted: "Suppose we heard an unknown man spoken of by many men. Suppose we were puzzled to hear that some men said he was too tall and some too short; some objected to his fatness, some lamented his leanness; some thought him too dark and some too fair. One explanation . . . would be that he might be an odd shape. But there is another explanation. He might be the right shape." It could be the case, in short, that "it is Christianity that is sane and all its critics that are mad—in various ways." It is the sheer depth and breadth of the Church, the complexity and multifacetedness of it, which narrow-minded enemies cannot grasp.

Christianity, Chesterton surmised, was, perhaps, too capacious to be easily comprehended.

However—and here is Chesterton's main point—it does not seem that Christianity is merely "sensible," standing as it were in the middle, taking in elements of both extremes. It does not seem to be the case that the Church is somewhat worldly and somewhat otherworldly, to some degree life affirming and to some degree life denying, a little optimistic and a little pessimistic. On the contrary, there seems to be, everywhere in the life of the Church, a quality of frenzy, excess, enthusiasm: Francis of Assisi was "a more shouting optimist than Walt Whitman" and St. Jerome, "in denouncing all evil, could paint the world blacker than Schopenhauer." One Christian saint could be more starkly ascetical than the severest Stoic, another Christian saint could celebrate life more ec-statically than a priest of Dionysus. In defending the celibacy of the clergy, the Church could be "ferociously against having children," and, in holding up marriage and family, it could be, at the same time, "ferociously for having children." The Church consistently and poetically placed the opposites side by side and allowed them to coexist in all of their purity, power, and intensity; Christianity encouraged the lamb and the lion to lie down together, without ever forcing the lion to become lamblike or the lamb lionlike. Chesterton offers us a wonderful image: The Church "has always had a healthy hatred of pink. It hates that combination of two colours which is the feeble expedient of the philosophers. It hates that evolution of black into white which is tantamount to a dirty gray."

Like Paul Tillich, the great Protestant theologian of the last century, Chesterton feels that moderation is a pagan not a Christian virtue. To stand blandly in the middle is to miss the thrill and the romance of Christianity, to overlook that strange event which stands at the heart of the Church and which separates it from any mythology or philosophy that preceded it. It is to overlook the Incarnation.

What emerges from even a cursory study of the great incarnational formula of Chalcedon is just this paradoxical principle. The early ortho-dox fathers resisted the temptation to be one-sided extremists in their ar-ticulation of the meaning of Jesus Christ. They would side neither with those who said Christ was only divine (the Monophysites), nor with those who claimed he was only human (the Nestorians), nor—and this is perhaps most intriguing—with those who held he was a little of both (the Arians). What Chalcedon declares is something altogether strange and unexpected, something that breaks the categories of philosophy and mythology, something that cannot be caught in the easy options of left, right, or center: Jesus Christ is fully, emphatically, robustly human *and* fully, emphatically, and robustly divine—*without mixing, mingling, or confusion.* Christ is not symbolized by a gray banner—somewhat white and somewhat black—rather, he is symbolized by a flag that is dramatically black and white, with all of the virtues of blackness and whiteness fully expressed. What the orthodox fathers of Chalcedon saw, in short, was the bi-polar extremism of the Christ event: humanity and divinity lying down together in personal union and utter differentiation.

And it is this strange juxtaposition, indeed this joke, which has, for two thousand years, galvanized the Christian imagination and animated the best of our art, architecture, literature, and theology. When Christians are seized by the paradox of the Incarnation, they understand themselves, the world, culture, and the divine in a wildly paradoxical manner; when Christians no longer "get" the joke of the Incarnation, they slide into the weary and ordinary categories of left, center, and right. When they can no longer hear the music of Chalcedon, they settle into either a destructive one-sided extremism or a hopelessly dull moderation.

Let me illustrate this incarnational principle—which Chesterton saw everywhere in Christian life—by looking at one of the classical doctrinal formulations of the Church. Our greatest theologians, from Origen, through Augustine and Aquinas, to Rahner and Tillich in our century, have maintained that God is not *a* being, even the supreme being, but rather Being itself. Aquinas, for instance, said that God is not the *ens summum* (the highest being) but rather *ipsum esse subsistens* (the subsistent act of being itself). What this means, of course, is that God is, at one and the same time, infinitely beyond the world *and* intimately connected to the world. As the sheer act of being, God is, simultaneously, *modally different* than any of the particular beings in the universe *and* closer to the world than the world is to itself. To use more classical terms, God is both unsurpassably transcendent *and* unsurpassably immanent. And please note that *it is not the case that God is, to some degree, transcendent and, to some degree, immanent, in one sense beyond the world and in another sense one with the world.* No, God's transcendence must be proclaimed with unlimited vehemence, and God's immanence must be celebrated with boundless enthusiasm—precisely because of the strangeness of God's nature. To make the same point in the more poetic language of pseudo-Dionysius or Meister Eckhart, God is both great and small, both light and dark, both inviting and intimidating. Or to put it in Augustine's magnificent phrase, God is *intimior intimo meo et superior summo meo* (closer to me than I am to myself and higher than what is highest in me).

What is perhaps not immediately evident is that all of these doctrinal statements concerning the being of God *flow from the radicality of the Incarnation.* In their attempts to name the divine, Christian theologians have consistently broken and rearranged the categories of classical (or modern) philosophy because they have, through Christ, been placed in the presence of a power that is stubbornly both/and. The God who makes the world from nothing, the God whose "thoughts are above our thoughts and whose ways are above our ways," the God whose name cannot be pronounced and whose image cannot be reproduced—has become a creature, has "pitched his tent among us," has established an intimacy with us beyond our imagining. When Christian mystics and theologians attempted to speak of the divine power that prompted this unheard-of event, they stammered and stuttered their way toward the kind of language I outlined above, toward the poetry of bi-polar extremism. When theologians forget the strangeness of the Incarnation, they settle into the predictable and mutually exclusive categories of philosophy or mythology.

My concern is that the poetry of the Incarnation is not much in evidence in the weary debates today between liberals, moderates, and conservatives. What are the themes so often emphasized by liberals in the Church? The presence of God in the world, the benevolence and availability of the divine, the basic goodness of the human and the creaturely, a concern for social justice and God's transforming grace, a passion for equality and human dignity. And what are the motifs so consistently underlined by conservatives? The radical otherness of God, the glory and majesty of the divine, the reality of sin and human weakness, the power of the divine judgment on the world, a suspicion of all social and political utopias. And what is the stance of the "moderate"? He will choose certain themes from each camp or he will attempt to "blend" them, using the excesses of one to correct the excesses of the other. As should be clear from the Chestertonian analysis I have offered, both liberals and conservatives are, precisely in their extremism, correct but one-sided, and moderates are, quite simply, dangerously incorrect. All three camps miss the music of Chalcedon.

Authentic Christians must be, at one and the same time and with unabashed fervor, radically liberal and radically conservative, passionately left-wing and passionately right-wing, excessively optimistic and excessively pessimistic. Some conservatives express dissatisfaction with the New Age movement and creation spirituality because, in their stress on the immanence and availability of the divine, they seem neopagan or gnostic. This style of critique, it seems to me, is wide of the mark. The Christian should not prudently correct New Age spirituality; rather, he should mock it by outdoing it. "You haven't begun sufficiently to emphasize the presence of God in the world; you aren't nearly New Age enough; you haven't even glimpsed the truth and beauty that healthy paganism appreciated in the world." An orthodox Christian could trump any neopagan assertion with the still shocking novelty of St. Francis of Assisi blithely preaching to the birds and calmly asserting that sun and moon are brother and sister to him. Again, it is not that the New Age thinker places an excessive emphasis on the immanence of God and the goodness of the world; on the contrary, he doesn't emphasize those themes *enough*. The orthodox believer does not want to calm and moderate the New Age advocate; he wants to join him and push him further.

On the other hand, some liberal critics feel that conservative theorists, in their emphasis on sin and the necessity for revelation, share a too pessimistic view of culture and the project of the Enlightenment. Again, this approach, I think, is wrong-headed. Just as God's immanence and availability cannot be overemphasized, so God's distance and, concomitantly, the world's darkness, cannot be stressed too strongly. God is indeed other, distant, threatening, overwhelming, and the world, as a consequence, does stand dramatically in need of grace and revelation.

The incarnational Christian should, once again, not moderate the conservatives, but rather outdo them, intensify them, turn them up a notch. "No matter how far you say God is from human culture and endeavor, know that he is further; no matter how hopeless the human project seems, it is worse than you can imagine." An orthodox believer could trump the most thoroughgoing pessimist with the image of St. Bernard kneeling on the cold floor of the monastery at Clairvaux, weeping in contrition for his sins.

The authentic Christian wants, not the optimist alone and not pessimist alone, and by no means some monstrous blend of the two. No, she wants the optimist at full volume and the pessimist at full volume. Is this madness? No, it is, I would argue, the bi-polar extremism that has always characterized Christianity at its best.

Is it difficult to hold these extremes together? Of course it is—as difficult as holding the humanity and divinity of Christ in creative tension. Bi-polar extremism requires patience, prayer, creativity, and imagination—the very qualities so much in evidence in our greatest theologians, spiritual writers, and saints. It is possible, I would state in conclusion, only in the context of a community of love. Only when we Christians are able to share our insights, experiences, ideas, and hopes around a table of fellowship and conversation will we be capable of rising to the challenge of Chalcedon. Only when we respect the widely divergent ways in which the immanent/ transcendent God has formed us can we even hope to approach the adequacy of theological expression and the fullness of spirituality implied in the virtue of bi-polar extremism.

Chapter Two

THE TROUBLE WITH A
BEIGE CATHOLICISM

IHAVE LONG SUSPECTED THAT THE CATEGORIES OF LIBERAL AND CON-
servative have run their course. Whatever descriptive power they once had
is gone, and now we are largely under their tyranny. Whenever we read theologians or hear speakers on religious topics, we feel compelled to file them
under one or the other of these broad and awkwardly political headings
and, as a result, we miss, not only the nuances of their positions, but also
what might be the *real* differences between them. For, in calling into question the liberal–conservative split, I am not proposing a false irenicism that
overlooks important divergences in theological approach. In fact, I am trying to get at those differences. But I want to name them more clearly and
accurately so as to facilitate the Church's conversation. My suspicion is that
behind the liberal–conservative smokescreen, far more intriguing and eccle-
sially significant agreements and disagreements go on.

"RELIGIOUSNESS A" AND "RELIGIOUSNESS B"

Instead of liberal and conservative I would propose what I take to be
the more descriptive categories of beige and colorful, bland and spicy,
abstract and concrete, epic and lyrical. Just to be clear from the outset,
I am by no means making a simple substitution: what we used to call

"conservative" we will now call "colorful" and what we used to call "liberal" we will now call "bland." As I hope to show in the course of the chapter, the beige and the spicy can be found in both traditional liberalism and traditional conservatism.

Perhaps the best place to begin an explanation of this new distinction is with Soren Kierkegaard. In his *Philosophical Fragments*, the melancholy Dane launches a spirited attack on the philosophical theology associated with Hegel, what he calls "religiousness A." The basic assumption behind this approach is that all people are implicitly religious and require but a teacher or a guide to render their implicit faith explicit. Like Socrates in the Platonic dialogues, this teacher cajoles the student, drawing forth from him the knowledge that he already secretly possessed. Since his role is merely educative or demonstrative, he is not an indispensable figure in the life of the student: once he has done his job, he can (and indeed should) move on. He is like the ladder that is left behind once the height has been reached.

To this construal, Kierkegaard sharply contrasts what he calls "religiousness B." The presumption behind this method is that human beings are not implicitly religious at all, just the contrary. What they require, therefore, is not merely a teacher who will draw from them their hidden spirituality, but rather a savior who will provide both the content of, and the condition for, their faith. On this assumption, the "moment" of the savior's arrival is of permanent significance, and the densely textured uniqueness of his teaching, gestures, vision, and style is crucial. In the framework of "religiousness A," a student draws on his own terms a general truth from the teaching of his master, whereas in the context of "religiousness B," the sinner is reshaped, remade, redeemed by the irreducible particularity of the savior.

What becomes clear in the course of Kierkegaard's analysis is that he thinks the Hegelian–Socratic interpretation has tragically undermined authentic Christianity, turning it into a bland game of religious philosophy. What gives the lie to a "religiousness A" construal of Christianity is, for Kierkegaard, the shock of the cross. If we are all implicitly religious, and if Jesus is the teacher who gently shows us the deepest truth about ourselves, why did we kill him when he came? Is it not in fact the case that we were, and are, implicitly opposed to what he brings? Are we not like Saul of Tarsus, hardly waiting to hear the message of Jesus, but rather walking boldly and confidently in the wrong direction, away from Jesus, indeed in opposition to him? Did not all the disciples in fact, to varying degrees, mistake him, misunderstand him, find him hard to take? Is this the expected reaction to the one who is only rendering explicit the deepest truth about them? Is the disciples' discomfiture not in fact the normal reaction to one who is painfully remaking them and reshaping them from within? All of this leads Kierkegaard to the conclusion that true Christianity is the great and unique instance of "religiousness B" in the sea of philosophies, spiritualities, and theologies that could be gathered under the heading of "religiousness A." What fundamentally characterizes the former is a relative prickliness, colorfulness, and spicy uniqueness; whereas what marks the latter is a relative abstractness, generality, and cultural accommodation.

Now presented in strictly Kierkegaardian "either/or" terms, these descriptions are too sharply drawn, but they provide, I submit, a far more helpful framework for conversation than do liberal and conservative. And in many ways the story of twentieth-century theology is that of the battle between these two interpretive possibilities. Perhaps the defining conversation in the Protestant theology of our century was the one that took place between Paul Tillich and Karl Barth. Serving as a chaplain and preacher during the First World War, Tillich discovered that the traditional language of Christianity—incarnation, creation, redemption, God—often fell on deaf ears. These once-evocative words had become weary symbols, void of transformative power. Accordingly, he developed a theology that would speak to and from the lived experience of the anxiety-ridden people of the modern age. Religion begins, he famously claimed, in the feeling of ultimate concern, and authentic theology consequently should have a correlational quality, relating the anguished questions of human existence to the "answers" found in the Scripture and tradition. Thus, for example, *God* is translated as "that which unconditionally concerns us" and *creation* becomes "the sense of being borne up by the ground of being." Not surprisingly, Tillich looks for inspiration to the theology of the early nineteenth-century Protestant thinker, Friedrich

Schleiermacher, for whom religion begins in the "pious consciousness" of being "absolutely dependent."

Now Tillich's colleague, the Swiss Reformed theologian Karl Barth, had, to say the least, serious objections to this experiential approach. In it he saw another form of Kierkegaard's culturally accommodating and secularist "religiousness A." If religion begins in our general experience of being ultimately concerned or totally dependent, then Jesus is, at best, a teacher and not a savior. He gives but a flavor and specification to what is a generally available consciousness. In a commentary on Tillich's method of correlation, Barth opined that such a method would work well in "paradise or in heaven, but not here below." In those blessed states, we would be in the presence of God and hence would know which questions to ask. The problem is that in our present condition, our minds and wills are warped by sin, and thus the very questions we ask are skewed and distorted. What we require, says Barth, is a savior who will place in our hearts both the right questions and the right answers, who will inaugurate us into his way of experiencing.

And perhaps the defining conversation of twentieth-century Catholic theology was that between Karl Rahner and Hans Urs von Balthasar. Concerned that neo-scholastic Catholic thought effectively precluded a dialogue with the modern world, Rahner attempted, throughout his career, to reconcile traditional Thomism with the critical and subjectivist philosophies of Kant, Hegel, and Heidegger. Accordingly, he began his meditations almost exclusively from the standpoint of the human experience of transcendence and mystery. In our thinking and willing, in our anxious questioning, in our very finitude, we human beings tend outward to the all-embracing mystery of Being itself. And this self-transcending orientation is what, for Rahner, constitutes a compelling starting point for the religiosity of the skeptical modern person. In Rahner's writings, the specifically Christian doctrines and stories are situated in the context of this general religious consciousness, the latter providing the interpretive horizon for the former.

Balthasar maintained throughout his career a deep respect for Rahner, often collaborating with him and at one point remarking that Rahner far outstripped him in speculative power. But he also felt that there was a fundamental divergence in their theological method and style. When asked to articulate this difference, Balthasar invoked two giants of modern German culture: "Rahner went with Kant and I went with Goethe." It would be worth our while to unpack this pithy observation. In embracing Kantianism, Balthasar felt, Rahner was seeking the distinctively modern ideal of grounding knowledge, not so much in empirical observation or received tradition, but in subjective consciousness, just as Descartes sought a foundation in the certitude of the cogito. The poet and playwright Goethe was a violent opponent of this modern subjectivist rationalism. Goethe was convinced that, in his mania for certitude, the modern scientist/philosopher drew the world into the narrow confines of his rational consciousness, accepting only what he could clearly see, measure, and take in on his own terms. Thus, the analytical botanist ripped plants from the earth, dissected them, and surveyed them under the bright light of his concerns and questions. Authentic knowledge, Goethe said, came, not from this invasive and arrogant rationalism, but from a respectful contemplation of form. Thus Goethe recommended that the true botanist ought to spend time with the plants he sought to know, observing them patiently, drawing them, watching how they develop in their natural setting, allowing *their* form to emerge in its complexity and in its own way. What he called for, in short, was a sort of humility in the presence of the object to be studied.

The subtitle of Balthasar's great work on theological method is the very Goethean *Schau der Gestalt* (Seeing the Form). He begins his theological project, not with an evocation of a general religious experience (our perspective), but with a careful, respectful, and contemplative gaze upon the form that stands at the center of Christianity, the crucified and risen Jesus. In the spirit of Goethe, he stays with the form, kneeling in its presence, seeing it in its proper liturgical context, refusing to subject it to the limits of his consciousness and his questioning. What Balthasar critiques in the method of Rahner is just this tendency to restrict the form, sequestering it in the confines of the generic human experience of openness to the Mystery and not allowing the form itself to break, surpass, and reconfigure that mode of receptivity. Balthasar says that the Kantian method of Rahner is like trying to show someone the windows of

Chartres Cathedral from outside the cathedral. From that exterior van-tage point, the windows are drab, lifeless, indistinct. Their power and beauty appear only from within the mysterious darkness of the church. Another key Balthasarian distinction is that between an "epic" and a "lyri-cal" theology. An epic approach, like Rahner's, seeks a grand overarching perspective *above* the particularity of revelation history in order to under-stand it; while a lyrical method, like Balthasar's own, stays closer to the ground, listening, seeing, and responding to the individual and unrepeat-able events of that history. Again, the former is more abstractly Kantian and the latter more poetically Goethean.

It is interesting to note that Balthasar was a friend and fellow citi-zen of Karl Barth. In many ways, Balthasar's project within Catholicism mirrored Barth's within Protestantism, namely, a warning against the dangers of "religiousness A." Balthasar says, in a distinctly Kierkegaardian vein, that the principal problem with Rahner's theology is that it lacks a coherent account of the cross. Indeed, if we are all standing in the pres-ence of absolute mystery, if we are all naturally oriented to the Incarna-tion, Balthasar wonders with Kierkegaard *why we killed him when he appeared in history?* For Balthasar, Kant needs to be corrected by Goethe, and "religiousness A" needs to be countered by "religiousness B."

COMING OF AGE IN AN "A" CHURCH

These debates concerning rival theological methods have, by no means, re-mained abstractly academic. In fact the tension between them is the ground for significant disagreements today in pastoral practice, ecclesial attitude to-ward the culture, and methods of evangelization. I would like to demon-strate this thesis by engaging in a bit of personal reflection, reminiscing on what it was like to grow up in a "religiousness A" Catholic Church.

I was born in 1959 and began first grade in 1965, the year the coun-cil ended. Accordingly, my education and formation as a Catholic was, al-most entirely, post-Vatican II. When one reads the memoirs of Catholics who came of age in the forties and fifties, one encounters either joyfully nostalgic memories of a vibrant Catholic culture or nightmare memories of a Gothic world of superstition, bizarre behavior, and ruler-wielding nuns. Whether it was loved or despised, that Catholic world was, at the very least, colorful. When I recall my Catholic youth in the late sixties and seventies, I think of the color beige.

It seemed to be an overriding concern of the teachers, nuns, and priests who formed my generation to make our Catholicism as non-threatening, accessible, culturally appealing, as possible. Nuns and clergy eschewed distinctive dress and frowned on special titles; doctrinal peculiarities were set aside in favor of generally humanistic ethical values; liturgies were designed to be, above all, entertaining; homilies were delivered by priests who had far more questions than answers; troubling biblical texts dealing with the divine anger and judgment and the reality of sin were scarcely mentioned; Jesus was presented exclusively as friend and brother. There was, above all, a hand-wringing and apologetic quality to the Catholicism of my youth. It seemed as though the project was to "translate" uniquely Catholic doctrine, practice, and style into forms acceptable to the environing culture, always downplaying whatever might be construed as "odd" or "supernatural." Thus, the biblical and theological tended to be replaced by the political, the sociological, and, above all, the psychological. When I attended the twenty-fifth reunion of my eighth-grade graduating class, we reminisced about the "banners and collages," which were the decidedly nondoctrinal staple of our religion classes and which for most of us effectively symbolized our Catholic youth.

Now all of this was, in a sense, understandable. The energies unleashed by the council were powerful, and the inevitable pendular swing away from the tightly defined Catholicism of the forties proceeded predictably. And I certainly harbor no feelings of resentment toward that Church (how, after all, could one resent something so tame and benign?), but I do look back at it with a certain boredom. What I see in all of the theological, liturgical, and practical expressions outlined above is a typically "religiousness A" move in the direction of the generic and the abstract. In its excessive desire to reach out to the culture and dialogue with it, the Catholicism of my youth tended to mute or even altogether to suppress its particularity, its strangeness, that very spicy uniqueness that makes it fascinating.

This drift toward the abstract can be seen too in the architecture and art of the period. The Catholic churches that were built during my youth fell into an easily recognizable pattern. They were usually great open spaces, cavernous rooms with little color, decoration, or imagery. Altar, ambo, and sanctuary furnishings were simple, blocky, unadorned. If there were statues or Stations of the Cross, they were reduced to the bare essentials, a few lines hinting at figure or gesture. Cultural critic Dr. Robert Orsi has observed that in the hymnals, textbooks, and missalettes of the sixties, religious art had become almost entirely abstract: In place of richly colored and densely textured saints there were now stick figures and vague shapes. A "religiousness A" aesthetic had come to dominate.

The influence of Tillich and (especially in Catholic circles) Rahner was, though often indirect, enormous. When we approached a religious theme, we were urged to begin, uniformly, not with art, history of doctrine, or biblical narrative, but with experience. We sought to work our way toward the biblical and dogmatic from the experiential and never vice versa, so that the latter became inevitably the measure and norm of the former. This typically "religiousness A" hermeneutic conduced, as one would expect, to a relative banalization and watering-down of the biblical, experience now forming the Bible and not the Bible experience.

ASSESSMENT AND CONCLUSIONS

Now what do we make of all this? Having made the basic distinction between these two fundamental approaches and having shown some of the effects of choosing one over the other, do I advocate a jettisoning of "religiousness A?" No, but I do recommend the subordination of "A" to "B." As a Catholic, I reverence the doctrine of the *imago Dei*, the deep conviction that there is a likeness unto God that can be found in the very structure of human experience and consciousness. It is this doctrine that grounds and legitimizes all forms of "religiousness A," from Origen to Tillich and Rahner. But notice that I specified the idea of the *imago Dei* as a *doctrine*, that is to say, as something that flows from a concrete and specific revelation. Generic "religiousness A" is valid, but only inasmuch it is conditioned and interpreted by the specificity of "religiousness B."

Is this option for "B" over "A" simply an arbitrary choice? No, I think it is rooted in the nature of Christianity as a religion of conversion and mission. Let me explain with the help of the great nineteenth-century Catholic thinker John Henry Newman. In his work *The Grammar of Assent*, Newman makes a key distinction between "real" and "notional" assent. The latter is the mind's acquiescence to general ideas, to concepts and abstractions. This sort of intellection is obviously necessary for the development of any philosophical system or worldview. Moreover, it figures, at some point, in even our most practical enterprises. But, argues Newman, it does not lead to decisive action because it does not engage the heart and the imagination. Real assent, on the other hand, is the mind's acquiescence to particulars, to the concrete, to the vividly imagined. Thus, though I might give notional assent to the Apostles' Creed, I give real assent to Chesterton's *Ballad of the White Horse*; though I notionally accept the *Summa* of Aquinas, I really accept Chartres Cathedral. And it is this real assent that fires the soul and compels it to act. Newman says that no one, strictly speaking, dies for an idea, but many people over the centuries have given their lives for friends and family and homeland.

The theme of Jesus' "inaugural address" is conversion: "The Kingdom of God is close at hand; repent and believe the Good News." And the motif of his final words is mission: "Go therefore and teach all nations." The Christian life is lived in between, and under the conditioning of, these two imperatives. Having seen the form, having been seized by the beauty of revelation, our only proper response is a change of life and a commitment to become a missionary on behalf of what we have seen. In the scriptural tradition, no vision or experience of God is ever given for the edification of the visionary; rather it is given for the sake of mission. Moses, Jeremiah, Isaiah, Peter, and Paul are visionaries *because they are missionaries*.

If Newman is right then, Christianity is, first and foremost, a religion of the concrete and not the abstract. It takes its power, not from a general religious consciousness, not from an ethical conviction, not from a comfortable abstraction, but from the person Jesus Christ. It is

Christ—in his uncompromising call to repentance, his unforgettable gestures of healing, his unique and disturbing praxis of forgiveness, his provocative nonviolence, and especially his movement from godforsakenness death to shalom-radiating resurrection—that moves the believer to change of life and gift of self. And it is the unique Christ—depicted vividly in the poetry of Dante, the frescoes of Michelangelo, the sermons of Augustine, the stained-glass windows of the Sainte Chapelle, and the sacred ballet of the liturgy—who speaks transformatively to hearts and souls across the Christian centuries. Thus, there is room for "religiousness A" in mission-oriented Christianity, but it must never be given primacy or pride of place.

I promised at the outset that I would show how the spicy–bland distinction did not simply correspond to the liberal–conservative split. Let me demonstrate this by looking ever so briefly at the life and career of Dorothy Day, the great founder of the Catholic Worker Movement. In study after study, article after article, one finds the puzzled commentator scratching his head over the "contradiction" of Dorothy Day, this woman who prayed in front of the Blessed Sacrament, attended daily Mass, took frequent retreats, spoke in pious language and accepted the traditional dogmas of the Church, *and who, at the same time,* lived with the poor, opposed any and every war, sharply criticized the economic and political status quo, and advocated a "radical Catholicism." How could she have been, simultaneously, so conservative and so liberal? What this question reveals, of course, is simply the gross inadequacy of those categories in the presence of a saint. But when seen in the context of the "A" and "B" distinction, the life of Dorothy Day becomes luminously coherent. She was a person who had made Jesus Christ in all of his concreteness the center of her life. Her "conservative" piety is expressive of this continual act of centering, and her "liberal" social commitment is her living out of the unambiguous message and style of Jesus. When a lesser person, on the one hand, chooses the piety and not the radical commitment or, on the other, roots the life of love in a principle and not in Christ, we have, respectively, the traditional "conservative" and "liberal." And both, I would argue, can be placed clearly in the category of "religiousness A," since both, in different ways, accommodate themselves to the culture.

What I hope has become clear is that the adoption of the "B" framework enables us also to valorize elements of both liberalism and conservatism. As long as we are centered in Christ, we can take ideas, perspectives, plans of action, insights, styles from both the "left" and the "right." Anchored in Christ and filled with a sense of mission, we can take what we need from any source and get up in any pulpit available to us. We are not tied into a political framework dictated to us by the culture and thus we can range around creatively, provocatively, unpredictably, borrowing now from Aristotle, now from Einstein, now from Chesterton, now from Cicero.

Therefore, let us leave liberal–conservative behind us. And let us leave behind us too that Catholicism which had allowed its distinctive colors to bleed into beige. And let us embrace the spicy, troublesome, fascinating, and culture-transforming person of Jesus Christ. And let *the Church of Christ* thereby shape the world.

Chapter Three

PATHS AND PRACTICES: RECOVERING AN EMBODIED CHRISTIANITY

APPRENTICING TO THE MASTER

ONE OF THE EARLIEST TERMS USED TO DESCRIBE CHRISTIANITY IS the simple but evocative word *Way* (Acts 9:2). This signals something of great moment: Christianity, before all else, is a form of life, a path that one walks. It is a way of seeing, a frame of mind, an attitude, but more than this, it is a manner of moving and acting, standing and relating. It is not simply a matter of the mind but of the body as well. In fact, one could say that Christianity is not real until it has insinuated itself into the blood and the bones, until it becomes an instinct, as much physical as spiritual. Perhaps the most direct description is this: Christianity, the way of Jesus Christ, *is* a culture, a style of life supported by a unique set of convictions, assumptions, hopes, and practices. It is like a game with a unique texture, feel, and set of rules. As such, it is a milieu into which one must be introduced through a process of practice and *apprenticeship*.

When a young man came to a Renaissance painter in order to learn the craft of painting, he moved in with the master, watching him at close quarters, catching the rhythms of his movements and the overall pattern of his life. In time, he might be given a simple task to perform—say the crushing of pigments—and this he would do for many months or even years. Though he undoubtedly found the process tedious and longed to involve himself in the actual painting of a great canvas, the young man did his job and thereby learned, not only the rudiments of color but more importantly the patience and discipline required for the production of a work of art. Only gradually would he be initiated into the more complex dimensions of the artist's realm of activity: draftsmanship, composition, application of color, use of chiaroscuro, the depiction of philosophical and mythological themes. During this entire process, he would scrupulously follow the direction and style of his master who, in his youth, had learned the same techniques from his elders. Only at the end of his years-long training, having moved, body and spirit, into the milieu of the painter, would the novice perhaps develop his own approach, find his own path.

And something very similar unfolds when a child steps onto a baseball diamond to begin his initiation into the game. His coach moves him through a series of drills—throwing, catching, swinging the bat, fielding the ball—designed to place the requisite skills of baseball into his muscles and mind. When necessary, the master of the game might demonstrate with his own body the pivot or slide that he wants the novice to make. If he is imaginative, the coach invites his charges to watch videos of great baseball players, encouraging them to mimic the graceful swing of Ted Williams or the energetic base running of Roberto Clemente. He might introduce them to the lore of the game, relating stories of the 1976 World Series or the Yankees' 1927 season; he might pass on the wisdom and strategies of successful managers like Tony LaRussa and Leo Durocher and he might share the goofy eloquence of Casey Stengel. At the end of this process of apprenticeship, the young man, it is hoped, will see and think and move as a baseball player—and he will love the entire form of life that is baseball.

When I was nineteen, I entered an accelerated program in philosophy at Catholic University in Washington, D.C. This was the beginning of my apprenticeship to a whole series of masters and my entry into a world that I still find enchanting. One of my professors in the first year of the program required us all to write a two-page paper each week on a single argument from a Platonic dialogue. His critiques were ruthless and his grading was draconian: He would return these papers (that we thought ranked with the classics of Western thought) and they were covered with lines, question marks, exclamation points registering his shock, corrections of grammar, and, hovering over all of it, a desperately low grade. One of his most common remarks was "you are just repeating standard arguments here; you are not *philosophizing.*" What exactly philosophizing was none of us knew for sure, but the master's criticisms and humiliations were compelling us to find out.

In another seminar, a classmate of mine finished his ninety-minute critical presentation on the *Nichomachean Ethics* of Aristotle with the following rhetorical flourish: "What then are we to do with this text?" The professor, an avid Aristotelian, responded with devastating laconicism, "Perhaps we could read it more carefully." Once more, we were all being taught how to philosophize through a sort of *via negativa,* seeing precisely how *not* to approach a great thinker. In my final year, I took a course that bore the improbable title "The Analogy and Univocity of Being in the Middle Ages." About twenty of us met on Monday nights with a gentle genius whose native language, according to local legend, was Latin. Under his guidance we worked our way through the untranslated texts of Thomas Aquinas on this obscure but important issue in medieval epistemology, learning thereby an arcane and fascinating argot that linked us to our distant ancestors in the philosophical tradition.

The most memorable moment for me in the process of apprenticeship took place midway through my second year. After spending several months studying the issue of human freedom and divine foreknowledge, I raised a challenging question one day in class. My professor gave a brief response that I found inadequate and I pursued the issue. Looking at me with a combination of delight and surprise, he said, "Okay, make your case." With some trepidation, knowing that the entire class was listening avidly, I then began to philosophize—not so much commenting, learning, analyzing, but thinking on my own, following the argument where it led. Sensing my excitement, the professor kept guiding me, spurring me on with questions and comments. Suddenly, I was not studying a Platonic dialogue; I was in one, the teacher playing patient Socrates to my enthusiastic Thrasymachus. In that moment, still fresh in my memory all these years later, I entered, however tentatively and imperfectly, into the great conversation of Western philosophy; in the course of that exchange, I became a brother, however unworthy, to Parmenides, Augustine, Aquinas, Hobbes, and Kant.

What happened in the course of those three years was that I entered a new world. At the end of the program, I had, not simply new ideas and information, but new eyes and a new mind. I spoke a different language and related to my environment in a discernibly novel way. Those who knew me before my philosophical initiation realized that, afterward, something was radically and irreversibly changed in me. That is what a true apprenticeship does: it converts you.

The first words spoken by Jesus in the Gospel of John are addressed to two former disciples of John the Baptist: "What are you looking for?" They respond, somewhat surprisingly, "Where are you staying?" One might expect that, in the presence of this new Rabbi, they would have answered, "the truth" or "enlightenment" or "peace." Instead, they answer the question elliptically with another question—and this odd nonanswer is, in fact, the key to the exchange. What they seek, what they want to know, is not so much the teaching or wisdom or perspective of the Rabbi; they want to know *him*, more to the point, precisely where and how he lives. In the mystical vocabulary of John's Gospel, the verb *menein* (stay or remain) refers to the source of one's life and meaning. Thus, Jesus says that he *remains* with the Father, drawing his being from him, and he promises that he and the Father will *remain* with believers, feeding and nurturing them. Therefore, in asking where he "stays," the disciples are wondering about the form of life that sustains him, the source of his power. Obviously pleased by their response, Jesus says encouragingly, "Come and see." And then, John tells us, "They came and saw where he was staying, and they remained with him that day." In this simple and understated narrative, we see that the form of Christian discipleship is not primarily listening or learning but rather moving into the "house" of Jesus, discerning his mode of life, being with him at close quarters.

After this visit with the Rabbi from Nazareth, one of the disciples— now identified as Andrew—emerges with enthusiasm, running to his brother Simon and exclaiming, "We have found the Messiah." It seems clear that the body (staying with him) in a significant sense conditions the mind ("he is the Messiah"), the way of life shaping the conviction. Throughout his ministry, Jesus certainly teaches his disciples, but the instruction always takes place in the far more elemental context of *following* him, as though the learning would never take place uncoupled from the life. In a word, Jesus invites his friends into an apprenticing relationship with him, encouraging them to "catch" his way of being through proximity, imitation, and love. And the processes that we traced in our examples above—practicing, watching patiently, repeating, disciplining the body—are all at work as one is grafted onto Christ.

The Way of Jesus has, over the centuries, given rise to myriad expressions in theology, liturgy, architecture, poetry, ethics, and spirituality. Staying with Jesus has resulted in the *Summa theologiae* of Thomas Aquinas, the *Divine Comedy* of Dante, Köln Cathedral, the life of St. Antony of the desert, the silence and suffering of John of the Cross, and the radical nonviolence of Dorothy Day. What can be lost or forgotten is the connection of all of these to the originating apprenticeship, to the form of life from which they flowed. Thus, Dorothy Day's protest against a culture predicated upon militarism arose, not simply from her reflection, but from the conditioning of her body through a lifetime of spiritual exercises; and Thomas Aquinas said explicitly that the depth of his theological analysis came, not so much from the acuity of his mind, as from the intensity of his prayer. Both Dorothy and Thomas were disciples who had "come and seen"; both had stayed with the Master and learned through practice a new way of being in the world.

THE PROBLEM WITH MODERNITY

I have been dwelling on this embodied and distinctive character of Christianity precisely because I fear that, in recent years, it has been largely lost sight of. The culture that is Christianity, the sacred Way, expressed in movement, practice, and apprenticeship, has become, too often, a faint echo of the secular culture or a privatized and individualized set of convictions. The dense texture of the Christian Way has been worn thin, and its bright colors allowed to bleed into beige, and this attenuating has been due to an accommodation to the characteristically modern frame of mind: skeptical, rationalist, and dualist.

Let me illustrate this with one simple but vivid example. Every year, a group of students from the seminary at which I teach make a lengthy pilgrimage to the Holy Land. Their sojourn usually coincides with the Muslim penitential month of Ramadan. What strikes these American Catholic seminarians is how unavoidable, vivid, and "in your face" the practice of Ramadan is. Simply to walk outside one's residence and open one's eyes and ears is to know that something powerful is going on. Ramadan affects the way the people behave, move, gesture, do business, eat, and celebrate (one seminarian was especially impressed by the festiveness at the end of the month of fasting, which trumps any Fourth of July celebration he had ever experienced). The rhetorical questions that I have posed to my students when they share these impressions are as follows: If a foreign visitor came to largely Catholic Chicago during our penitential season of Lent, would he or she particularly notice anything? Would it be obvious in any sense that something of religious significance were underway? Would you see Lent in people's faces, bodies, movements? Does it change the way they buy and sell, advertise, eat and sleep? The answer to all of these questions is, alas, no. And that is the problem. What does indeed affect our bodies, what does mark the way we move and sleep and do business, what has profoundly written itself into our muscles and bones, is the modern ethos, the secular religion. And a beige, bland, attenuated Christianity is no match for such a powerful and focused counterculture.

BACK TO PRACTICES

A key insight of the American psychologist and philosopher William James is that the knowing mind is not to be isolated from the will, the passions, the desires, and the movements of the body. Sometimes, he says, knowledge comes in a flash of insight, but more usually it arrives as the result of a long and complex process involving attention, feeling, and above all, action. "We need only in cold blood *act* as if the thing in question were real, and keep acting as if it were real, and it will infallibly end by growing into such a connection with our life that it will become real." This is not "wishful thinking," but an acknowledgment that deep desire and the conformity of one's body can open one to a truth that would be, otherwise, unattainable.

A good friend of mine, an Irish priest, makes a yearly pilgrimage to Lough Derg, a penitential site in the northern part of the Irish Republic. In the Middle Ages, it was known as St. Patrick's Purgatory, and it was featured on maps from that period. Lough Derg is a place of intense Christian practice. The pilgrim arrives at an island in the middle of a small lake and is immediately instructed to remove his shoes. He is to spend the next three days barefoot. For the first day and night he performs a series of penitential and contemplative exercises—walking, kneeling, praying the rosary, confessing his sins—and he does this without benefit of sleep. During that first long night, if he begins to nod off, one of his fellow pilgrims pokes him awake. My friend has said that this fighting off of sleep is one of the most difficult and dramatic elements of the experience: "Sleep hunts you like an animal," he says. The next day, the same round of practices is repeated and, at the end of that day, the pilgrims are permitted to sleep. They leave the island the next afternoon, following a morning of prayer and fasting. Now there's some Celtic spirituality for you!

When I first heard a description of this process I was a bit horrified by its severity, but I have to admit that I was fascinated at the same time. Part of my interest came from the surprising *bodiliness* of it. At the end of a Lough Derg weekend, you would know, in your flesh, that you had been through something. And my friend confirmed this when he reflected on the curious practice of going barefoot: "Whatever happened to me during that experience," he said, "came up through my feet." It didn't so much "occur" to him or "dawn" on him; it invaded him bodily. And he would never have been so affected had he not actually gone to the place and walked the walk. In the spirit of William James, he *acted* his way to a deeper truth about himself and God.

Now what are some ways that we can *practice* the faith? How do we learn with our bodies and souls how to walk the Way, apprenticing to the

Master? Dorothy Day said that everything a baptized person does should be either directly or indirectly related to the corporal and spiritual works of mercy. A typically blunt and uncompromising remark from the founder of the Catholic Worker, the woman who, much to my delight, consistently confounds the keepers of the pure flames of liberalism and conservatism. I think what she means is that real Christian love has a form. It is not a bland abstraction about being kind or just, but rather a set of very concrete *things to do*. When someone says, "I'm for peace and justice," a legitimate comeback is "Whose peace and which justice?" After all, every political thinker from Plato to Karl Marx has a proposal about the nature of justice and peace. Dorothy Day's challenge is to put a distinctively Christian form to such abstractions: Christian justice and peace looks like something—it is giving food to the hungry (yes, that hungry man whom you meet downtown), and sheltering the homeless (yes, that street person whom you see at your rectory door), and visiting the sick (yes, that disabled child on your block), and counseling the doubtful (yes, that student struggling with his faith), and bearing patiently the troublesome (yes, that annoying woman whom you would love to be rid of).

Dorothy Day was uneasy with Roosevelt's New Deal precisely because it turned concern for the hungry, homeless, and unemployed over to the government, rendering at best abstract the particular Christian's own work of charity. I think that she would be delighted if we moved today from the bland rhetoric of peace and justice to the hands-on practices of the works of mercy. I think she would be pleased if we taught our kids the corporal and spiritual works and, more to the point, showed them how to perform those works, taking them to nursing homes and homeless shelters and into the rooms of the sick and the psyches of the suffering. When idealistic young people came to the Catholic Worker House in New York, full of romantic fantasies about being with the poor, Dorothy always told them, "There are two things you should know about the poor: they tend to smell and they are ungrateful." What she was communicating to them was the hard truth that the corporal and spiritual works of mercy cost—and that they will mark the body and soul. These exercises, these practices are, I think, ways of apprenticing to the Master, means of access to the culture of Christianity.

Another set of practices has to do with prayer. In the fall of 1993, I attended the Parliament of the World's Religions. It was a wonderful and colorful gathering of representatives from practically all of the faiths and spiritualities of the planet. At one of the sessions, I found myself next to an exotic figure, a man swathed in the robes of a guru, his head covered with a hood, his forehead marked with the distinctive Hindu symbol of the circle, and, in his hand, something like a rosary of prayer beads. When the talk was over, this mysterious figure raised his hand to pose a question. I turned to him expectantly, waiting to hear a mystic comment in the dulcet tones of India. Well, he sounded just like me. It turns out that he was an ex-priest from Cleveland! I had to smile because, though I couldn't prove it, something told me that when that man was a Catholic priest, he wouldn't have been caught dead wearing a cassock or Roman collar or carrying a rosary. Somehow, distinctive clothing, bodily practices, concrete forms of prayer are okay when they're found in an exotic context—but they are hopelessly retrograde when found in our own religious setting.

Can I use this little anecdote as a justification for saying a word in support of the much-maligned rosary as a practice? First, the rosary is concrete, densely objective—it is something that you hold in your hand. Anthony de Mello said that the simple feel of the rosary put him in a mystical frame of mind. How Jamesian! Second, the rosary is a way of disciplining what the Buddhists call the "monkey mind," the mind that leaps impatiently from branch to branch: "What's my next appointment? Why did she say that to me? What am I going to do about this? Do I have my tickets?" As long as that mind—skittish, superficial, obsessive—is dominating, we never move to the deeper realms of the soul. The rosary prayer, precisely as a mantra, is meant to dull and quiet the monkey mind and allow the depths to rise. Thirdly, the rosary slows us down. Even my Irish grandmother, who prayed the rosary at ninety-five miles an hour, took fifteen minutes to get through it! All the spiritual traditions witness to the fact that the soul likes to go slow. Again, the surface of the psyche is in constant motion, hurrying to its next thought, its next objective, its next accomplishment. But the spiritual center likes to see, to hear, to savor. Repeating the Hail Mary 50 times (or 150 times if the entire rosary is prayed), moving in a circle, not getting particularly anywhere, is the sort of thing the deep soul loves to do. And so does the body for that matter—just think of a slow romantic dance. In this regard, the rosary is like the stations of the cross or that ancient prayer form now in vogue: the walking of the labyrinth. Dr. Ewert Cousins has said that the genius of Catholicism is that it never threw anything away. How sad that so many Catholics run to the religions of the East and to the New Age to find embodied practices of prayer, when we have them in spades in our own ecclesial attic!

CONCLUSION

Christianity—like baseball, painting, and philosophy—is a world, a form of life. And like those other worlds, it is first approached because it is perceived as beautiful. A youngster walks onto the baseball diamond because he finds the game splendid, and a young artist begins to draw because she finds the artistic universe enchanting. Once the beauty of Christianity has seized a devotee, she will long to submit herself to it, entering into its rhythms, its institutions, its history, its drama, its visions and activities. And then, having *practiced* it, having worked it into her soul and flesh, she will know it. The movement, in short, is from the beautiful (it is splendid!) to the good (I must play it!) to the true (it is right!). One of the mistakes that both liberals and conservatives make is to get this process precisely backward, arguing first about right and wrong. No kid will be drawn into the universe of baseball by hearing arguments over the infield-fly rule or disputes about the quality of umpiring in the National League. And no person will be enchanted by the world of Christianity if all he hears are disputes about *Humanae vitae* and the infallibility of the Pope.

Christianity is a captivating and intellectually satisfying game, but the point is to play it. It is a beautiful and truthful Way, but the point is to walk it.

Part II

LITURGY

Chapter Four

LEX ORANDI, LEX VIVENDI:
THE LITURGY AS A SOURCE
FOR THE MORAL LIFE

A PREOCCUPATION OF MANY THINKERS OF THE MODERN PERIOD
was to discover a universal form of reason, a way of knowing that would
allow disputants to rise above their sectarian squabbles—which had become, by the seventeenth century, not only intellectually distressing but
politically ruinous—and come to agreement on basic truths. We can see
this project with special clarity in Descartes's resolution to call into question the whole of the confusing and conflicted tradition and to start
afresh on the basis of the *cogito*, an intuition at once deeply personal and
in principle available to all. It also becomes apparent in Kant's insistence
that a transcendentally aware philosophy could become as clear and transculturally valid as Newtonian physics. The modern universalizing style
is also on display in Schleiermacher's interpretation of theology as a reflection, not so much on the particularity of Christian doctrine, but on
the general experience of absolute dependency.

This frame of mind strongly influenced the modern understanding
of ethics as well. In his moral philosophy, Kant sharply distinguished the
exterior realm of custom, nature, and particular practice from the interior
dimension of the categorical imperative, insisting that the former has precisely nothing to do with the formulation of correct moral judgment and

the latter everything. Of course, the principal feature of the imperative (at least in its first formulation) is universality: "always act in such a way that the maxim of your will could become a universal law." This deontologism of Kant is usually seen as the polar opposite of consequentialism, but in fact certain consequentialisms bear a strong family resemblance to Kant's system in the measure that both are conditioned by the modern passion for the universal. A particularly clear illustration of this is in the moral theology of Timothy O'Connell. At the heart of O'Connell's system is the claim that the moral quality of a person's life is determined, not so much by his particular actions, but by the fundamental option taken at the deepest ground of his being, an option for or against God.[1] Any concrete calculations concerning the consequences of individual acts are, in fact, trumped, overshadowed by this basic orientation. Since grace is everywhere, the possibility of making the fundamental option is universal, and therefore, Christian ethics is finally human ethics, with a particular style of motivation: "Whoever says 'yes' from the depths of his being to anything, says 'yes' to everything. . . . In the deepest sense of the word, they have been saved." James McClendon archly comments, "Saved, in this case, without the gospel, without faith in Christ, without discipleship, without the way of the cross! Here moral universality has been purchased for Christian ethics, but at the expense of the particularity that comes from Jesus of Nazareth and his Way."[2] McClendon's comment applies, of course, as much to Kant's ethics as to O'Connell's, and it provides a helpful bridge to what I wish to explore in this chapter. I want to show that a properly Christian ethics is grounded in the dense particularity of the way of life opened up by Jesus Christ, especially as that form becomes evident in the fundamental Christian practice of the liturgy.

THE LITURGY AND MORAL FORMATION

Though I will be exploring the role of the liturgy in moral formation, I want to be clear from the outset that I labor under no illusion that this is the primary purpose of the liturgy. The proper *telos* of the liturgy is the praise and worship of God. At the same time, it is precisely because it is an act of worship that the liturgy also functions powerfully in the shaping of the moral self. Thomas Aquinas argued that the Mass is an act of justice, since in thanking and praising God, we render to him, in a necessarily inadequate but real way, what is due to him. By this very act, we are aligned with God, put into right relation to him. Dietrich von Hildebrand elaborated on the same connection in his study *Liturgy and Personality*. He held that the liturgy, by its very spiritual excellence, positively shapes the personalities of those who participate in it, so that one might adapt the famous adage and say *lex orandi, lex vivendi* (the law of praying is the law of living). In the first chapter of John's Gospel, two disciples of John the Baptist approach Jesus. When the Lord turns on them and says, "What are you seeking?" they reply with another question: "Where do you stay?" Obviously satisfied with this response, Jesus answers, "Come and see" (John 1:39). We hear then that they remained with him the rest of that day, commencing their time of discipleship and formation in the Way. The liturgy constitutes a privileged "staying with" the Lord Jesus, a participation in the world that he opens up. It is, as such, the practice that most completely embodies the kind of person that a disciple ought to be.

Now the advocate of modernity might intervene here and complain that such an approach will prove necessarily sectarian, or even, at the limit, relativistic. William Placher, one of the most articulate of the postliberal critics of modernity makes an illuminating distinction between the range of truth—which must of course be universal—and the access to truth, which can be, and usually is, particular.[3] Thus, at the very heart of Christian faith is the contention that the universal truth of things— God's own Logos—became known to us through the one whom Balthasar called the *concretissimus*. The range of the truth contained in Jesus is, of course, limitless, while the access to that truth was as finite and historically conditioned as the first-century Jew who suffered under Pontius Pilate. The same principle can be applied to the universal moral truth on offer in and through the uniquely textured particularity of the liturgy.

The Gathering

Throughout his massive study *Christian Origins and the Question of God*, New Testament scholar N. T. Wright argues that Jesus' proclamation of

the Kingdom of God was not a statement of abstract spiritual truth but
the announcement of a specific program that would have been clearly understood by the people to whom he spoke.[4] To say that the Kingdom of
God is at hand was to claim that Yahweh was commencing his great work
of gathering the tribes of Israel, forgiving their sins, and establishing
them as the "true pole of the earth," which is to say, the focal point for the
gathering of all of the peoples of the world into God's right order. In his
open table fellowship, his praxis of forgiveness, his works of healing, and
especially in his subversive act of cleansing the temple and calling for the
building of a new one, Jesus was acting out the Kingdom that he was announcing. Then, in a totally unexpected way, the gathering was affected,
the Kingdom fulfilled, through the event of the Paschal Mystery. Around
the body of the crucified and risen Jesus, around *Iesous Kyrios*, the tribes
of the world were to be gathered into friendship with God and peace with
one another.

As the privileged icon of the Paschal Mystery, the liturgy of the
church affects, fosters, and relies upon the gathering of the faithful. In
their dysfunction, human societies and institutions rest upon divisions,
separations, stratifications, plays of power, political antagonisms. The
Mass lures us onto a different ground. To the liturgy are invited people
from varying social strata, different economic and educational back-
grounds, a variety of races, both genders. This is, of course, an eschatological symbol, an icon of the Kingdom of God, a showing-forth of the
Christ in whom "there is no slave or free, no Jew or Greek, no male or fe-
male" (Gal. 3:28). When Dorothy Day was considering conversion to
the faith, she was deeply moved by the way the Church gathered for
worship: The Catholic Mass, she noticed, was the place where the immigrants and the poor knelt side-by-side with the wealthy, all equal in the
sight of God. Now this eschatological equality has nothing to do with a
political egalitarianism that would level all distinction and differentiation. Just as the gathered tribes of Israel remain unique tribes, so
Catholics assembled for the liturgy maintain their distinctiveness and
complementarity. When we come together for Mass, we do so as a body
of differentiated and interdependent organs; accordingly, laity, ministers,
musicians, deacon, and priest cooperate through a hierarchically struc-

tured but nondomineering order. This dynamic play between equality and ordered mutuality shapes the behavior and moral imagination of those who participate in it.

The ritual proper begins with a chant accompanying the procession of the ministers. Music and singing are not incidental to the liturgy or merely decorative; instead, they express and encourage the harmonic (many as one) relationship of those gathered, and, more importantly, they evoke the transcendent harmony in which the Mass is situated. There is, therefore, a tight connection between the opening chant and the sign of the cross that immediately follows it. The entire prayer of the Mass takes place within the musical *communio* of the trinitarian persons, within the love shared by Father, Son, and Holy Spirit. Catholic Christians do not pray *outside* of God, as mere petitioners or supplicants; on the contrary, we pray *in* God, *within* the relationality of the Trinity, standing with the Son as we invoke the Father through the Holy Spirit. The liturgy could not be practiced if God were simply a monolith, a supreme being among the many beings. Rather, the dynamic participation in the divine life is possible only because God is a family or *communio* of love, a play of Speaker, Word spoken, and Speech; of Singer, Song, and Singing; or in Bernard's arresting metaphor, of Kisser, Kissed, and Kiss. In the "space" opened up between these subsistent relations, we can, as it were, stand; or better, with the symphony of these primordial tones we can harmonize.

The British novelist Charles Williams, who along with C. S. Lewis and J. R. R. Tolkien was a member of the Oxford writers' group the Inklings, held that the core idea of Christianity is co-inherence, the sharing of being.[5] This principle is obviously on display in the one-in-the-otherness of the trinitarian persons, but it can also be glimpsed in the participation of all created things through the divine power and in the interdependence of the members of Christ's body. Christian metaphysics is neither a nominalist individualism nor a Spinozan monism, but an affirmation of the primordiality of relationship, being for the other. John Paul II has expressed the ethical implication of this ontology as "the law of the gift": that one's being increases and intensifies in the measure that it is given away in love.[6] This metaphysics and its accompanying morality are taught as worshippers gather under the sign of the trinitarian love.

After we have been situated in the spiritual space of *communio* and co-inherence, we are invited to call to mind our sins. G. K. Chesterton remarked, "There are saints in my religion, but that just means people who know that they are sinners."[7] In the biblical tradition, those who come close to God become more not less aware of their imperfection. Upon being called to the prophetic office, Isaiah protested, "Lord, I am a man of unclean lips" (Isa. 6:5), and upon seeing the miraculous draught of fishes, Peter said, "Leave me, Lord, I am a sinful man." Much as the smudges on a pane of glass become more apparent in the direct light, so the flaws of the soul spring more fully to consciousness in the light of God's holy presence. Thus the person who has entered into the dynamics of the liturgy, who has been situated in the context of the trinitarian relationality, becomes, perforce, a confessor of sin. All of this might seem rather obvious, but in the context of our ethical culture, it has a revolutionary power. The popular imagination is captivated by a casual Nietzscheanism, by which I mean a near-total valorization of the power of the will as such and a concomitant occlusion of the objectivity of the good. And if subjective choice itself is the ground of value, then there can be no flaw in the will except perhaps a failure of nerve, or in existentialist jargon, inauthenticity. The roots of this conviction stretch as far back as late-medieval voluntarism and its conception of freedom as absolute spontaneity, and its consequences are readily apparent today in our apotheosizing of personal decision. In its 1992 decision in the matter of *Casey v. Planned Parenthood of Southeastern Pennsylvania*, the U.S. Supreme Court determined that "at the heart of liberty is the right to define one's own concept of existence, of meaning, of the universe, of the mystery of human life."[8] The will trumps, determines, and gives value to, quite literally, everything. Therefore, when the church of Jesus Christ follows the liturgical practice of admitting to the fallenness of the will, it effects a tremendous cultural reversal.

The title to Augustine's greatest work has a double sense in Latin, for *confessio* can mean the confession of sin as well as the profession of praise. And as we have seen, the two dimensions of *confessio* are mutually implicative (it is the saint who knows that he is a sinner); therefore, it is reasonable that directly after the admission of sin, the liturgical community sings its praise of God. The Gloria of the Mass—at once both metaphysically precise and poetically evocative—is one of the most magnificent prayers in the Catholic tradition. I want to focus simply on the opening line, since it provides a remarkably succinct description of the well-ordered life. "Glory to God in the highest and peace to his people on earth," the liturgical assembly prays. The implication is that when God is given the central place in human affairs—when he is glorified in the highest—the political, social, and cultural life of human beings falls into peaceful harmony. Augustine commented that we should love God for his own sake and everything else for the sake of God, implying that trouble ensues when anything creaturely is given ultimate importance. At the beginning of the second part of the *Summa theologiae*, Thomas Aquinas shows that none of the finite goods that lure the will—money, material things, pleasure, power, fame—can ever satisfy the soul's longing for the infinite good and that therefore the proper use of those limited values is conditioned upon the soul's unambiguous orientation to God as the highest good.[9] In the *Nichomachean Ethics*, Aristotle argued that a friendship can endure only in the measure that the two friends, together, give themselves to a transcendent third—beauty, truth, God—that they love in common.[10] If their love remains focused only upon one another, their friendship will devolve into a mutual egotism. This philosophical and theological principle comes to plastic expression in the rose windows of the Gothic cathedrals. At the center of the rose, invariably, is a depiction of Christ, and then, wheeling around that center in ordered harmonies, are the myriad other medallions and pictures. The implication, once more, is that the placing of God in the center of one's concerns conduces to the proper arrangement of all one's other desires and interests.[11] In singing the Gloria, the liturgical community acknowledges this truth that peace here below is contingent upon the transcendent orientation of the will.

THE OPENING UP OF THE BIBLICAL WORLD

In his seminal book *The Nature of Doctrine: Theology in a Postliberal Age*, George Lindbeck distinguished between an experiential-expressivist and a cultural-linguistic model of doctrine.[12] In accord with the first conception, dogmas and theological statements are symbolic expressions of universal religious feelings. Schleiermacher's explanation of Christian doctrine as a manifestation of the sense of absolute dependency would be a classic instance of this form. According to the second type, doctrines are the rules that structure the grammar of distinctive religious language games. On Lindbeck's reading, the theology of Karl Barth, with its unapologetically biblical focus, manifests this cultural-linguistic understanding. For the Schleiermacherian tradition—represented in the twentieth century by both Paul Tillich and Karl Rahner—the theological enterprise is an act of hermeneutical archeology, the unearthing of the grounding experiences that lie behind and enliven the often abstract language of doctrine. For Barth, on the other hand, the point is not to get behind the language of Scripture and theology, but rather to explore the world that they open up and to learn thereby how to think, feel, imagine, and choose in a different way. Barth's persistent protest was that liberal theologians, in their eagerness to make religious talk intelligible, effectively domesticated it, drawing it into the reassuring confines of generic experience. In point of fact, he held, the purpose was just the opposite: to draw our world into the biblical world.

Many readers have complained that Tolkien's *Lord of the Rings* gets off to too slow a start, as they are compelled to move through one hundred pages describing Bilbo Baggins's birthday party. But Tolkien, in a rather Barthian vein, explained that this discipline was necessary in order to acclimate the reader to the absolutely novel universe that he had created; he had to learn how Middle Earth looks, sounds, smells, and how its denizens speak and choose. Relatedly, Tolkien consistently protested when people too readily sought to make of his story an allegory applicable to the present political and cultural scene. When people balked at the lengthy opening section of *The Name of the Rose*, Umberto Eco, in a very similar way, countered that his readers had to go through something like a Benedictine novitiate—long, a bit tedious, full of history and information—if they were to understand the universe in which his characters moved.[13]

In my judgment, the liturgy of the Word is fully intelligible only in this sort of cultural-linguistic framework. After we have been gathered under the sign of the trinitarian love, after we have confessed both our sin and our praise, we sit down in order to listen to the divine Word. If the biblical narratives, songs, poems, and histories simply express what we already know apart from them, then their place in the liturgy seems, at best, redundant. We listen to them, in fact, because we could not otherwise enter into the universe of meaning and experience that they create; we listen to them because we trust that they will revolutionize the world that we ordinarily inhabit. To develop this insight thoroughly would be to write an entire systematic theology, but I would highlight a few points. It is in the twinned stories of Israel and Jesus Christ that Christians learn their distinctive way of being in the world. In the creation narratives of the book of Genesis, for example, they know that they are a people whose being is received as a grace; in the liberation narratives of the book of Exodus, they realize that they have entered into a covenental relationship with a God who both relentlessly pursues them and respects their freedom; in the prophetic literature of the books of Isaiah, Jeremiah, Ezekiel, and Daniel, they know that the heart of the moral life is the hearing of the cry of the widow, the orphan, and the slave, and that this ethical commitment is undermined most thoroughly by the worship of false gods; in the narratives concerning Jesus, the God made flesh, they know that God's most intimate involvement with us enhances rather than diminishes our being; and in the still overwhelming story of Jesus' death on the cross and subsequent resurrection, they know that the deepest ground of existence *is* love, the radical being-for-the-other. All of this literature opens up the world of co-inherent love that, in turn, shapes the Christian moral self.

Alasdair MacIntyre has observed that the moral life of every society is ordered according to certain archetypes of human flourishing. Thus, in the ancient Greek and Roman societies, the soldier and the statesman were especially lionized, and in the Middle Ages, the scholarly monk and the pious king were particularly admired. In our culture, he says, the manager and the therapist—the untanglers of, respectively, unwieldy bureaucracies and unwieldy psyches—are the moral ideals.[14] For the Christian, none of these figures is determinative; rather, the ideal moral self as embodied, to varying degrees of perfection, in the great biblical prophets, patriarchs, heroes, and apostles, and, paradigmatically, in Christ himself, is normative. The kind of person that a Christian aspires to be is not intuited through universal reason, abstracting from particularity, but is rather displayed in the biblical narratives themselves. Aristotle argued that we come to know right moral action by watching the good man as he chooses and moves. I am making much the same argument here, except that the good man in question is not Aristotle's coolly moderate aristocrat, but rather Christ and those figures who, in different ways, constellate around him. It is therefore by attending to the stories in the context of the liturgy that the Christian understands the form of the moral life.

On experiential-expressivist assumptions, the homily is an act of correlation, the establishment of a link between the questions arising from general experience and the answers implied in the Scripture. But in a cultural-linguistic framework, the homily affects, not so much a correlation, as a reconfiguration; it attempts to draw the world of ordinary experience into the biblical world through an accurate description of the former and an imaginative and iconic display of the latter. This absorbing of the universe of the listener into the universe of the Bible is described succinctly in Justin Martyr's account of the structure of the liturgy, dating from around the year 150: "The memoirs of the apostles and the writings of the prophets are read. . . . When the reader has finished, he who presides over those gathered admonishes and challenges them to imitate these beautiful things."[15] In Balthasar's language, the homily is a demonstration of the peculiarly beautiful "theologic" that obtains in the biblical narratives, a way of thinking often radically at odds with conventional modes of assessing and deciding.

Having been drawn into the richly textured universe of the Bible, the worshippers are now in a position to profess their faith in it. The creed is statement of the fundamental pattern of the biblical form of life, and therefore the recitation or singing of it is far from an exercise in abstract theologizing. Instead, it is an existential declaration that that pattern should become the structuring pattern of one's own life. Once again, to develop this insight adequately would require the writing of an entire theology, but I will focus on just one aspect of it. The opening statement of the credo—I believe in one God, the Father the Almighty, the maker of heaven and earth—is a reaffirmation of the Old Testament Shema ("Hear O Israel, the Lord your God is God alone"), a declaration that formed the people of Israel and provided the ethical foundation for their lives. Joseph Ratzinger has commented that this proclamation of monotheistic faith is subversive in nature, since it implies that no nation, state, political party, leader, ideology, or culture, indeed nothing in the created realm, can be of ultimate concern.[16] The Credo therefore, like the Shema, relativizes and places in question all rival gods, all powers that would seek, in a final sense, to order human life.

The liturgy of the Word concludes with the offering of the prayers of the faithful, and this liturgical exercise, too, has a strong ethical overtone. What the members of the worshipping community have come to know through the gathering and then through the display of the biblical world is that they are not merely a collectivity of like-minded people, but rather a body, an organism of interdependent cells, molecules, and systems. The *communio* of the trinitarian persons is mirrored in the *communio* of the fields of force that constitute the body of Christ. But a principal way that this corporate identity is expressed is in the act of praying for one another, in the explicit acknowledgment that the suffering of any one member of the body is the suffering of all. Stanley Hauerwas has insisted that the prayers we offer for others are also a spur to activity on their behalf. Once the worshipping community knows who is sick or suffering, they are compelled to act.[17] Dorothy Day said that everything a baptized Christian does should be directly or indirectly related to the corporal and spiritual works of mercy, those acts by which the body of Christ is built up. Among the latter is praying for the living and the dead, and it is with this work that the first great part of the liturgy draws itself to a close.

THE LAW OF THE GIFT

The essential dynamic of the Christian life can be expressed, as we saw, in terms of the law of the gift: One's being is confirmed and enhanced in the measure that one gives it away in love. The life of the prodigal son dried up when he demanded to make the goods of his father his own possession; it was restored when he returned to the circle of grace. Jesus said that clinging to one's life is the surest means of losing it, and he told his followers, "What you have received as a gift, give as a gift." When the prophet Elijah found the widow of Zaraphath at the end of her strength and with oil and wheat sufficient only for a last meal before death, he told her to make him a cake. And when she took the risk of the gift, she found that her provisions were replenished. The deepest ground of this principle is, as we've seen, in the gift-character of existence. God is a *communio* of persons whose very to-be is a sheer relationality, a giving and receiving of gifts, and creation is nothing but the overflow from the intensity of the divine generosity and communality: *bonum diffisivum sui*. The liturgy of the Eucharist is an ecstatic display of this graceful quality of both divine and created being.

Before proceeding with an analysis of this part of the Mass, however, we have to deal with an important objection raised by a number of postmodern philosophers in regard to the coherency of the category of gift-giving. Jacques Derrida and Jean-Luc Marion have entered into this conversation, but the aporia of the gift was first raised by Marcel Mauss in 1950.[18] His argument is simple but penetrating. It appears to belong to the nature of a gift that it be, on the part of the giver, utterly gratuitous and non-self-interested, and on the part of the recipient, without obligation of reciprocity. However, when a person consciously gives a gift to another, it seems as though he inevitably establishes his own moral superiority vis-à-vis the recipient and awakens in him the obligation to reciprocate, at the very least through gratitude. Even the anonymous gift can fill the giver with a sense of pride in regard to the many nongivers around him, and it can still fill the recipient with an open-ended and therefore more frustrating sense of obligation. The upshot is that all gift-giving is caught in the rhythm of an economic exchange, a ceaseless quid -pro quo, and remains, to that degree, at odds with itself, incapable of meeting the demands of its own nature. But if this is the case, then any claim that gift-giving is ontologically basic seems absurd. Any gift that God might give would turn into *Gift*, poison for his creatures.

The only way around this objection is to insist on the radical self-sufficiency of God vis-à-vis creation, or to state the same thing more technically, on the merely logical quality of God's relation to the world that he has made. Aquinas specified that a real relation is one that affects the being of the two elements that enter into the relationship (like a cathedral wall and a flying buttress), while a merely logical relation is one that signals a shift, not *in re*, but only in one's mode of understanding (as when a person moves from the left to the right side of a stationary pillar). Creation, for Aquinas, is a mixed relation. It is real in the fullest sense of the term as far as the creature is concerned, for it affects the creature's being in the most radical way, but it is purely logical as far as God is concerned, since God neither gains nor loses any actuality through the relationship.[19] The merely logical character of God's rapport with the world—so criticized by many contemporary theologians—is, in point of fact, the way past the dilemma of the gift pointed out by Mauss and others. God cannot be caught in an economic exchange because he can in no ontologically real way benefit from either our gifts or our gratitude; nor can he be hurt by the lack thereof. Because he is not really related to the world, God can—indeed must—give in a totally non-self-interested manner, and if love means willing the good of the other as other, then God's acts of self-offering on behalf of the world are loving in the fullest possible sense. Further, whatever gift is given back to God by a creature must necessarily redound to the benefit of the creature, since it cannot add to the divine being. The gifts of God, therefore, even as they awaken gratitude in those who receive them, involve neither party in the vicious cycle of a mutually obliging economic exchange; rather, they ground a loop or cycle of grace between the divine and the nondivine. Our being is enhanced in the measure that it participates in and approaches (albeit asymptotically) the perfection of God's gift-giving. It is this metaphysical and spiritual law that governs the second half of the liturgy.

After the prayers of the faithful, the gifts of bread, wine, and water are presented by the people and are then offered to God by the priest in the Berakah. These offerings represent, of course, the very lives of those who have gathered for worship. Though modernity is predicated upon the assumption that the autonomous individual is basic, Christian metaphysics has a different orientation, for it assumes the radically received character of creaturely being. Everything that we have, indeed our very existence, has been given to us as a grace, and the moral concomitant of this ontological conviction is the offering of our being in an act of gratitude. It was in the light of this perception that Paul could tell the Thessalonian church to "dedicate yourselves to thankfulness" and that Ignatius of Loyola, over and against the language of the rights of the autonomous individual being formulated by his contemporary Thomas Hobbes, could pray, "Take Lord, receive, all my liberty, my memory, my understanding, my entire will. You gave them to me, and I give them back to you." The giving back to the source what the source has given to us—the inclusion in the loop of grace—is what the offertory of the liturgy symbolizes and embodies.

Between the preface and the eucharistic prayer proper comes the Sanctus prayer. The triple repetition of "holy" places us, once again, in the context of the trinitarian *communio*, and the association of our song with the song of the angels signals a higher creaturely *communio* in which we are called to participate. Focused together in their praise of the transcendent third, the angels achieve a peaceful coexistence—symbolized by their harmonious singing—which serves as a model of the beautiful community here below. Aquinas dedicated over twenty rather lengthy questions in the *Summa theologiae* to a consideration of the angels, and the liturgy, with similar seriousness and persistence, compels us to contemplate the angelic order.

With the great prayer of consecration, the liturgy reaches its climax, for here the law of the gift is on fullest display. What had been given to us was given back to God and then, transformed through God's power into the very body and blood of Jesus, it is presented back to God. The coinherence of God and the world, the mutual indwelling of created and uncreated freedom, is consummately realized in this exchange. But, once again, since nothing offered to God benefits him, the eucharistic sacrifice breaks, as it were, against the rock of the divine self-sufficiency and becomes food for us. The faithful do not simply contemplate God's love made flesh; they eat it and drink it, thereby becoming conformed to it. For so many of the Fathers of both the East and the West, the proper goal of the Christian life is nothing as bland as moral excellence or growth in virtue, but rather *theiosis*, deification, becoming God. This is why, of course, the doctrine of the real presence is so important for the moral and spiritual life. Were Christ's eucharistic presence merely symbolic, a function of our meaning-making capacity, then we would not be transformed through a participation in it. The condition for the possibility of deification through the Eucharist is that Christ has ontologically changed the elements of bread and wine through *his* meaning-making capacity.[20]

As the faithful come forward for the reception of Christ's body and blood, the corporate quality of the Church is made specially manifest. The Church, as we saw, is not simply a congregation of spiritually interested people, but instead, according to Paul's vivid suggestion, a body of interdependent members, drawing its life from Christ the head. Therefore, when they come together to the altar to partake of Christ, the faithful are, necessarily, drawn together and animated in their identity as a co-inherent company. They realize that they are connected to each other by bonds of love that transcend any social, cultural, or political divisions that might separate them. And they thereby come to know that the true ethical universality is had, not through the abstraction of the categorical imperative, but through the *concretissimum* of Christ's living body.

THE SENDING

After the faithful have been gathered under the sign of the trinitarian love, after they have confessed their sin and their praise, after they have been drawn into the particularity of the biblical world, after they have been included in the rhythm of the law of the gift even to the point of deification, they are sent out. No biblical figure is ever given an experience of God without receiving, at the same time, a commission. Moses spies the burning bush, hears the sacred name of Yahweh, and is then told to go back to Egypt to liberate his people; Isaiah enjoys a mystical encounter with God amidst the splendor of the temple liturgy and is then sent to preach; Saul is overwhelmed by the luminosity of the risen Jesus and is subsequently called to apostleship. Balthasar has argued that the beautiful, by its nature, calls and sends: It stops the viewer in his tracks (aesthetic arrest) and then plants within him a desire to speak to others of what he has seen.[21] This electing and commissioning quality is unsurpassably evident when the beauty in question is the divine perfection. What we have been tracing here is the process by which the liturgy effectively calls the faithful, drawing them into the world of Jesus Christ. The final moment in the liturgical celebration is the sending that necessarily follows the call.

The priest blesses the people with the sign of Christ's cross and then he says, "The Mass is ended, go in peace to love and to serve the Lord." They have been deified through a contemplation of the divine beauty and through the eating and drinking of the divine *communio* and now they are sent out to bring others to that same splendor and to that same circle of co-inherence. The implications of this sending for Christian ethics are weighty. In the classical ethics of Aristotle, the moral subject orders his life in accord with the ends that he has discovered through theoretical and practical reason and with the help of the virtues that he has cultivated through careful habituation. He remains rather serenely in command of his life, engaging, to use Michel Foucault's language, in a "care of the self." Though Christian theologians have certainly made use of the classical ethical form, they can hardly rest easy with its construal of the moral self. The Christian ethical actor is someone who has been called, named, ordered, and sent by a Person outside of himself. Emmanuel Levinas catches the biblical tone when he comments that Abraham does not, like the Aristotelian philosopher, say, "Here is what I shall do," but rather, "Here I am, Lord; I am ready."[22] In Levinas's French, Abraham, when called by Yahweh, replies, *"me voici,"* placing himself in the accusative. The Christian moral self, as shaped by the liturgy, listens, therefore, to the voice of the Other who is God and of the suffering others with whom God, in Christ, has identified himself: "Whatsoever you do to the least of my brothers, you do to me." He does not so much dispose himself to act as he allows himself to be acted upon; his moral choice is not so much in the nominative as in the accusative case.

The three magi, after encountering the Christ child and offering him their gifts of gold, frankincense, and myrrh, returned, the Bible tells us, "by a different route." The church fathers commented that this is only natural, since no one comes to Jesus and goes back the same way he came. So the worshipper who comes to Christ's liturgy to be gathered, transformed by contact with the scriptural world, and divinized in the loop of grace, is sent home by a different route. The worship of God conduces to the transformation of the self: *lex orandi, lex vivendi.*

NOTES

1. Timothy O'Connell, *Principles for a Catholic Morality* (New York: Seabury Press, 1978), 105f.

2. James William McClendon, *Ethics: Systematic Theology,* vol. 1 (Nashville: Abingdon Press, 1986), 53–54

3. William Placher, *Unapologetic Theology: A Christian Voice in a Pluralistic Conversation* (Louisville: Westminster John Knox Press, 1989), 123–24.

4. See especially N. T. Wright, *Jesus and the Victory of God* (Minneapolis: Fortress Press, 1996), 199–202.

5. Charles Williams, *Charles Williams: Essential Writings in Theology and Spirituality,* ed. Charles Hefling (Cambridge: Cowley Publications, 1993), 17–18.

6. See George Weigel, *Witness to Hope: The Biography of Pope John Paul II* (New York: Harper Collins, 1999), 136–37.

7. G. K. Chesterton, *Alarms and Discursions* (London: Methuen, 1924).

8. *Casey v. Planned Parenthood of Southeastern Pennsylvania,* 112 Sup. Ct. 2791 at 2807.

9. Thomas Aquinas, *Summa theologiae,* Ia IIae, q. 2.

10. Aristotle, *Nichomachean Ethics,* bk. 8, ch. 3 in *The Basic Works of Aristotle,* ed. Richard McKeon (New York: Random House, 1941), 1061.

11. Robert Barron, "God as Artist," *Angelicum* 80 (2003): 409.

12. George Lindbeck, *The Nature of Doctrine: Religion and Theology in a Postliberal Age* (Philadelphia: Westminster Press, 1984), 31–41.

13. Umberto Eco, *The Name of the Rose: Postscript* (New York: Harcourt Brace, 1983), 520.

14. Alasdair MacIntyre, *After Virtue* (Notre Dame: University of Notre Dame Press, 1984), 30.

15. Cited in *The Catechism of the Catholic Church,* 1345 (New York: Doubleday, 1995), 374.

16. Joseph Ratzinger, *Introduction to Christianity* (San Francisco: Ignatius Press, 1990), 73–76.

17. Stanley Hauerwas, *Sanctify Them in the Truth: Holiness Exemplified* (Nashville: Abingdon Press, 1998), 163.

18. See John D. Caputo, *The Prayers and Tears of Jacques Derrida: Religion without Religion* (Bloomington: Indiana University Press, 1997), 161ff., and Robyn Horner, *Rethinking God as Gift: Marion, Derrida, and the Limits of Phenomenology* (New York: Fordham University Press, 2001), esp. 12–15.

19. See Robert Sokolowski, *The God of Faith and Reason: Foundations of Christian Theology* (Notre Dame: University of Notre Dame Press, 1982), 8–9.

20. Herbert McCabe, *God Still Matters* (London: Continuum, 2002), 120–22.

21. Hans Urs von Balthasar, *Theo-drama: Theological Dramatic Theory*, vol. 2, *Dramatis Personae: Man in God* (San Francisco: Ignatius Press, 1990), 21–35.

22. Captuo, *Prayers and Tears*, 205–11.

The Liturgical Act and the Church of the Twenty-First Century

In April of 1964, Romano Guardini wrote an open letter to Johannes Wagner in connection with the Third German Liturgical Conference. The missive bore the title *Der Kultakt und die Gegenwärtige Aufgabe der Liturgischen Bildung* (The Cult Act and the Present Task of Liturgical Education). Toward the end of this somewhat rambling text, Guardini delivered himself of the line that has inspired much hand-wringing and impassioned commentary over the past thirty-five years: "would it not be better to admit that man in this industrial and scientific age, with its new sociological structure, is no longer capable of a liturgical act?" What I would like to do here is to take up this provocative question, seeking first to understand it from Guardini's perspective and then to ask it again in our present context. Are we so-called postmoderns in the same bind as Guardini's moderns, or are we, perhaps, more "capable" of the rhythms, gestures, and attitudes that constitute the *Kultakt*? As a bridge between these two sections of this chapter, I will briefly explore Thomas Aquinas's doctrine of worship as an act of religion, which is to say, a virtue in connection with justice. It is my conviction that Thomas's spare account of liturgy as a moral act illumines both Guardini's liturgical theology and our postmodern situation.

GUARDINI'S *KULTAKT* AND THE MODERN PERSON

What I have noticed in so many of the commentaries on Guardini's 1964 letter is a quality of dismay, even shock: How could one of the pioneers of the liturgical movement have said something so discouraging, especially in the immediate wake of the publication of *Sacrosanctum Concilium*, seen by many as the culmination of all of the fondest hopes of the liturgical reformers? And how, as *Gaudium et Spes* itself was in the process of preparation, could this Vatican II *peritus* have so disparaged the modern person? The usual tack of the mainstream interpreters is to say that Guardini had, by 1964, grown a bit cranky and reactionary and had begun to turn away from the optimism of his youth. One can find a similar interpretive key used to explain the supposed anomalies in the later writings of Ratzinger, de Lubac, Balthasar, Congar, and others. But what strikes me is how remarkably congruent the 1964 question is with the entire corpus of Guardini's writings on liturgy and modernity which spans six decades.

In the course of his letter, Guardini identifies three elements that are essential to the *Kultakt*: attention/contemplation, the integration of body and soul, and communality/participation. He then implies, without providing a detailed justification, that the typically modern attitude is at odds with all three, thereby prompting the famous rhetorical question. I would like to supplement the necessarily sketchy treatment in the letter of 1964 by exploring these three themes and their relation to modernity as articulated in Guardini's earlier and more substantive writings.

One of Guardini's most powerful influences was Goethe, and not simply in the great man's poetry and drama, but especially in his science. Along with Hamaan and Herder, Goethe was one of the earliest critics of the aggressively analytical form of rationality characteristic of modernity. This invasive and finally arrogant mode of reason was exemplified, for him, in the method of Newton. The Newtonian scientist would rip a plant from the ground, place it under bright lights, dissect it, and compel it to answer his questions. Goethe felt that this method might yield certain insights, but would never give rise to real knowledge of the object, precisely because it wrestled the object into submission, forcing it into the small, well-lighted space of the subject. In contrast, Goethe proposed a far more contemplative form of science, one that allowed the object to remain in its natural environment and to follow its own rhythms, raising and answering its own questions. Essential to the Goethean method is quiet, attentiveness, and humility before the object of study. In the sixth of his *Letters from Lake Como*, entitled "Mastery," Guardini shows his preference for this approach: "I have come to realize so clearly these days that there are two ways of knowing. The one sinks into a thing and its context. The aim is to penetrate, to move within, to live with. The other, however, unpacks, tears apart, arranges in compartments, takes over and rules."[1] As he meditates on this distinction in the setting of Lake Como, he realizes that what accounts for the beauty and integrity of the traditional architecture of the place is just this Goethean concern for the living rapport between earth, water, and building materials. And what he fears is the increasing prominence of the mastering Newtonian attitude, according to which "materials and forces are harnessed, unleashed, burst open, altered and directed at will."[2] The result of this invasion, he thinks, is an easily discernible decrease in the quality of more contemporary architecture and design.

It is the Goethean that Guardini urges again and again as the proper attitude in the liturgical context. In a remarkable series of meditations on liturgical elements and objects—the altar, the lit candle, holy water, the church door, bread and wine—Guardini insists that the meaning of these things will emerge only to the one who gazes at them with endless patience and reverent attention.[3] And we find something similar in the well-known chapter on liturgy as play in his early text *Vom Geist der Liturgie* (The Spirit of the Liturgy). As playful or purposeless, the liturgy is like a work of art that has no other raison d'être than to be itself. But such useless things demand a particularly focused attentiveness: "People who contemplate a work of art should not expect anything of it, but they should be able to linger before it, moving freely, becoming conscious of their own better nature."[4] So the participant in the sacred ballet of the liturgy must put aside his more Newtonian tendencies and learn again how to gaze. The desire to master nature—the stated goal of the archetypically modern method of Descartes—is therefore antipathetic to a properly liturgical consciousness.

The second theme that emerges in the 1964 letter—the union of body and soul—also has a long history in the works of Guardini, but it is nowhere more fully developed than in his 1923 text *Liturgische Bildung* (Liturgical Education). In the chapter entitled "Body and Soul," Guardini launches into a spirited attack on all forms of Neoplatonic, Manichaean, or Puritanistic dualism that would denigrate or set aside the body in favor of the spiritual faculty. "What assumes a liturgical posture, what prays, sacrifices and acts is not 'the soul,' not 'interiority,' but the human being. The entire human being bears the liturgical action."[5] Drawing on Thomas Aquinas, Guardini holds that the soul, though it has its own spiritual integrity, nevertheless remains *forma corporis* and the "living entelechy of the body."[6]

Now it is not only Neoplatonism and its descendents that propose a type of dualism. One of the great marks of the modern Cartesian project is a radical separation of body and soul, the latter knowable through a clear and distinct intuition and the former belonging to the dubious realm of the sensible. And this drastic separation between the *res cogitans* and the *res extensa*, of course, gave rise to the characteristically modern prejudice in favor of the *Innerlichkeit* that arouses Guardini's suspicions. Hence Spinoza, Kant, and Hegel all favor a religion of reason over and against the sensual and historically conditioned positive religions; and Schleiermacher, sharing that same prejudice, seeks the source of faith in the deepest ground of one's interiority, in the feeling of absolute dependency. An exaggerated *Innerlichkeit* was, for Guardini, a problem in certain forms of preconciliar piety, but it was, even more dramatically, a problem at the heart of the modern project, particularly in its religious expression.

And the third motif from the letter of 1964—the primacy of community in the liturgy—is also a consistent theme in Guardini's texts. Guardini belonged to that generation who, inspired by the Tübingen school of the nineteenth century, reclaimed the concept of the *Corpus Christi mysticum* in connection with ecclesiology. Moving away from secular political models, Guardini and his colleagues employed organic images in their articulation of the nature of the Church. Thus we find this splendid text in *The Spirit of the Liturgy*:

The faithful are actively united by a vital and fundamental principle common to them all. That principle is Christ himself; His life is ours; we are incorporated in Him; we are his Body, *Corpus Christi mysticum*. The active force which governs this living unity, grafting the individual on to it, granting him a share in its fellowship . . . is the Holy Ghost. Every individual Catholic is a cell of this living organism or a member of this Body.[7]

The liturgy is the place where the identity of this living body is on display and acted out. And this is why "the liturgy does not say 'I' but 'We,'" and why the "we" includes, not only those present at the celebration, but all believers in Christ across time and space, including those who have found their dwelling place among the *Communio sanctorum*. Guardini's contemporary, Henri de Lubac, made this same point even more dramatically when he argued, in his book *Catholicisme*, that every dogma of Christianity—Incarnation, redemption, creation, Eucharist, the Church—is social and not individualist in nature.

What was motivating this strong reemphasis on communality and connectedness? To a large extent, it was the stress placed by modernity on the primacy and autonomy of the individual, both in knowledge and action. In the *Discourse on Method*, Descartes makes it abundantly clear that his intercourse among the various cultures and his conversations with his fellows led, at the epistemological level, only to confusion and frustration. Only when he retreated into that famous heated room in Ulm, and withdrew into the silence of his interiority, did Descartes find the indubitable knowledge he was seeking. Hobbes, breaking with a centuries-long tradition that saw the common good as the focus of political life, held that authentic political science must be grounded in the "rights" of the fearful individual; and Kant maintained that the starting point for morality is not in the outside realm of motivation, consequences, and interdependent activity, but in the luminosity of the moral law shining at the heart of the individual will. All of this obviously shaped the modern consciousness, even in the arena of theology and spirituality. To take but one example among many, Paul Tillich's theology of correlation sought a correspondence between the truths revealed in the biblical tradition and the anxious concerns of the post-Freudian twentieth-century individual. Thus, it is not difficult to see why Guardini felt that, in his individualism, the modern person was incapable of the essentially communal act of the liturgy.

We have filled out a bit the sketch that Guardini offered in his letter of 1964, but if we want to get to the heart of his argument concerning the incompatibility of the modern consciousness and the liturgical act, we have to move beyond the three elements mentioned in the letter and find the Ur-problem of which they are but expressions. Guardini's principal complaint about modernity has to do with the abuse of power. The characteristically modern person, in his darkest incarnation, exercises raw power, unanchored to nature, ethical values, or the commands of God, and this has made him, paradoxically, the slave of power: "People today hold power over things, but we can assert confidently that they do not yet have power over their own power."[8] Once power is seized for its own sake—Descartes's mastery over nature again—it becomes a fetish and then a sort of Frankenstein's monster, threatening the very one who created it: "When we examine the development as a whole, we cannot escape the impression that nature as well as man himself is becoming ever more vulnerable to the domination—economic, technical, political, organizational—of power."[9] There is, to be sure, something distinctive to the modern abuse of power, but in its essence, it is nothing new. Guardini sees power as the central category in the biblical story of the Fall. Made in the image and likeness of God, the human being was given nearly free rein in the garden of creation, naming the animals and eating the fruit of all the trees but one. This prelapsarian liberty and ranginess is an icon of the proper exercise of human power. Linked to God and obedient to his commands, the first humans were the lords and stewards of creation and not its masters.

At the heart of the serpent's temptation, on Guardini's reading, is a lure in the direction of pure and arbitrary power: "The serpent, a symbolical figure for Satan, confuses man by misrepresenting the fundamental facts of human existence: the essential difference between Creator and created; between Archetype and image; between self-realization through truth and through usurpation."[10] The same theme is hinted at in *Letters from Lake Como*, where Guardini insistently complains about a technological culture that succeeds only in getting us places faster without giving us the foggiest notion of what we should do when we get there. The will to power, in Nietzsche's phrase, or the *libido dominandi* in Augustine's language, is the result of the ontological confusion that follows from severing the link between creature and Creator.

Christianity proposes a solution to this ontological/moral problem, indeed the only possible solution, for it speaks to us of the humility of God. In the face of the various abuses of power, sages and philosophers had indeed proposed the virtues of moderation and self-control, but these are only pseudosolutions, since they are "attempts to erect a stand, an order within disordered existence." Salvation in the proper sense, Guardini argues, had to involve a remaking of creation itself from within by the one powerful enough to effect such a transformation. In other words, it required a God humble enough to become a creature. When Jesus, the Son of God, obeyed the will of his Father even to the point of death, he disclosed the true nature of power as humility, a turning to the other in love, and in this he broke the spell of arbitrary power that had bedeviled the race since Eden. It is important to note that Jesus is not simply a creature acknowledging his radical dependence on the Creator; he is God himself showing that obedience belongs to the very nature of God, that ultimate power and the *kenosis* of love coincide.

In light of this Christology, it is easy to see why Guardini was so enamored of the idea of the mystical body. The hold of arbitrary power over us can be dissolved only in the measure that we are grafted onto the living embodiment of the divine humility. It is never simply a matter of taking in a new teaching; it is becoming someone different through organic participation. And, as we have seen, such participation is effected precisely in the sacraments, including and especially the eucharistic liturgy. Thus we come to the heart of the matter and to the fullest illumination of Guardini's 1964 letter. At the center of the liturgy is the establishment of a new order, an ontological realignment, a correction of the disorder born of the abuse of power:

> Man is not constructed to be complete in himself and, in addition, capable of entering into relations with God or not as he sees fit. His

very essence consists in his relation to God and what he understands by that relationship; how seriously he takes it and what he does about it are the determining factors of his character. . . . God is the Reality on whom all other realities, including the human, are founded. When existence fails to give him his due, existence sickens.[11]

Liturgy is the act by which we participate in Christ, the humility of God, and thereby render God what is due to him, reestablishing the right *ordo* between Creator and creature. The reason that the modern person finds this act so difficult is that it is healthy, and his existence has become sick through self-aggrandizement.

AN AQUINAS INTERLUDE

The language of rendering to God his due calls to mind the theologian whose thought would have been profoundly formative for any Catholic of Guardini's generation, namely Thomas Aquinas. Thomas discusses the worship of God in the course of the massive second part of the *Summa theologiae*, which deals with the moral life or the journey back to the cause from which all things have come. Accordingly, worship, like any other moral act, is situated, for Thomas, in a richly ontological context: somehow it has to do with the establishment of a right order in being. Exploring Aquinas's treatment of this motif will shed light, I hope, on Guardini's idea of the liturgy as a reordering of the creature in relation to God.

What we call *liturgy*, or the formal public worship of God, Thomas places under the heading of religion, which is further specified as one of the potential parts of justice, that is to say, a virtue annexed to, but falling short of, the fullness of justice. Following Cicero, Aquinas says that justice is the virtue by which we "render to another his due" and that religion, the act by which we "offer service and ceremonial rites or worship to some superior nature," is a specification of this virtue in regard to God.[12] Now it is at this point that Aquinas affects his customary Christian radicalization of a classical philosophical source. While Cicero can speak of the divine as a "superior nature" to which obeisance and honor are due, Thomas must speak of God as the Creator of all finite existence ex nihilo and hence as the one to whom absolutely everything is due.

In his great texts on creation from the first part of the *Summa theologiae*, Aquinas is at pains to describe creation as an absolutely unique act, distinguishing it carefully from all forms of motion, change, or manipulation. Since God is the sheer act of to-be, whatever exists apart from God owes the entirety of its being to God, participating in the source of existence as the light in the atmosphere participates in the light of the sun. Since all finite reality comes from God, there is, in creation, no substrate upon which God works or no subject that receives the causal influence of God. Creation is not in time, since time is a creature; it does not occur in the arena of space, since space is a creature. Unlike any of the mythic or philosophical accounts of beginnings, there is nothing that God has to fight against or wrestle into submission. Rather, as John Milbank has seen, *creatio ex nihilo* is an utterly nonviolent act. When, in the disputed question *De potentia Dei*, he is pressed to specify the "locus" of the act of creation, Thomas adopts Zen-like language: "that which receives creation is created by the very act that it receives."[13] Later in that same text he utilizes what can only be called metaphysical poetry: "Creation is a kind of relation to the Creator with freshness of being." And since the creature is nothing else than this divine act by which it comes into being, it must follow that the creature, as such, *is* a relationship to the divine source, an unalloyed receptivity, an acceptance of the nonviolent intervention of God. Gerard Manley Hopkins expressed much the same thing when he spoke, in "The Grandeur of God," of "the dearest freshness deep down things."

What therefore is worship, the just act by which we thank God for the gift of our total existence, but the ritual affirmation of our creatureliness, our sheer relationality to the to-be of God? What is it but the gesture which sums up our being, rightly construed? This is why Thomas speaks of religion as the "chief of the moral virtues": As the acting-out of our deepest ontological identity, it is the act which informs, conditions, and directs all the other acts that order us to God. And therefore it is not inappropriate to characterize the liturgy as the proper setting for the

Christian moral life, the place where the virtues, in their authentically Christian form, appear and find their purpose. As many have pointed out, the interpretations of the virtues proffered by Aristotle and Cicero are transformed in a Christian setting, and here we can see the reason for it. The pagan virtues, including religion itself, are transfigured by their contextualization in the liturgy, that is to say, in the ritual acknowledgment of creation from nothing.

How might the follower of Aquinas respond to Guardini's question concerning the compatibility of the religious act and the modern consciousness? He or she might situate the question in the broader context of the breakdown of the participation metaphysics that made possible the distinctively modern construal of the subject. When the creature is seen as deriving its existence in the most intimate sense possible from God, then creaturely being, though really distinct from God, is in an analogical relationship to the divine reality. But this means, in turn, that creaturely being is, by nature, ecstatic and not autonomous. It furthermore implies that every creature is connected through the center of its being to every other creature, so that Francis's statement about brother sun and sister moon could be not only a charming bit of poetry but a rather exact metaphysical remark. Now when this conception began to unravel, first through Duns Scotus's introduction of a univocal sense of being and then through the Reformers' distantiation of God, a properly secular realm emerged, that is to say, an arena of finite being that could ground itself. The breakdown of an analogical conception of being led also to a fundamentally antagonistic social ontology, the link between creatures having been eliminated. Thus, Descartes was right in holding to the autonomy and self-validation of the individual, and Hobbes was right in seeing social life as, by nature, "nasty, brutish, and short." What makes the modern successors of Descartes and Hobbes incapable of the liturgical act? The disciple of Aquinas might respond: the loss of a participation/creation metaphysics and hence the attenuation of any sense of an ecstatic and communitarian self.

Both Guardini and Aquinas signal the unavoidable difficulty of the liturgical act, really, for any sinner of any era. In the measure that the self-elevating ego is dominant—through pride, power, concupiscence, the *li-*

bido dominandi—the metaphysical rectitude of the liturgical act will be hard to sustain. But the modern person, in his conscious and unapologetic claim to autonomy, is perhaps uniquely ill-disposed to it.

The Liturgical Act in the Twenty-First Century

What is the resonance of Guardini's question when we hear it posed in our midst, at the dawn of the twenty-first century? And how would we answer it? In light of the numerous postmodern critiques of modernity—many of which were remarkably adumbrated in Guardini's early texts—we are, I would submit, a bit less surprised and dismayed by his question than were many of his contemporaries. We are far less sanguine about the modern person and her capacities, especially in regard to the radicality of Christian life. At the end of the bloodiest century on record, we are, to say the least, skeptical about the gloriously autonomous human subject. We know that those who wreaked havoc on earth in the twentieth century were not those who looked to God but those who explicitly denied him and relied on their own freedom. And we see precisely what Guardini saw in the 1920s: An embrace of power disconnected to truth (the exclusive primacy of the "can" over the "ought") led by a short road to moral chaos and the piling up of corpses. Simply in light of this postmodern awareness of the dire practical consequences of autonomous subjectivity, we are more capable of the liturgical act, more willing to engage in the great practice of the God-centered self.

But I would like to make this general observation more exact by looking at two prominent themes in the writings of post-liberal theologians: antifoundationalism and the critique of experiential-expressivism. It has become a commonplace among post-liberals that the liberal project of grounding knowledge on some one unshakable foundation is deluded. There have been two great versions of this liberal proposal, the empirical, associated with Locke, Hume, and the logical positivists, and the rational, associated with, among many others, Descartes and Kant. According to the first, certain knowledge is guaranteed, finally, by the objectivity and verifiability of sense experience. But it is generally acknowledged among postmoderns that all sense experience, even the simplest and most "objective" is in fact "theory laden," shaped by expectation, context, point of view, the assumptions of one's community, and so on. For the second form of foundationalism, sure knowledge is grounded in some commonly held inner intuition or conviction—Descartes's cogito, Kant's a priori forms, Schleiermacher's feeling of absolute dependency, Tillich's ultimate concern, and so forth. But here again, postmodern critics have called radically into question any claim to a universal intuition independent of language, way of life, and the conditioning of one's tradition. (Whatever Schleiermacher meant by "the feeling of absolute dependency," he had that feeling, not because he was human, but because he was Christian.)

These criticisms are important for our purposes because they serve to question the autonomous subject. In either of its basic forms, foundationalism claims a ground for knowledge and action in the experience of the self, in what the subject sees or knows through its own perceptive powers. But a creation metaphysics disallows just this sort of self-reliance. The created self, as we have seen, is inescapably an ecstatic self, one that finds literally nothing in itself to stand on. And the liturgy is the arena for the expression of this self that finds its one foundation in the Creator God. Therefore the post-liberal antifoundationalist remains, at least in principle, more capable of the ecstacy of a properly liturgical act.

The second trend within post-liberalism that I would like to explore is the movement away from what George Lindbeck has called an "experiential-expressivist" model of doctrine toward what he terms a "cultural-linguistic" one. The first, assumed by most forms of theological liberalism, relates doctrine to experience as effect to cause, the latter giving rise to the former as its symbolic expression. Because it rests on essentially foundationalist assumptions, this approach, despite its enormous popularity, has been characterized by Lindbeck and others as theologically inadequate. What Lindbeck proposes as an alternative is the so-called cultural-linguistic model which, in a certain sense, relates doctrine to experience as effect to cause, the former shaping and determining the latter, much as the rules of a game determine the play of the participants. This second approach, closely tied to St. Paul's insistence that *fides ex auditu*, allows us to give an account of the densely textured particularity of Christianity, for the doctrines, beliefs, practices, and rituals of the Church really produce a new form of life in those who move in accordance with them.

In the liberal framework, something like liturgy is important only in the measure that it provides a means of expression for deep-seated experiences of the sacred; whereas on the cultural-linguistic reading, the liturgy is indispensable to the shaping and transforming of those who participate in it. When Guardini calls for the awakening of a Goethean contemplative gaze in the liturgical context, when he insists that we look meditatively on candles, altars, bread, wine, and water, so that we might be changed by them, he is presupposing what Lindbeck called a cultural-linguistic framework. If all of the movements and objects of the liturgy are but expressions of an underlying religious sensibility, why gaze so attentively on them? In point of fact, why not reduce them to a bare minimum, the better to rest in the peace of our inner experience? This supposition appears even more clearly when Guardini argues that the liturgical act amounts to a sort of metaphysical and psychological realignment, a rendering to God what is due. We don't shape the liturgy; it shapes us. And inasmuch as Thomas Aquinas takes the virtue of religion to be the chief of the moral virtues, he is assuming that the liturgical act is much more than an expression of an underlying experience; he is presuming that it makes us good.

Can we see the three negative qualities mentioned in Guardini's 1964 letter—lack of a contemplative attitude, the favoring of *Innerlichkeit* over body/soul unity, and exaggerated individualism—as typical by-products of experiential-expressivism? And can we therefore appreciate in the post-liberal criticism of that style an important point of contact with the mind and spirit of Guardini?

CONCLUSION

Perhaps at the end of these reflections, I can return, briefly, to the beginning, to the question that the postconciliar liturgical establishment has found difficult to understand. It seemed to them that Guardini was recommending an abandonment of the great project: If liturgy itself is out of step with modernity, the work of reform has been a waste of time. But this very construal of his remark indicates the epistemological problem at the heart of too much postconciliar reflection: the privileging of modernity and its assumptions over the radical, surprising, and finally, transtemporal convictions of the Church. It was Edward Schillebeeckx who commented ruefully that the Catholic Church embraced the modern at the very moment that the modern was losing confidence in itself. Thus the liturgical establishment got it precisely backward: Guardini was not implying that we abandon the liturgy or its reform, but he was implying that we ought perhaps to abandon modernity. And this does not mean, of course, that we should turn our backs on the contemporary world, or much less, on the concerns and hopes of contemporary men and women. It means that the metaphysical and above all epistemic convictions of modernity mix awkwardly at best with the "world" opened up by the liturgy.

The project is not shaping the liturgy according to the suppositions of the age, but allowing the liturgy to question and shape the suppositions of any age. Is the modern man incapable of the liturgical act? Probably. But this is no ground for despair, for our goal is not to accommodate the liturgy to the world, but to let the liturgy be itself—a transformative icon of the *ordo* of God.

Notes

1. Romano Guardini, *Letters from Lake Como*, trans. Geoffrey W. Bromiley (Grand Rapids, Mich.: William B. Eerdmans, 1994), 43.

2. Ibid., 46.

3. See Romano Guardini, *Sacred Signs*, trans. Grace Branham (St. Louis: Pio Decimo, 1956), 21–68.

4. Romano Guardini, *The Spirit of the Liturgy* (New York: Herder and Herder, 1998), 69.

5. "Was in der liturgischen Haltung steht, was betet, opfert und handelt, ist nicht 'die Seele,' nicht 'die Innerlichkeit,' sondern 'der Mensch.' Der ganze Mensch trägt das liturgische Tun." Romano Guardini, *Liturgische Bildung*, 1923.

6. "Die Seele ist lebendige Entelechie des Leibes." Ibid., 31.

7. Romano Guardini, *Spirit of the Liturgy*, 37.

8. Romano Guardini, *The End of the Modern World* (Wilmington, Del.: Intercollegiate Studies Institute, 1998), 109.

9. Ibid., 125.

10. Ibid., 137.

11. Ibid., 92.

12. Thomas Aquinas, *Summa theologiae*, IIa IIae, q. 80, art. 1.

13. Thomas Aquinas, *Quaestiones Disuptatae de potentia Dei*, q. 3, art. 1, ad. 17.

Chapter Six

THE TROUBLE WITH BEIGE CHURCHES: A CRITIQUE OF THE INFLUENCE OF CARTESIAN MODERNITY ON CONTEMPORARY ECCLESIAL ARCHITECTURE

I WAS BORN IN 1959 AND HENCE CAME OF AGE DURING A RATHER ICON-oclastic period within Catholicism. The churches that were built in the immediately postconciliar era were, for the most part, large empty spaces, marked by very little symbolism, narrativity, art, statuary, or painting, and most of the ecclesial buildings renovated during that time were stripped of these elements. The rationale offered for this practice was that, in light of the liturgical prescriptions of the Second Vatican Council, emphasis should be placed on the essential elements of altar, ambo, and, above all, the action of the gathered assembly. One of the dominant metaphors employed during that period was Jungmann's trope of the cluttered building that needed cleaning out.[1] Though Jungmann intended this image to have a broad reference to liturgy, ecclesiology, theology, and pious practice, it seemed especially apt with regard to church buildings themselves.

It is my conviction that much of this work has been disastrous for the Church and that the real motivating principle behind it was not the

Vatican Council nor, as is sometimes claimed, the great liturgical movement of the thirties and forties, but rather philosophical modernity.
What I shall attempt in this chapter is an exploration of the modern and
a demonstration of the fundamental tension between modernity and
Christian revelation. Next, I shall try to specify this claim by showing
that the church architecture of the past forty years, precisely in the measure that it has been shaped by modern presuppositions, is incapable of
bearing the weight of Christianity. Finally, by looking back at certain features of Gothic architecture, I will attempt to indicate a way forward for
designers and builders of Catholic churches today.

THE MARKS OF THE MODERN

I am well aware of the difficulty inherent in any attempt to describe the
features of an entire era and mode of thought. Like any other cultural period, modernity is rife with what David Tracy has called "plurality and
ambiguity." Yet, given the peculiar passion for methodological clarity evident in all of the shapers and founders of modernity, this type of description is at least relatively feasible. To grasp the salient characteristics of the
period, it is still best to turn to the writings of its paradigmatic figure—
René Descartes. With his customary verve and literary grace, Descartes
lays out, in his *Discours de la Méthode*, a program that almost every major
thinker followed until the middle of the last century.[2] I would like to
highlight four elements in this Cartesian approach: subjectivism, rationalism, dualism, and antitraditionalism.

As the young Descartes surveyed the intellectual scene at the beginning of the seventeenth century, he saw a sort of wasteland of confusion and contradiction. With regard to the profoundest questions, the
most important thinkers—Plato, Augustine, Thomas Aquinas, Cicero—
seemed to be in radical disagreement and there appeared no obvious way
to adjudicate their disputes. Moreover, the customs, practices, and convictions of various cultures were irreconcilably at odds with one another.
Most tellingly, in the midst of the religious wars that were exhausting the
coffers and willpower of Europe's governments, it was painfully obvious

that there was no hope of common ground in regard to issues of revelation and salvation. Determined to find certitude in the midst of this confusion, Descartes adopted the strategy of methodical doubt: Whatever he could doubt, he would, not stopping until he had found that which he couldn't question. So he swung the wrecking ball of his skepticism, knocking over customs, traditions, systems of thought, sense experience itself, until he discovered that the one thing he couldn't knock down was the wrecking ball itself. This realization gave rise to what is surely the best known one-liner in the history of philosophy: cogito ergo sum (I think, or perhaps better, I doubt; therefore I am).[3] The ground of certitude was not in anything objective, but rather in the depths of Descartes's subjective consciousness.

The Cartesian reliance on subjectivity as foundational can be seen in almost all of the great modern thinkers. Kant affects a Copernican revolution in epistemology and metaphysics, orienting reality to mind rather than mind to reality; and the starting point for his ethics is not behavior, virtue, or nature, but the categorical imperative discernible in the very structure of the will.[4] Similarly, Hegel engages in a careful phenomenology of mind and, at the conclusion of his mammoth philosophical project, apotheosizes human consciousness. This modern turn to subjectivity is especially evident in many of the leading Christian theologians of the past two hundred years. In his *On Religion: Speeches to Its Cultured Despisers*, Friedrich Schleiermacher reoriented Christian dogmatics, rooting it in the purportedly universal "sense and taste for the infinite."[5] All theological claims—God's existence, providence, grace, redemption—are correlated to, and intelligible in terms of, this subjective sensibility. Schleiermacher's influence was strongly felt in the twentieth century, especially in the works of Paul Tillich and Karl Rahner. Tillich sought to render Christian dogmas persuasive to skeptical moderns by correlating them to the sense of being "ultimately concerned," and Rahner grounded his theology in the experience of standing in the presence of absolute mystery.[6] George Lindbeck has characterized these Schleiermacherians as "experiential-expressivists," since they construe doctrines as expressions of underlying experiences.[7]

The second great mark of Cartesian modernity is rationalism. As we saw, Descartes was impressed by the fact that most of the intellectual disciplines—philosophy, science, literature, and so on—were character-ized by confusion and contradiction. Only austere, rational mathematics seemed to remain unchangingly reliable across the centuries. Hence, Descartes laid out his method along mathematical lines: begin only with a luminously self-evident starting point; break problems down into their component parts; proceed from step to step only according to a rigorous logic; and finally, check your work carefully.[8] This rationalist, geometrical *méthode* would, he thought, clear up the intellectual confusion of his time. One of the chief consequences of this option for the mathematical was a marked preference for the abstract over the concrete. To a large extent, the certitude of geometry and mathematics is a function of their tran-scendence of particular and exceptional cases. Hence, Descartes holds that reality is most effectively analyzed under the simple (and desperately abstract) rubric of *res cogitantes* (thinking things) and *res extensae* (ex-tended things).

This Cartesian option for the rational and the generic profoundly marked the development of modern religious thought. It can be seen, for example, in Kant's reduction of religion to a universally knowable moral-ity, as well as in Deist accounts of the scientifically verifiable truth that hides behind all particular religious claims. Indeed, the title of Kant's greatest book on the subject fairly clearly gives away the game: *Religion within the Limits of Reason Alone*.[9] And so many of the theological writers of the last two centuries have followed this rationalizing lead. Rudolf Otto spoke, not so much of particular religious traditions, but of the "holy" or the "numinous" that lies behind all of them; and Tillich, as we saw, explored the "ultimate concern" that animates, not only all religions, but all cultural expressions as well.[10] Moreover, numerous modern the-ologians engaged in various forms of rationalistic demythologization, sweeping aside the miraculous, prophecies, the supernatural—or else ex-plaining them away as evocative poetry.

A third quality of the Cartesian approach is a radical dualism. There were, to be sure, various types of dualism prior to Descartes—Plato's is an obvious example—but there is a unique texture to the modern form. The ground of it is the pristine quality of the *cogito*, which, in its clarity and dis-tinctness, is sharply different from the dubious sensible realm of the body.

In developing his anthropology, Descartes considered the soul or the mind as a "ghost in the machine," a pure spirit in an, at best, awkward relationship to a body.[11] The bifurcation between mind and matter is a dominant motif in modern thought, especially in regard to religion. In Spinoza, Leibniz, Kant, and Hegel, we find a clear preference for universal rational religiosity over any of the historically conditioned forms of revealed or positive religion. Indeed, to a person, these thinkers considered the particular claims and practices of the various religious traditions as the prime source of violence and all harbored the dream that in passing beyond them, peace would reign. A corrolary of this dualism is a certain disdain for the imagination and ritual. We can see it in Kant's disgust over liturgy and prayer, as well as in Hegel's relegation of religious *Vorstellung* to a position subordinate to the conceptual clarity of philosophy.

And this dualism has certainly been on display in the properly theological discussions during the modern period. When Hans Urs von Balthasar spoke of the need for a kneeling theology over and against a sitting theology, he was critiquing forms of theological reflection born, not from embodied prayerful practice, but from sheer speculation. A dualism can be discerned in the sometimes aggressive critique of practices and devotions rooted deeply in the bodies and imaginations of ordinary believers.

A fourth characteristic of the Cartesian style is antitraditionalism. The image that Descartes used to describe the state of European intellectual life was that of the cluttered, confusing, and dangerous medieval city, full of collapsing buildings, dead-end streets, and blind alleys. Would it not be better, he asked, simply to tear down that old wreck of a town and construct a new one on the basis of a coherent design and according to the purposes of one architect and planner?[12] Thus his project involved the sweeping away of received traditions, religious convictions, philosophical programs, and time-honored practices and the reconstruction from scratch of a new, streamlined, and rationally respectable system.

Nowhere is this Cartesian impatience with intellectual clutter more apparent than in Kant's *Religion within the Limits of Reason Alone.* As we have seen, Kant reduced authentic religion to the pursuit and cultivation of moral goodness and, in accord with that reduction, swept away, with breathtaking thoroughness, practically everything else preserved by the Christian tradition. Twentieth-century Protestant antitraditionalism is on display in Harnack's reductionistic Christology and in Bultmann's demythologizing hermeneutics, and a contemporary Catholic version of it can be seen in the project I mentioned at the outset of this chapter, namely, Jungmann's cleaning out of the cluttered house of liturgical theory and practice. In my own formation in the period just following the Second Vatican Council, a Cartesian suspicion of the tradition was clearly in evidence. In workshops and courses—whether in theology, liturgy, architecture, pastoral practice—a familiar pattern emerged: the benighted preconciliar perspective has been eliminated and replaced by a new vision forged at Vatican II. This was, of course, despite the fact that the leading figures at the council—Rahner, de Lubac, Congar, Guardini, Ratzinger—remained profoundly appreciative of the tradition.

Thus modernity—subjectivist, rationalist, dualist, and antitraditionalist—has made its influence felt from the writings of Descartes, through the speculation of some of the most important intellectual figures of the past 300 years into the theory and practice of ordinary believers of the present day. How we might assess this state of affairs is the concern of the next section.

MODERNITY AND CHRISTIANITY

Like all cultural periods, modernity is, from an evangelical standpoint, ambiguous, that is to say, to some degree receptive and to some degree hostile to the preaching of the word of Christ. Two of the great and permanent achievements of modernity are the development of the physical sciences (and the technology that resulted from this) and the emergence of democratic polities. Both were made possible by the Cartesian shift that I described in the last section, and, in the measure that they have enormously benefited humanity, they are both congruent with the deepest intuitions of revelation. However, I am convinced that the more closely we consider the characteristics of the modern mentality, the more we see its fundamental irreconcilability with the mind and practice of

Christianity. To state it a bit more precisely, modernity has a very hard time bearing the weight of Christian revelation and accepting the content of Christian proclamation. I would like to justify this claim by revisiting the four elements we isolated above.

We saw that a corollary of the rationalism of modernity is a preference for the abstract and the generic. This formalism puts modernity at odds with the irreducible specificity of Christian revelation, the stubborn fact that God has spoken himself thoroughly in a particular first-century Jew, crucified under Pontius Pilate. Hans Urs von Balthasar wrote an article entitled *Das Ganze im Fragment* (The Whole in the Fragment), describing the Christian paradox that the Word that informs the whole of existence became flesh and spoke in a very specific human voice.[13] What animated so many of the modern thinkers, as we saw, was a desire to shed the husk of the particular biblical narratives in order to uncover the abstract and universal religious truth underneath. Thomas Jefferson, in a paradigmatically modern move, excised from the Gospels all of the supernatural and miraculous elements, leaving behind what he took to be the pure moral doctrine.[14] But, for Christians, the narratives in their specificity are not expendable; rather, they are the heart of the matter. In a word, the meaning of a biblical story *is* the biblical story; this Jesus *is* the Word: *das Ganze im Fragment*. It is interesting to note in this context the "thin" quality of the Christologies presented by the leading liberal theologians of the past century. Thus, while Karl Rahner's transcendental anthropology is carefully and densely presented, his Christology remains largely formal and abstract.

The third quality of modern thought, namely dualism, also sits uncomfortably with Christianity. As John Henry Newman indicated, the central principle of the Christian religion is the Incarnation.[15] That God became flesh is the claim that undergirds Christianity's sacramentalism, its liturgical prayer, its theological reflection, its penitential practice, its hope in the resurrection of the body, and all of its dogmas. What follows from this is the willingness to use the myriad expressions of a playful and very embodied imagination in the evangelical project. Thus Chartres Cathedral, Dante's *Divine Comedy*, Michelangelo's frescoes on the ceiling of the Sistine Chapel, Bernini's colonnade outside of St. Peter's, Mozart's

Requiem, Bach's *St. Matthew's Passion*, Newman's sermons, Chesterton's essays, Flannery O'Connor's short stories—all flow from, and give expression to, the Incarnation. All witness to the Christian conviction that the body does not have to be bypassed or bracketed in order to reach the soul, just the contrary. Thomas Aquinas gave voice to this idea when he commented that the soul is in the body, not as contained by it, but as containing it, thereby implying not only that the soul can be reached through the body, but that any address of the soul necessarily implicates the body. The modern attempt to separate the core of religion from its embodied and particular husk clearly violates this incarnational principle.

Finally, the antitraditionalism of modernity is inimical to a vibrant Christianity. Unlike nature mysticisms and New Age spiritualities, Christianity is a revealed religion, which is to say, one rooted in concrete historical events. Furthermore, the interpretation of this historically grounded revelation has, itself, a history. As Newman has indicated, the "idea" of Christianity has unfolded itself over time, through the lively interplay of conversation, objection, question, and authoritative clarification.[16] The Christian tradition is thus like a growing plant (which occasionally sends off errant shoots) or a flowing river (that from time to time gives rise to tributaries destined to dry up). The point is that one could never get at the truth of the Christian idea by cutting down the plant, or searching out the source of the river, precisely because that idea *is* the plant, *is* the river. Therefore Descartes's project of wiping clean the slate of the intellectual tradition in order to start from scratch is, as far as Christianity is concerned, simply untenable.

MODERNITY AND ECCLESIAL ARCHITECTURE

As I mentioned at the outset of this chapter, I am convinced that many of the Catholic churches built and renovated during the past thirty years were inspired largely by philosophical modernity. What I should like to do in this section is to back up this claim by looking at contemporary church architecture in light of the four qualities that I have isolated and analyzed.

When I was coming of age in the 1960s and 1970s, I constantly heard the mantra that the Church is the people, not the building. In line with *Lumen Gentium's* insistence that the Church is the people of God, nearly exclusive stress was placed on the gathered community and their prayer, while the ecclesial structure itself was seen—in the blunt but admirably clear words of *Environment and Art in Catholic Worship*—as "a shelter or skin for a liturgical action" that "does not have to look like anything else, past or present."[17] The image for the church building that that quotation brings to mind is not that of the temple or the *domus Dei*, but rather the tent meeting, thrown up when the people come together, struck as soon as they continue their pilgrim way. Ecclesial design and renovation were carried out during the postconciliar period in accord with this people-centered, subjectivist schema. Thus sanctuaries, seating areas, and sight lines were arranged so that the members of the assembly could see one another; and art, decoration, statuary were reduced to a bare minimum or eliminated altogether lest the attention of the people be diverted from their own action. One justification that I heard proposed for a barren, barnlike church constructed in the 1970s was that it was meant to be dull, coming to life only when the people assembled for worship in it. But this sort of explanation is congruent only with a fundamentally experiential-expressivist model of doctrine and faith. If, as we have seen, Christianity is not a set of convictions that comes welling up from within experience, but rather a way of life that comes to us from a whole series of cultural, artistic, and doctrinal cues, then the emptied-out, assembly-centric ecclesial building is symbolically inadequate. In the great tradition of Catholic ecclesial architecture, church structures are decidedly not simply gathering spaces, but rather repositories of the Christian story and therefore conduits to an entirely new world of psychological and religious experience.

For sake of brevity, I will analyze together the closely related qualities of rationalism and dualism in regard to ecclesial architecture. One of the implications of the option for mathematical rationalism is, as we saw, a preference for the generic over the concrete, and evidence of this preference is readily available in contemporary church building. First, we notice the prevalence of clean lines and simplified geometrical forms (as in so much of Bauhaus architecture), as well as the absence of the kind of decorative vocabulary that would serve to specify the nature of the building. In her *Venus in Exile: The Rejection of Beauty in Twentieth-Century Art,* Wendy Steiner points out that a passerby would be hard-pressed to guess the nature of Le Corbusier's modernist Dominican convent in La Tourette.[18] Judging from its external appearance it could be anything from an office building to a parking garage. But nowhere is this option for the generic more evident than in the beigification of so many of our contemporary churches. It seems to have been a concern of ecclesial architects in recent years to drain the church of color, narrativity, and decorative playfulness. In order that the eye might be directed to the central action of the liturgy, anything that might distract or (God forbid) delight the eye seems to have been, in many cases, eliminated. The option for a dialectical as opposed to analogical imagination is furthermore apparent in the almost total absence of saints, angels, nature, and the cosmos in our churches. We remark that when design and statuary do appear in a contemporary church, they tend to be, in line with the dictates of modern rationalism, relentlessly abstract, narrativity and specificity eclipsed by sheer formalism. But all of this attenuates, as we have seen, the profoundly antidualist and incarnational convictions of authentic Christianity.

Descartes made practically a fetish out of what he called "clear and distinct ideas," that is to say, concepts that appear unambiguously in the light of reason. The modern period reached its high point during the late eighteenth century, and this epoch came to be known as the Enlightenment, indicating illumination after centuries of obscurantism. What strikes me upon entering almost any contemporary Catholic church is its "clean, well-lighted" quality. Everything can be seen; everything is lit up and open for investigation. In line with this rationalism, liturgists during the postconciliar period endeavored carefully to explain and clarify all of the movements and symbols of the liturgical action.

Two early critics of modernity—Pascal and Goethe—signaled their distaste for a one-sided embrace of rational clarity. Goethe pilloried the Newtonian scientist who sought to understand nature through the exercise of an invasive reason that posed its own questions and displayed

77

the objects of its investigation under the bright light of analysis. Far better, he thought, to watch nature with a kind of contemplative reverence, allowing an object to reveal itself slowly and on its own terms. And Pascal observed that though the mind loves the clarity of strong, direct light, the heart is far more enamored of the indirection and warmth of candlelight, a medium that allows for a play of illumination and shadow. Shouldn't there be room in our churches for a similar play of light and darkness? Shouldn't there be nooks, crannies, corners, chapels—places where one could slip in to pray? Shouldn't our churches appeal as much to instinct, emotion, passion, and heart as to mind?

And this brings us to the last of the marks of modernity, that is to say, antitraditionalism. Perhaps nowhere was the Cartesian spirit more apparent than in the wholesale cleaning-out of churches in the wake of the Second Vatican Council. It is not an exaggeration to refer to the often indiscriminate removal of altars, altar rails, reredos, crucifixes, statues, paintings, pews, and sculptures as a sort of vandalization. There are only two periods of Christian history that are roughly comparable in this regard: the iconoclastic outbreak during the ninth century and the Reformation of the sixteenth century. In all three instances, a theological elite, legitimately eager to purify the tradition, rather aggressively uprooted it. In his *The Stripping of the Altars*, Eamon Duffy has powerfully reminded us that the ravaging of Catholicism in sixteenth-century England—the emptying out of churches and the cancellation of countless practices and devotions—was carried out against the will of the vast majority of churchgoers.[19] What makes Duffy's analysis so disturbing is that he sees the Church of the postconciliar period in the distant mirror of that time.

To be sure, the clarification of the liturgical essentials and the removal of obvious clutter and repetitive symbols from churches were a desideratum, but Cartesian demolitions are never a good idea in the household of the Church. In terms of Newman's metaphors, the plant should be pruned, but not torn up, and the river should be tended and not allowed to dry up. Just as doctrine and practice have unfolded over the centuries, so ecclesial architecture has grown organically throughout the ages, an older style often incorporated into the new, or elements of one approach integrated with another. The Cartesian prejudice is that the good city is constructed from scratch by one mind, but anti-Cartesians know that this sort of tyranny usually produces a city of charmless functionalism. They prefer the city (or church) that reflects the influence of a variety of minds, playfully intersecting, creatively conversing, sometimes at odds with one another. In regard to ecclesial architecture, this sort of pluralism not only produces churches of greater charm and interest, but it also reverences more fully the complexity and variety of the Catholic tradition. Ewert Cousins has commented that the genius of Catholicism is that "we never threw anything away."[20] As they go about their necessary work, church designers and renovators ought to keep that profoundly anti-Cartesian sentiment in mind.

LOOKING BACK IN ORDER TO GO FORWARD

In this final section, I shall explore some of the theology present in the architecture and decoration of the great Gothic cathedrals. I would like to state something clearly at the outset: I am neither recommending that we start constructing imitation Gothic churches nor claiming that the Gothic is the premier or privileged style for ecclesial building. The purpose of this exploration is not to glorify medieval architecture, but rather to uncover certain elements of the Gothic form that effectively bear the Christian tradition and that might thereby serve as signposts for the church designers of the future. Chesterton said that if, at a fork in the path, you have taken the wrong road, the best way forward is to go back as fast as you can. This little adage is misunderstood if it is construed in a blindly reactionary way, for the point is to go forward. What Chesterton's dictum helps me to see in this context is that a journey back before the Cartesian fork in the road might be a prerequisite for more authentic progress. Accordingly, I shall look briefly at three features of Gothic cathedrals—the rose windows, verticality, and the façade—and I shall attempt to unpack their spiritual meaning in the hopes of sparking the imaginations of ecclesial builders and designers today.

When, as a child, the nineteenth-century artist and restorer Viollet-le-Duc first saw the north rose window at Notre Dame, he said to his mother, "Listen, it is the rose that is singing."[21] What the young man was sensing in the window, by a remarkable intuition, was the harmony or *concordia* that medieval philosophers took as the mark of the beautiful. Thomas Aquinas said that the beautiful occurs at the intersection of *integritas* (unity), *consonantia* (harmony), and *claritas* (radiance), at the point, in short, where a unified harmony becomes radiantly evident. The rose window, a brilliantly illuminated wheel of numerous elements in ordered arrangement around a central feature, is thus an almost perfect illustration of this medieval aesthetic principle.

But it also has a more precise focus, for its final purpose is to speak of the beauty of a life harmoniously gathered around Jesus Christ. At the center of the north rose at Notre Dame is a depiction of Christ and then, wheeling around him are the various medallions and decorative details, all of which are connected by spokes to the central motif. This is a picture of the well-ordered soul. When Jesus is the center of one's life, one's mind, will, imagination, body, sexuality, and passion tend to find their place in a pleasing pattern around him. And when something other than Christ—sex, money, power, ego—is placed in the center of the soul, a splintering occurs, the soul's powers becoming a jumble of competing and irreconcilable forces. This latter phenomenon is narratively displayed in Mark's account of the Capernaum demoniac, that single man who speaks, nevertheless, in the voice of the many: "What do you want of *us*, Jesus of Nazareth" (Mark 1:24)? Thus the rose window is far more than a decorative detail; rather, it is a spiritual symbol that draws the viewer into a new dimension of experience, the beautiful life that is, in Paul's words, "Christ living within." I would love contemporary churches to be filled with such densely textured symbolic evocations of the Christian story and the Christian life.

Another feature of the Gothic cathedral that I would like to analyze is the façade. What we spontaneously call the front of a Gothic church—the façade and towers—is in fact the back, for the building is meant to face the east, and it is the apse that is (usually) oriented. This suggests symbolically that the people of God face the rising sun for they have oriented their lives to Christ, the risen Son of God. But to set one's face is to set one's back; to declare what you are for is to declare, ipso facto, what you are against. Hence, the façade and towers, facing the west or the realm of the setting sun, stand for the Church's opposition to all those forces that are opposed to Christ. They are the "no" of the Christian community toward violence, hatred, division, self-absorption. And this is why there is a bristling, looming, slightly unsettling quality to the Gothic façades: they are the fighting face of Christianity.[22]

John Courtney Murray has argued that a central motif of the Gospel of John is the ever-increasing *agon* (struggle) of Jesus against the powers.[23] From his birth to Calvary, Jesus excites opposition: Herod and all Jerusalem trembled, the scribes and Pharisees schemed against him, the demons taunted him, and at the end of the day, everyone—the Jewish leadership, the Roman establishment, his own disciples—turned on him. The cross is simply the full and final expression of the sinful world's rejection of the author of life. When the risen Jesus appears to his disciples, he offers his peace, but he also shows his wounds, reminding them of what their betrayal and denial did to him. This means that the Church—which is the very body of Christ continuing to appear in the midst of sin—must itself have a sharp, oppositional quality, precisely *because* it proclaims the love of Jesus. As Stanley Hauerwas has commented, "If there is no enemy, there is no Christianity."[24] A church that simply blends into the environing culture and society, adopting its perspectives, values, and language, is dysfunctional.

And therefore church buildings ought to be, at least in part, strange, off-putting, challenging. They ought to remind us vividly that the world that we move in is not, *tout court*, the world that God desires. In the measure that so many of our contemporary churches mimic the bland suburban architecture that surround them; inasmuch as they fit seamlessly into the culture, radiating acceptance and domesticity, they fail to bear the challenging power of Christ in a symbolically adequate way. An element that I particularly miss in contemporary church design is the use of the exterior of the building in the announcement of the Christian faith. When one approaches a Gothic cathedral, he knows unambiguously that he is dealing with a Christian church—and a church, more to the point, that is making demands upon him even before he steps inside. I believe that one should have the same sense in confronting a church built today.

A final feature that I would like to explore is that of verticality. Perhaps the first thing that any visitor to a Gothic church remarks is the dizzying vertical thrust of the place, every line and arch compelling the gaze upward. I have frequently seen groups of tourists making their way through the nave of a Gothic cathedral, and moving, not with confidence, but slowly, meditatively, drifting like a school of lazy fish, their eyes trained on the distant heights of the structure. There is something purposely disorienting about a Gothic interior, because it is designed to move a person out of the world of his ordinary experience into a whole series of greater worlds. One feature that sharply distinguishes a Gothic from a modern church is the presence of nature in the decoration of the former. Even a casual glance at the interior and exterior of Chartres reveals plants, trees, tendrils, roots, animals, birds, planets, and stars; and on the points of the four principal towers of Laon Cathedral are sculptures of the oxen that carried supplies and food to the building site. The medieval architects had been formed by the biblical conviction that the created cosmos reflects the glory of the Creator, and they were therefore altogether pleased to include depictions of that cosmos in the house of God.[25]

But there are even wider horizons, for God's creation includes the properly supernatural order, the realm of the angels and saints. And this dimension is amply represented in Gothic architecture. On the façade of Reims Cathedral, we find some of the most moving figures in all of Western sculpture: angels with mysterious and slightly unsettling smiles. An angel ready to announce the Good News to the four corners of the earth stands perched on the roof of Chartres, just over the point of the apse. In the tympanum surrounding the main portal of Notre Dame de Paris, there are numerous angels watching the drama of the Last Judgment, some in pious concentration, others giggling and pulling faces, still others leaning over the balcony like theatergoers straining for a better view. The point of all of this is deeply biblical: The human drama unfolds in the context of a much richer and higher drama, the contours and texture of which we can only dimly glimpse. The angels, though ontologically other, *have to do with us*; our stories are intertwined. An insight common to all the spiritual masters of the Christian tradition is that our lives are not about us. Thomas Aquinas expressed this idea when he said that what God loves the most is not any particular creature, but rather the whole of the created universe. In drawing us up out of ourselves and even out of the circle of the worshipping assembly, the Gothic churches witness to this truth. I would welcome the return of the cosmos to our bland and altogether too anthropocentric ecclesial buildings.

Conclusion

In his letter to the Romans, St. Paul made the simple observation that "faith comes from hearing" (Rom. 10:17). This phrase has become a sort of motto of the Christian post-liberal movement, for it implicitly contradicts a central tenet of liberalism, that doctrine, dogma, and religious practice are conditioned by an underlying subjective experience. If faith comes from hearing, it comes from outside of consciousness, experience, and expectation. And if that is the case, then symbol, ritual, color, drama, narrativity, and design—all those elements that shape subjectivity—are of essential, indispensable importance.

What I have argued in this chapter is that far too many contemporary church buildings have been formed by the modern/liberal mentality and that the sign of this formation is the beigification that I have been bemoaning. What I am calling for are church structures that not only house and gather the worshipping assembly, but that tell the Christian story boldly, unapologetically, and with panache.

Notes

1. Josef Jungmann, *The Early Liturgy to the Time of Gregory the Great* (Notre Dame: University of Notre Dame Press, 1959), 2.

2. René Descartes, "Discourse on Method," in *The Philosophical Works of Descartes*, trans. Elizabeth S. Haldane and G. R. T. Ross (Cambridge: Cambridge University Press, 1979).

3. Descartes, "Discourse on Method," 101.

4. See especially Immanuel Kant, *Foundations of the Metaphysics of Morals* (Indianapolis: Bobbs-Merrill, 1978), 9–10.

5. Friedrich Schleiermacher, *On Religion: Speeches to Its Cultured Despisers* (New York: Harper Torchbooks, 1958), 39.

6. Karl Rahner, *Foundations of Christian Faith* (New York: Crossroad, 1984), 44–89.

7. George Lindbeck, *The Nature of Doctrine: Religion and Theology in a Postliberal Age* (Philadelphia: Westminster Press, 1984), 31–32.

8. Descartes, "Discourse on Method," 92.

9. Immanuel Kant, *Religion within the Limits of Reason Alone* (New York: Harper Torchbooks, 1960), esp. 139–77.

10. Paul Tillich, *Systematic Theology*, vol. 1 (Chicago: University of Chicago Press, 1967), 11–14.

11. Descartes, "Discourse on Method," 106–18.

12. Ibid., 89.

13. Hans Urs von Balthasar, *Das Ganze im Fragment. Aspekte der Geschichtstheologie* (Einsiedeln: Benzinger, 1963).

14. Thomas Jefferson, *Jefferson's Bible: The Life and Morals of Jesus of Nazareth* (New York: American Book Distributors, 1997).

15. John Henry Newman, "An Essay on the Development of Christian Doctrine," in *Conscience, Consensus, and the Development of Doctrine*, ed. James Gaffney (New York: Image Books, 1992), 290.

16. Ibid., 72–75.

17. *Environment and Art in Catholic Worship*, sec. 42. A publication of the USCC, 1978.

18. Wendy Steiner, *Venus in Exile: The Rejection of Beauty in Twentieth-Century Art* (New York: Free Press, 2001), 118.

19. Eamon Duffy, *The Stripping of the Altars: Traditional Religion in England 1400–1580* (New Haven: Yale University Press, 1992).

20. Ewert Cousins, private conversation with the author.

21. Robert Barron, *Heaven in Stone and Glass: Experiencing the Spirituality of the Great Cathedrals* (New York: Crossroad, 2000), 29.

22. Ibid., 56.

23. John Courtney Murray, *An Eight Day Retreat*, unpublished manuscript.

24. Stanley Hauerwas, *Sanctify Them in the Truth: Holiness Exemplified* (Nashville: Abingdon Press, 1998), 191.

25. Ibid., 49.

Part III

AT THE FEET OF
THE MASTERS

Chapter Seven

Thomas Aquinas's
Christological Reading
of God and the Creature

I T IS A CENTRAL CONVICTION OF MINE THAT THOMAS AQUINAS IS A spiritual master, that is to say, someone concerned with the cultivation of the human relationship with God. Like his patristic forebears, Aquinas did not clearly distinguish between theology and what we would call "spirituality." For him, the whole theological task—the naming of God and the world in relation to God—is an expression of the saving power at work in Jesus Christ, soul-doctoring if you will. One is meant to be changed by contact with the works of Thomas, the rhythm of question and answer continually pushing, pulling, cajoling the reader in the direction of deeper vision. This "spiritual" reading of Aquinas is justified by the hermeneutical importance of what I choose to call the "icon" of Christ. Thomas is not an Aristotelian commentator occasionally borrowing insights from the tradition of Christian revelation; he is, in the richest sense possible, a Christian theologian who reflects on God and creation from the standpoint of the Incarnation and who borrows liberally from spiritual, mystical, theological, and philosophical systems in order to illumine further what has occurred in Christ. It is decidedly not the case that Thomas fits Jesus artificially into a theological system constructed on other foundations. When we read the methodological texts of the *Summa*

theologiae with care, attending to the overall structure of the work, we notice the inescapable centrality and determining quality of Jesus Christ for
Aquinas. It is in light of the event of the Incarnation that Thomas interprets both God and the human, seeing the former as an uncanny, surprising, and ever greater act of love, and the latter as, at its best, an act of
sheer openness to the inrushing of God. To put it succinctly, he sees, in
Christ, the meeting of two ecstasies, and this coming-together is the lens
through which he reads everything else.

In the course of this chapter, I will attempt to justify this claim by
looking closely at texts from the *Prima pars* and the *Tertia pars* of the
Summa theologiae. Next, I will try to demonstrate a more "soulful" reading
of key texts in the disputed question *De potentia Dei* concerning the simplicity of God and the sheer dependence and receptivity of the creature.
My hope is thereby to recover the deepest spiritual intention of these
texts: to lure you onto the *via* (a word that Thomas loved) which is Christ.

REVELATION

It is, of course, a common criticism of Thomas Aquinas, especially from
Protestant theologians, that he underplays revelation and favors, instead,
a philosophically tinged apologetic approach to Christianity. One has
only to consult Luther's eloquent denunciations of scholasticism or Paul
Tillich's well-known essay on the two types of philosophy of religion to
see this critique played out. Though this charge might be justly leveled
against the *Summa contra gentiles* (a text in which a philosophical doctrine
of God is entirely in place in book 1 and Christology and Trinity are discussed in book 4), it is wide of the mark with regard to Thomas's mature
work in the second *Summa*.

When we turn our attention to the very first article of the first
question of the first part of the *Summa theologiae*, we see, clearly articulated, the theological radicality of Thomas's project. He wonders whether
there is a need for *sacra doctrina* (holy teaching) besides the range of philosophical disciplines practiced in the medieval university. Aquinas's pithy
response merits close attention: "it was necessary for human salvation

that there be a certain doctrine following from divine revelation besides the philosophical disciplines investigated by human reason. Firstly, indeed because the human being is ordered to God as to an end which surpasses what reason can grasp."[1] First, we see that revelation is required, not for the satisfaction of the mind alone, but precisely for salvation, the healing of the soul, the enhancing of the rapport with God. When Luther accused scholasticism of proposing a one-sided and arrogant *theologia gloriae* (theology of glory) and of overlooking the *theologia crucis* (theology of the cross) that is invariably *pro nobis*, he must have forgotten this elemental text of Aquinas. For Thomas, whatever God proposes to us about himself is for us and for our salvation. But at the heart of Thomas's response is a paradoxical theological anthropology: We human beings are, by nature, oriented to an end that surpasses our natural capacities of reason and will. There must be a science beyond Aristotelian physics and metaphysics because those disciplines are built up by human reason—they are our artifacts—and we are destined to find ourselves only in an ecstatic surrender to a power that surpasses whatever we can achieve or make or know. In the *Milieu divin*, Teilhard de Chardin speaks of a divinization of activities—our active cooperation with the purposes of God—and a far more important divinization of passivities—our willingness to be hollowed out, to be drawn painfully beyond ourselves, by the mysterious power of God.[2] There is something of this in this first article of the *Summa*. The rational Aristotelian sciences—built up by human reason—are to be practiced and reverenced, but such activity can never constitute the deepest realization of humanity, since we are destined finally to let go and be drawn toward a knowledge that we cannot control. From the start, we see the theme of ecstasy, obedience, and surrender, virtues that, as we will argue, are most fully evident in the human being Jesus Christ.

In article two we find the often remarked upon discussion of the "scientific" nature of *sacra doctrina*. Though it appears prima facie to be a rather dry and abstract concern, Thomas's elaboration of it helps enormously to disclose the spiritual quality of theology. Thomas holds that *sacra doctrina*, like music, is a subalternate science, since it proceeds from principles "known in the light of a higher science." But what precisely is the higher *scientia* from which *sacra doctrina* proceeds? Thomas's answer: *scientia Dei et beatorum*, the science or knowledge of God and of the saints, that is to say, the illumination enjoyed by God himself and those blessed who see the essence of the divine. Theology, in short, is a kind of participation in, and anticipation of, the beatific vision, the ecstatic seeing that is the goal of the spiritual enterprise. Obviously one of the problems that we face in interpreting such a text is that we do so from a post-Cartesian and post-Newtonian perspective, assuming that *scientia* is, at its best, an objective and distanced form of knowing. When Thomas Aquinas speaks of *scientia*, he undoubtedly has, to some degree, the rational Aristotelian discipline in mind, but, it seems to me, he speaks in this context much more with a biblical–spiritual resonance, assuming that "knowing" has far more to do with existential intimacy than with conceptual clarity. The authentic theologian, in short, is the one who seeks more fully to understand and more clearly to express the experience of radical union with God.

But is the spiritual nature and teleology of Thomas's project not compromised, as many of his critics have alleged, by his prodigal use of philosophical method and sources? Once again, his treatment of this issue is surprising and illuminating. The overly enthusiastic advocates of natural theology notwithstanding, Thomas in no sense bases his theology on philosophical premises or findings. As we saw, the basis for the enterprise is God's own self-knowledge. Aquinas is clear that theology does not depend upon philosophy but rather *uses* it "as something inferior and ancillary" due to a "defect" in the human minds that theology wishes to address. In a word, the function of philosophy in theology is not foundational but pedagogical. It is worth exploring a bit precisely what Thomas means when he speaks of this *defectum* in our reason. In his commentary on the Gospel of John, he speaks, in a rather patristic vein, of the Incarnation as a salve for the eyes of the soul, a healing balm that enables fallen minds to understand. The *debilitas* or *defectum* in the mind is the inordinate tendency, born of sin, to orient ourselves to the things of this earth rather than to the power that lures us from above. In light of this clarification, we can understand Thomas's insistence on the pedagogical necessity of lesser sciences in order to prepare us for the fullness of theological truth. "It may well happen that what is in itself the more certain may seem to us the less certain on account of the weakness of our intelligence, which is dazzled by the clearest objects of nature as the owl is dazzled by the light of the sun."[3] Theology does not depend upon rational science for its supposed clarity; rather, it uses that science in order to "lead by the hand" the mind that is unaccustomed to the brilliance of the Light itself. Rational argumentation is not so much a foundation for theology but a tool used by the theologian in order to prepare the fallen mind for vision. When his opponents accused Thomas of diluting the wine of theology with the water of Aristotle, he turned the metaphor around: "I am hardly diluting wine with water; rather, I am transforming water into wine."

CHRISTOLOGICAL FOCUS

But here we come to the heart of the matter: What exactly is the content of the revelation that animates *sacra doctrina*? In order to respond to this question, we have to leave the confines of the *Prima pars* and examine some texts at the beginning of the *Tertia pars* dealing with the person and work of Jesus Christ. In the prologue to the final major section of his masterpiece, Thomas says: "Inasmuch as our savior, the Lord Jesus Christ . . . demonstrated to us in his own person the way of truth by which we might be able to arrive at the beatitude of immortality through resurrection, it is necessary, in order to bring the work of theology to completion, that we now consider the Savior of all."[4] We recall that the purpose of revelation is to elevate the human mind and heart, to orient them to the realm which is beyond the range of finitude, to that supernatural end which is proper to us. Here we see that Jesus is the "way of truth," the path that leads us to that beatitude attainable only through resurrection, that is to say, through being drawn beyond the confines of nature and finitude. The conclusion is unavoidable: The illuminating revelation by which the Thomistic theological endeavor begins and by which it is conditioned is Jesus Christ, the definitive *via* to God. He is the *consummatio* of the theological project, not only its end but its beginning, the one in whom the whole endeavor holds together. He is the light in which we see who God

is (transcendent, ungraspable yet alluring power) and who we are in relation to God (spirits oriented toward transcendence through obedience).

This becomes clearer when we begin to crawl through the texts at
the beginning of the *Terita pars*. In question one, article one, Thomas
wonders about the "fittingness" of the Incarnation, and the *sed contra* of
this article is one of the most interesting methodological passages in the
Summa. On the basis of Paul's Epistle to the Romans, Thomas argues
that the *invisibilia* of God are made known through the *visibilia* of creation, and, as the argument progresses it becomes clear that the *visibilium*
he is speaking of is not so much the realm of sensible objects but Christ.

> By the mystery of the Incarnation are made known at once the
> goodness, wisdom, the justice, and the power of God. . . . His good-
> ness for he did not despise the weakness of his own handiwork; his
> justice since on man's defeat he caused the tyrant to be overcome by
> none other than a human being . . . his power or infinite might, for
> there is nothing greater than for God to become incarnate.5

The sheer effervescence of the divine goodness and the sheer range
and surprise of the divine power would not be fully known apart from
the unheard of act by which God becomes a creature. That God is benevolent and powerful was certainly known by philosophers and theologians
prior to the Incarnation, but the intensity and unsurpassability of that
benevolence and might were not suspected before Christ. It is the shocking condescension of the Incarnation, God's stooping low to join us as
one of us, that "blows open" the mind, expanding it to a relatively adequate sense of God's uncanniness and otherness. To borrow from the
work of my former professor Robert Sokolowski, I could say that the radically nonworldly character of God's being is paradoxically enough revealed precisely in the act by which God enters the world. Were God a
being in or alongside of the universe, one of the natures in the world, God
could not *become* a creature without ceasing to be God or compromising
the ontological integrity of the creature he becomes.6 In short, that God
is *totaliter aliter* (totally other) and *semper maior* (always greater), that he is
alluring yet totally ungraspable mystery, is given to us in the event of

Christ. And therefore in this unheard of surprise, revelation, as Thomas described it in the first question of the first part, truly takes place.

This theme of the superabundance of God is further developed in the *Respondeo* of article 1. Thomas reminds us that the term *conveniens* is used to describe a quality that flows from the nature of the thing in which it inheres. Thus it is "fitting" that a human being thinks, since thinking is in accord with our rational nature. But, says Thomas, it is the nature of God to be good, and the good, as Dionysius says, is *diffisivum sui*. Thus it "belongs to the supreme good to communicate itself supremely to the creature, and this happens in the richest sense by his so joining created nature to himself that one person is made up of these three: the Word, a soul and flesh."[7] Once again, the key terms are *maxime* and *summo modo*. The divine might be known and described apart from Christ on the basis of "natural" speculation, but it is only in light of the Incarnation that the supreme and surpassing goodness of God is seen. And therefore it is only in the light of Jesus that we realize the radicality of the transcendent destiny that is ours, the intensity of the goodness that we are invited to share.

This insight is marvelously summed up in Thomas's Johannine commentary when he remarks, again to the great surprise of natural theologians: "creatures were not sufficient to lead to a knowledge of the Creator. . . . Thus it was necessary that the Creator himself come into the world in the flesh, and be known through himself."[8] The language here is striking. The presumption seems to be that some knowledge of God is attainable through creatures alone but that real knowledge of the divine, that is to say, knowledge that saves us and provides the basis of *sacra doctrina* is possible only through the kenotic act of the Creator himself.

Earlier we noted the *pro nobis* character of revelation and *sacra doctrina*: God discloses something of his own self-knowledge precisely for the purpose of raising us up to a share in the divine being. This implies that knowledge of God's being and human being are correlative: The more adequately we understand who God is, the more adequately we grasp precisely who we are and ought to be. Human fullness is in proportion to the *scientia* of God. This coming-together of knowledge concerning the divine and the human flows, of course, from the moment of revelation that we have been considering: It is in Christ, the God-human, that the double manifestation occurs. But what precisely is disclosed about human beings in Jesus? A short answer is this: When we are radically open to and dependent upon the divine, God in all of his ecstasy can appear. Or to turn it around, when God fully manifests himself, we appear as who we authentically are: sheer transparencies to the sacred ground.

I would like to demonstrate how Christ illumines the human reality by looking at just a couple of texts. In *quaestio* 7, article 1 of the *Tertia pars*, we find Thomas treating of "the grace of Christ as an individual human being." He states that there is a superabundance of habitual grace, that is to say, a real participation in the life of God, present in the soul of Jesus, and he offers three justifications for his position: ". . . on account of the union of his soul with the Word of God. For the nearer any recipient is to an inflowing cause, the more does it partake of its influence . . . on account of the dignity of his soul, whose operations were to attain so closely to God by knowledge and love . . . and on account of the relation of Christ to the human race."[9] The deepest center of Jesus' human life—his soul—is pressed unsurpassably close to the Word of God: He is a human being utterly formed by and in union with the creative Logos; he is, if you will, the obedient one par excellence. Further, he is closest to the "inflowing cause" which is God. We have seen, precisely in the Incarnation, that God is an ecstasy beyond the human capacity to grasp. What emerges here is that Jesus' full humanity amounts to an openness to this inrushing and outflowing of the divine power. And then we see that the "dignity" of his soul consists in the intensity of its intellectual and voluntary operations, its knowledge and love of God. Is Christ not the archetype of that elevation of human knowing and loving—that *scientia*—which takes place through God's self-disclosure?

The second text I would like to consult is the first article of question 18. Here Thomas distances himself from the Monothelite position of Appolinarius and affirms, unambiguously, the orthodox view that in Christ there are two wills, human and divine. It is in the play between the first objection and response that the key clarification is made. The objector maintains, sensibly enough, that since the will is the "first mover" or commander in whoever wills, Christ's divine will must have swallowed up his human will, effectively eliminating it, rendering it practically powerless. Aquinas's response to this objection is worthy of careful consideration: "Whatever was in the human nature of Christ was moved at the bidding of the divine will; yet it does not follow that in Christ there was no movement of the will proper to human nature, for the good wills of other saints are moved by God's will. . . . For although the will cannot be inwardly moved by any creature, yet it can be moved inwardly by God."[10]

Thomas grants that the human will of Christ was totally subordinate to the divine will, but he refuses to admit that such passivity amounted to a blotting out of the human. To justify this claim he refers us to question 105 of the *Prima pars* where he had argued that God, precisely as the ultimate good, is irresistibly present to each act of our will. Willy-nilly, in every act of our freedom, we are desiring the unsurpassable ground of the good which is God, and hence the human will finds itself in surrendering as fully as possible to the divine good that is its magnet and raison d'etre. Authentic freedom for the human will consists, paradoxically, in enslaving itself to the divine power. Christ's human will, utterly at one with the divine freedom, is but the fullest expression of this noncompetitive relationship between creature and Creator. As Chalcedon insinuates and as Thomas explicitly states, Jesus is the paragon of humanity precisely inasmuch as he allows the divine reality most fully to inhabit and conquer his humanness: "The glory of God is a human being fully alive."

What we see here in short is a *mise en question* of our assumptions concerning relationships of intimacy, causality, and dependency. Creatures are characterized, at an elemental level, by a sort of mutual exclusivity, an over and againstness. But in the creature–Creator relationship, a new modality emerges: Dominance by the divine is tantamount to full flourishing in the one so dominated. The creature is most itself when it is least itself in the presence of the power of Being. If God has been disclosed in the Incarnation as ecstatic, ever surprising love, then the human (and by extension the creature) has been disclosed as imitative ecstasy. In Jesus of Nazareth, we have the coming-together of a divine power that wants nothing more than to give itself away and a human surrender in the presence of such a gift. It is my contention—and in some ways this is the central argument of this chapter—that this "icon" of divine–human ecstacy is the hermeneutical key to the project of *sacra doctrina* that Thomas Aquinas undertakes in the *Summa theologiae*. The God he describes is not so much the divinity of Aristotle—in fact it is interesting to note just how dramatically he twists and turns the categories of Aristotle—but rather the God and Father of our Lord Jesus Christ. Thomas's divinity is the power disclosed in the Incarnation as the ever greater and noncompetitive act of Being itself. And the creaturely realm he describes is also revealed through the Incarnation: the finitude that is a sheer transparency to the divine creativity, that which is most itself when it is least itself.

THE SIMPLENESS OF GOD

With these methodological clarifications in mind, let us turn now to a text that Thomas was writing practically simultaneously with the *Summa theologiae*, the disputed question *De potentia Dei*. It is in this work, composed for his "graduate students" and not for the "beginners" of the *Summa*, that Thomas gives his richest and most compelling account of the strangeness of both God and creature seen in the light of Incarnation.

That God is not a being but the sheer act of to-be itself is affirmed in a variety of Aquinas's writings, but the argument for this position as articulated in the *De potentia* is of special interest inasmuch as it constitutes an indirect demonstration for the existence of a creator God. The text is the *Respondeo* in article 2 of question 7, and it begins with the observation that sometimes several causes, producing a variety of effects, give rise, nevertheless, to one effect in common. To illustrate his point, St. Thomas uses the homely example of cooking: a group of elements—pepper, ginger, and so on—each making a unique contribution to the flavor of a dish, nevertheless unite in producing heat. But this phenomenon can be explained only through recourse to some one superior cause that has, as its proper effect, the common effect in question. In the second part of the *Respondeo*, Thomas applies this general principle to a particular case:

All created causes have one common effect which is being, though each one has a particular effect which distinguishes it from the others. Thus, heat makes something to be hot and a builder makes the house to be. Therefore they have in common the fact that they cause being although they differ inasmuch as the fire causes fire and the builder causes the house. There must therefore be some cause superior to all others, in virtue of which all cause being and whose proper effect is being. And this cause is God.[11]

God is that primordial cause by which causality itself exists. He is that grounding power which alone can explain the act—characteristic of all causes—of passing on being. Now from the standpoint of this remarkable demonstration—so unlike any of the *quinque viae*—Thomas endeavors to show the unicity of being and essence in God. "The proper effect of any cause proceeds from that cause according to a likeness of its nature. It is therefore necessary that being is the substance or nature of God."[12] In other words, because the proper effect of the first being is *esse* and because a proper effect always expresses and mirrors the nature of its cause, God must be *esse*. Because he gives, not a particular type of being but the act of to-be itself, God cannot be a *being*, a thing, an example or instance of *esse*. Rather, his very nature must be to-be, since to-be is his characteristic effect.

Thomas gives even more pointed expression to this insight in article 3: *Utrum Deus sit in aliquo genere* (whether God is contained in any genus). It is, of course, one of the marks of the Aristotelian science to categorize objects according to genus and species, naming things through comparison and contrast with others. What emerges in the course of this discussion is the surprising truth that God is in no sense either comparable to or contrastable from any of the things in the world. In the *Respondeo*, Aquinas offers three arguments in support of the proposition that God cannot be contained in any genus, and I shall consider the third. His *ratio* proceeds from the supreme perfection of the God who is the sheer act of to-be. As simply and absolutely actualized, God must contain within himself the perfections of all genera. Were he confined to a particular genus, he would be limited by the restrictions of that category and would be, consequently, only conditionally perfect. As the most intense reality, God must transcend the limitations of any "division" of being:

"Thus it is also evident that God is not a species, nor an individual, nor is there any difference in him; nor can he be defined, since every definition is in terms of genus and species."[13] It is here that we see, perhaps most clearly, the dismantling of the mythology of the supreme being that takes place throughout Thomas's writings. When Aquinas laconically tosses off the observation that God is not an *individuum*, he announces the radicality of the Christian conception of the sacred. God is not a supreme reality in, above, or alongside of the world. As that reality which simply *is*, God is prior to any of the splits that characterize less dramatic instances of being. He is neither above nor below the world; neither the same as nor different from the universe; neither greater nor less than the realm of creatures. Due to the sheer intensity, uniqueness, and incomprehensibility of his being, he is not to be contrasted with or compared to anything in the world. He is not a being among beings; nor is he an existent supremely removed from other existents. Thus the logical mechanism of the Aristotelian scientist breaks down in the presence of this reality which in principle remains invisible, unheard of, inconceivable, not so much through "distance" as through "strangeness." God is not so much somewhere else as some*how* else.

What emerges from this koan-like rhetoric is the insight that God—the nonindividual—is *totaliter aliter* and unspeakably close, *intimior intimo meo et superior summo meo*. Precisely because he is uncanny and incomparable, God can be, at the same time, the creative ground of all that is (the cause of causality) and the alluring mystery beyond grasping and knowing (the simple one). God can pour himself with reckless abandon into every nook and cranny of finitude, and he can draw finitude infinitely beyond itself. What we are dealing with, in a word, is the God of revelation disclosed in Jesus Christ, the ever greater and ever more surprising love. If Thomas had emphasized simply the *totaliter aliter* quality of the first reality, he would not have honored the "involving" dimension of the divine reality offered in revelation, and if he had emphasized only the immanent availability of God, he would not have honored the drawing, transcending, ever greater quality of the sacred that is also given in revelation. We saw that God is *pro nobis* in his self-offer and, in that same gift of self, infinitely beyond the grasp of the recipient of revelation. This salvific tensiveness is duly honored in the odd language of the God beyond God, the simple one.

THE NOTHINGNESS OF THE CREATURE

Our consideration of Thomas's christological method revealed that knowledge of God and the human are correlative: God's ecstatic otherness is disclosed precisely in the measure that the human creature becomes self-forgetful. In Christ's perfect obedience, the ever greater and always stranger love of God pours forth. Following Heidegger, Paul Tillich explicitly states that the human relationship to God is the lens through which the creaturely relationship in general can be understood. A human being can know, feel, and describe the dynamics that characterize all finite being in relation to the infinite. The full expression of the human in rapport with the divine is, for Tillich, Jesus of Nazareth, especially in the obedience and self-surrender of the cross. In that moment of utter transparency to the divine in love and obedience, the crucified Christ reveals what the creature ought to look like in the presence of the unconditioned reality of God. It is therefore from the standpoint of Christ that Tillich reads the ontology of the creature, concluding that the finite thing is most itself when it is least itself, in sheer transparency to the unconditioned ground of being.

I wonder whether *mutatis mutandis* an analogous claim might be made with regard to Thomas Aquinas's interpretation of creation. If *sacra doctrina*—the articulation of God and the world in relation to God—flows from revelation, and if revelation reaches its consummation precisely in the event of the Incarnation, does it not follow that Thomas's theological reading of creation—even of the nonhuman order—is necessarily colored by the dynamics of Christ's human rapport with God? Might we not see in his insistence on the sheer receptivity and passivity of the creature in the presence of the Creator a reflection of Christ's suppleness of mind and will in the presence of his Father? Is it not the case that the humanity of Jesus, in intimate union with the divine, provides the asymptotically approached model for the general creaturely rapport with God? It is with such a christological hermeneutic in mind that I would like now to move through some of the texts dealing with creation and the creature in the *De potentia*.

The problem of creation is broached in question 3 of the text and it spreads out over nineteen carefully argued articles. We will focus on but a few texts in articles 1, 2, and 3. The problem raised in article 1—*utrum Deus possit aliquid creare ex nihilo*—determines and conditions the whole of question 3, and Thomas's resolution of it is of decisive importance for his theology, as is signaled by the vehemence of the language used at the outset of the *Respondeo*: "It must be held firmly that God can make something from nothing and that he does so."[14] Thomas commences his argument proper by stating that every agent acts inasmuch as it is in act. Now a given agent is "particularly" in act in a double sense: first, in comparison with itself, and second, in comparison to other agents. In the first way, a natural cause is, in its own essence, only partially in act since it is a hybrid of matter and form, substance and accident, and so forth. In the second way, it is but partially in act in relation to other causes, since no one thing expresses the fullness of actuality that can be found in the composite of causes. Thus every finite agent is determined to produce being in only a limited way, according to this genus or that species. "And therefore the natural agent does not produce being as such but being pre-existing and determined to one thing or another, for example to the species of fire or to whiteness. . . . And for this reason, the natural agent acts through moving and thus requires matter as a substrate of the change or motion."[15] Since it is not sheerly actual, the natural agent can produce only modifications of being, merely transforming something already given.

But God is that agent which is in no sense natural and hence in no way restricted in his agency:

God on the contrary is totally actual, both in comparison to himself, since he is pure act . . . and in comparison to things which are in act, since in him is the origin of all beings. Consequently through his action he produces all of subsisting being, without a pre-supposition, as the one who is the principle of all being. . . . And for this reason he can make something from nothing.[16]

As the simple reality, the act of to-be itself, God cannot exercise his agency through an intermediary since there is, literally, nothing outside of God. God could not possibly use an auxiliary case in the act of creation since in creating he brings all of being into existence. Were there a substrate to creation, it would have to exist, *per impossibile*, outside of the act by which the totality of existence emerges.

The radicality of this doctrine of *creatio ex nihilo* is signaled in the exchange between the first objection and response. The objector argues that God cannot do what is contrary to the common conception of the mind, that is to say, to self-evident first principles. But, he continues, Aristotle reminds us that it is the common conception of philosophers that *ex nihilo nihil fiat*. Thus it would be contradictory to claim that God creates in the strict sense. By way of counterargument, Thomas says that the proposition *ex nihilo nihil fiat* was appreciated as self-evident with regard to natural agents that act through motion. However, in reference to the *agens supernaturalis* which creates the act of being itself, the proposition in question is by no means self-evident. In the wake of revelation, one can see that even the most obvious "truths" about the world are thrown into question, precisely because a new horizon of ultimacy has opened up. The "natural" is now no longer the final context for the playing out of the destiny of the universe and the agents within it; and we know this precisely through the elevation of consciousness that took place in revelation.

This novelty is even more dramatically highlighted in the play between the seventeenth objection and response, and it is here that we glimpse for the first time what I call the christological heart of the creation teaching. The objector maintains, sensibly enough, that if God makes something from nothing, he *dat esse* (gives being). But that which receives this being which God gives is either something or nothing. If it is nothing, then nothing is made (there being no proper recipient); if, on the other hand, it is something, it is outside of the creative act of God, since nothing can be, simultaneously, both recipient and that which is received. Thus it seems to follow that God must create from something preexisting. Once more, the objector is operating within the intellectual framework of Aristotle, for whom the formation of the world has to do with the prime mover's shaping of preexisting matter through attraction, drawing its potentialities to actuality.

Thomas's response to this powerful objection is beautifully understated. In two lines, Aquinas signals the overthrow of generally accepted ontology: "God simultaneously gives being and produces that which receives being. And thus it does not follow that his action requires something preexisting."[17] Again we remark the Zen-like language: that which receives being is the being that it receives. What Thomas indicates through this paradoxical language is that the being-to-being rapport is undermined in the context of creation. The creature cannot be a "something" outside of God that receives as a relational accident some influence from the Creator. Rather the creature *is* the act by which it is created. The relationship between Creator and creature, in other words, is primary and elemental and the "substances" involved—God and the world—are derivative, metaphysically secondary. The giver–receiver language, inextricably tied to a metaphysic of substance, cannot be applied to the act by which finitude itself is constituted. In question 7 Aquinas had shown that God is not a "thing," not an *individuum*; in this response to objection 17 he hints at something just as radical, namely, that the creature too is not a "thing" but a sheer relationship.

It is this last insight that is explicitly developed in article 3 of question 3. The query that Thomas poses is this: "whether creation is something really in the creature." To what degree, in other words, does the act of creation reach into the constitution of the thing created? He begins his *Respondeo* with a survey of various opinions that have been offered on the "locality" of creation, and then he offers his own solution, basing it, as he usually does, on a distinction. There are, says Thomas, two types of *creatio*, active and passive. The former, designating the action of God bringing the world into being, is identical to the essence of God and hence is *in* God. However, inasmuch as it involves no dependency of God on the creature (since God need not create) it is not "really" in God. In other words, the *operatio* by which God makes the world *is* God, but the *relatio* to the creature that occurs through this *operatio* is in God only logically. Now, taken in a passive sense *creatio* designates, not a change in the creature, but a relation to the Creator:

Creation cannot be taken as a movement of the creature prior to its reaching the terminus of its movement but must be taken as an accomplished fact. Consequently, creation itself is not an approach to being, nor a change brought about by the creator, but only the beginning of being and the relation to the creator from whom the creature has its being. And thus creation is nothing other than a certain relation to God, with the newness of being.[18]

Because there is no substrate to the process, creation is not a movement, and because there is no time "prior" to creation, the *inceptio* involved is not a temporal emergence into being. Rather, creation is the "beginning" of finite being in the sense that God's action is the *principium*, deepest ground and ontological constitution of the finite realm. And precisely as *inceptio*, creation is a *relatio*. The creature is not some thing that *has* a relation or experiences *inceptio*; rather, the creature is nothing other than a beginning, nothing other than a relation, nothing other than the openness to the simple reality. In a word, the creature *is* what Thomas calls passive creation, *is* this *quaedam relatio* to God that involves the "newness of being."

What becomes clear is the sheer radicality of the dependence of the creature on the God who creates ex nihilo. In one of his best-known poems, Gerard Manley Hopkins says that "there lives the dearest freshness deep down things." This comes close to what Thomas means by the act of creation: In the richest sense, the creature is not a being standing over and against the supreme being; rather, the creature is, in every aspect of its reality, nothing but a relation of dependency upon the God who continually *dat esse*, gives the activity of to-be. And thus we can understand Thomas's insistence on "newness of being." At every moment, the creature is constituted anew, afresh, by the inrushing of the divine gift; the creature has nothing to cling to, no neutral place to stand apart from the divine—and this very dependency is, paradoxically, the being of the creature, that which makes it itself.

And it is in light of these considerations that the properly christological orientation of Thomas's teaching emerges. We have seen that, seized by the novelty of revelation, he consistently undermines the assumptions of Aristotelian natural philosophy in his discourse concerning both God and the world. The *novum* of Christ breaks through in this "metaphysics of the Gospel," this peculiar insistence that the creature is most itself when it is least itself. Just as Jesus was the perfect human being precisely in his attitude of sheer openness to and dependency upon the will of God, so the creature is truest to itself in its uncompromised relationality, its "nonsubstantiality" before God. And again, such dependence is possible—both for the humanity of Christ and for the universe— because God is not a supreme being looming competitively and threateningly above the finite.

Conclusion

Thomas saw in the event of the Incarnation the strangeness of both God and creature and was thus led to a radical reimagination of the real. What Aristotle saw as a realm of substances in accidental relation to a prime mover, a supreme and self-absorbed substance, Thomas saw as an arena of creatures, that is to say, sheer relations to an immanent/transcendent act of self-emptying love. Did the coming-together of the natures of Christ—in personal union yet without mingling or confusion—signal to him that something else might be the case with regard to both the divine and the nondivine? And, if I might speculate a bit further, did he see that the world articulated by Aristotle and corresponding to a common-sense view of things, is the illusory world produced by sin? Is the blocky universe of mutually exclusive divine and nondivine substances not the universe overcome in the revelation of the Incarnation? And does Thomas not give us—in his theological undermining of both the supreme being and the supreme ego—a glimpse of a new world?

Notes

1. "... necessarium fuit ad humanam salutem, esse doctrinam quandam secundum revelationem divinam praeter philosophicas disciplinas quae ratione humana investigantur. Primo quidem quia homo ordinatur ad Deum sicut ad quendam finem qui comprehensionem rationis excedit." Thomas Aquinas, *Summa Theologiae*, Ia, q. 1, art. 1.

2. Pierre Teilhard de Chardin, *The Divine Milieu* (New York: Harper and Row, 1968), 50–93.

3. "... nihil prohibet id quod est certius secundum naturam esse quoad nos minus certum propter debilitatem intellectus nostri qui se habet ad manifestissima naturae sicut oculus noctuae ad lumen solis." Aquinas, *Summa Theologiae*, Ia, art. 5, ad. 1.

4. "Quia Salvator noster Dominus Iesus Christus...viam veritatis nobis in seipso demonstravit per quam ad beatitudinem immortalis vitae resurgendo pervenire possimus, necesse est ut ad consummationem totius theologici negotii ... de ipso omnium Salvatore ... consideratio subsequatur." Aquinas, *Summa Theologiae*, IIIa, prologus.

5. "... per incarnationis mysterium monstratur simul bonitas et sapientia et iustitia et potentia Dei ... bonitas quidem, quoniam non despexit proprii plasmatis infirmitatem; iustitia vero, quoniam non alium facit vincere tyrannum neque vi eripit ex morte hominem ... potentia vero sive virtus infinita quia nihil est maius quam Deum fieri hominem." Aquinas, *Summa Theologiae*, IIIa, q. 1 art. 1.

6. Robert Sokolowski, *The God of Faith and Reason* (Notre Dame, Ind.: University of Notre Dame Press, 1982), 31–40.

7. "... Pertinet autem ad rationem boni ut se aliis communicet.... Unde ad rationem summi boni pertinet quod summo modo se creaturae communicet. Quod quidem maxime fit per hoc quod naturam creatam sic sibi coniungit ut una persona fiat ex tribus, Verbo, anima et carne." Aquinas, *Summa Theologiae*, IIIa, q. 1, art. 1.

8. "Nam creaturae insufficientes erant ad ducendum in cognitionem creatoris ... unde necessarium erat ut ipse creator per carnem in mundum veniret, et per seipsum cognosceretur." In Jn. para. 141.

9. "... propter unionem animae illius ad Verbum Dei. Quanto enim aliquod receptivum propinquius est causae influenti, tanto magis participat de influentia ipsius ... propter nobilitatem illius animae, cuius operationes oportebat propinquissime attingere ad Deum per cognitionem et amorem ... propter habitudinem ipsius Christi ad genus humanum." Aquinas, *Summa Theologiae*, IIIa, q. 7, art. 1.

10. "... quidquid fuit in humana natura Christi, movebatur nutu divinae voluntatis; non tamen sequitur quod in Christo non fuerit motus voluntatis proprius naturae humanae. Quia etiam aliorum sanctorum piae voluntates moventur secundum voluntatem Dei...Licet enim voluntas non possit interius moveri ab aliqua creatura, interius tamen movetur a Deo." Aquinas, *Summa Theologiae*, IIIa, q. 18, art. 1, ad. 1.

11. "Omnes autem causae creatae communicant in uno effectu qui est esse, licet singulae proprios effectus habeant, in quibus distinguuntur. Calor enim facit calidum esse, et aedificator facit domum esse. Conveniunt ergo in hoc quod causant esse sed differeunt in hoc quod ignis causat ignem, et aedificator causat domum. Oportet ergo esse aliquam causam superiorem omnibus cuius virtute omnia causant esse et eius esse sit proprius effectus. Et haec causa est Deus." Aquinas, *De potentia*, q. 7, art. 2.

12. Ibid.

13. "Ex hoc ulterius patet quod Deus non est species, nec individuum, nec habet differentiam, nec definitionem: nam omnis definitio est ex genere et specie." Aquinas, *De potentia*, q. 7, art. 3.

14. ". . . tenendum est firmiter quod Deus potest facere aliquid ex nihilo et facit." Aquinas, *De potentia*, q. 3, art. 1.

15. "Et ideo agens naturale non producit simpliciter ens, sed ens praeexistens et determinatum ad hoc vel ad aliud, ut puta ad speciem ignis, vel ad albedinem, vel ad aliquid huiusmodi. Et propter hoc, agens nturale agit movendo; et ideo requirit materiam, quae sit subiectum mutationis vel motus, et propter hoc non potest aliquid ex nihilo facere." Aquinas, *De potentia*, q. 3, art. 1.

16. "Ipse autem Deus e contrario est totaliter actus, et in comparatione sui, quia est actus purus non habens potentiam permixtam, et in comparatione rerum quae sunt in actu, quia in eo est omnium entium origo; unde per suam actionem producit totum ens subsistens, nullo praesupposito, utpote qui est totius esse principium. . . . Et propter hoc ex nihilo aliquid facere potest; et haec eius actio vacatur creatio." Aquinas, *De potentia*, q. 3, art. 1.

17. ". . . Deus simul dans esse, producit id quod esse recipit; et sic non oportet quod agat ex aliquo praeexistenti." Aquinas, *De potentia*, q. 3, art. 1, ad. 17.

18. "Creatio autem . . . non potest accipi ut moveri, quod est ante terminum motus, sed accipitur ut in facto esse; unde in ipsa creatione non importatur aliquis accessus ad esse, nec transmutatio a creante, sed solummodo inceptio essendi, et relatio ad creatorem a quo esse habet; et sic creatio nihil est aliud realiter quam relatio quaedam ad Deum cum novitate essendi." Aquinas, *De potentia*, q. 3, art. 3.

The Christian Humanism of Karol Wojtyla and Thomas Aquinas

Karol Wojtyla and Thomas Aquinas are separated by 700 years. One is a diocesan priest and bishop in the twentieth and twenty-first century, the other was a thirteenth-century Dominican friar. One came of age in the maelstrom of one of the darkest periods of recorded history, caught between the pincers of two maliciously anti-Christian totalitarianisms, the other in a conflicted but still relatively stable Christian culture. One entered into the philosophical conversation as the modern world was giving way to the postmodern, while the other dialogued and debated in an unambiguously premodern context. Despite these significant differences, the two thinkers can illumine one another precisely because of the overwhelmingly important thing that they had in common, that is, their faith in the God–man Jesus Christ. Both believed that the mystery of creation and the mystery of God are most richly disclosed in the Incarnation, and hence both took that event as the lens through which all of reality is properly surveyed.

In this chapter, I will concentrate on the Christian humanism that emerges in the writings of Wojtyla and Aquinas, a perspective that is a thoroughgoing paradox. For both thinkers, the human being is fully alive precisely in the measure that he conforms himself to the radical obedience of Jesus Christ, which is to say, Jesus' utter surrender in love to the Father. For both, authentic human freedom is had in an act of self-forgetting and self-abandonment. What makes this a paradox and not a contradiction is the oddness of the person to whom the surrender is offered: a God whose entire being is a being for the other, a God who is nothing but the giver of gifts. I will develop this insight in two basic stages. First, I shall examine some key texts of Thomas Aquinas dealing with Incarnation, creation, and the nature of God, in the hopes of explicating Thomas's understanding of God as noncompetitively and noncontrastively transcendent to the world. Next, against this background, I shall examine some themes in the theological ethics of Karol Wojtyla, endeavoring to show that, for him, robust human flourishing is possible only through a Christ-like abandonment to God, or to state it more abstractly, that freedom is most itself when it is placed in correlation to the truth.

THE DISTINCTION IN THOMAS AQUINAS

In his dismissive assessment of Thomas Aquinas, Bertrand Russell said that Thomas was a competent commentator on Aristotle, but no more, and that this modest achievement was out of all proportion to his enormous reputation.[1] Such a construal is possible only for someone who read Aquinas inattentively, for what makes Thomas so interesting is precisely the way he twists and turns Aristotle's language, struggling to make it speak a truth that Aristotle himself never envisioned. Thomas Prufer said that Aquinas spoke "a fractured Aristotlese," implying that, when Aquinas employed it, the rhetoric of the philosopher broke under the weight of something it could not quite bear, that is, the Incarnation of God. It is my contention that the entire theology of Thomas—especially as he articulates it in the second *Summa*—is conditioned by this great fact and hence becomes unintelligible apart from it. Therefore, if we want to understand his view of God, cosmos, and the human, we must turn first to the texts on the enfleshment of the Son of God.

The opening question of the third part of the *Summa theologiae* is this: whether it is *conveniens* (fitting) that God become a creature.[2] After entertaining objections on both metaphysical and aesthetic grounds, Thomas answers that the Incarnation was supremely fitting because God is the ultimate good and the good, as Pseudo-Dionysius argued, is *diffi-sivum sui* (diffusive of itself), and there could be no greater self-gift than that God would become a creature out of love. In a word, the Incarnation was fitting because it was peculiarly characteristic of the one whose very nature is self-offering. Now, to press the matter a bit, this act on the part of God could be seen as good only in the measure that it benefited the one who received it. In so many of the ancient mythologies, gods and goddesses "become" human, but this takes place in an invasive and manipulative way. What stands behind Thomas's discussion, of course, is the great antipagan formulation of the Council of Chalcedon, that the Incarnation takes place through the hypostatic joining of two natures, divine and human, that remain, even in the union, distinct and integral. This means that God "becomes" a creature without ceasing to be God or violating the integrity of the creature he becomes. The closeness of God does not undermine humanity, but rather enhances it.

Robert Sokolowski has pointed out with great insistence that such a state of affairs could hold only if there is an absolutely basic distinction between God and the world. Were God in any sense a creaturely or finite nature, a thing *in* the world, he could not become a creature without some sort of compromising either of his own being or that of the thing that he becomes.[3] This is true because there is a mutual exclusivity at the ontological level between any two finite natures: an antelope "becomes" a lion only by being devoured, and a house becomes ash only by being destroyed. But since in Christ God enters into creation in the most intimate sense without undermining creaturely integrity, without ontological violence, God must be utterly unlike that which he enters. Were he of the same type as a worldly nature, he couldn't establish the closeness to a worldly nature that is described in the doctrine of the Incarnation. And here we begin to sense the high paradox of the central Christian claim. This divine otherness that we have been describing cannot be construed simply and one-sidedly as "transcendence," as though God were, in Karl Barth's phrase, a distant planet or a Greek philosophical idol.[4] Were God simply "spatially" or even "quantitatively" other—a highest or supreme being among many—he would still be a worldly nature and still therefore incapable of effecting the Incarnation. The God of Jesus Christ must be qualitatively other, not so much somewhere else, but some*how* else, this peculiar otherness allowing him to establish an unheard of intimacy with that which he is not.

Kathryn Tanner has expanded upon Sokolowski's formula by speaking of God's noncompetitive and noncontrastive transcendence to the world. She implies that God is other but precisely not the way that one worldly nature is contrastively over and against another.[5] God's to-be does not face down the to-be of a creature, competing with it for time, space, or ontological primacy. God differs from the world to be sure, but he differs differently than creatures differ from one another. When in the *Proslogion*, St. Anselm "defines" God as "that than which no greater can be thought," he is giving voice to this same paradox.[6] If God were a being in or alongside of the world (like a classical god or goddess), he would not be that than which no greater can be thought, since he plus the rest of the world would be greater than he alone.[7] God must exist in such a way that the universe's existence neither adds to nor subtracts from his own being; while retaining his complete otherness, he must be, in Nicholaus of Cusa's phrase, the *non Aliud*. And this is why, furthermore, Thomas Aquinas rarely used the phrase *ens summum* (highest being) when speaking of God, preferring instead the more mysterious *ipsum esse subsistens* (the sheer act of to-be itself). The unreceived energy of existence is, obviously, radically unlike any existing thing, even as it enters "by essence, presence, and power" into all existing things, from archangels to atoms.

What Sokolowski calls "the Christian distinction" is especially on display in Aquinas's doctrine of creation. In the mythologies and cosmologies of the ancient world, the universe comes into being through some act of primordial violence, one god defeating another, or a divine principle wrestling some recalcitrant force into submission. The rational cosmologies of Plato and Aristotle retain a good deal of this mythic quality. Plato holds that matter is shaped by the Demiurge in accord with the patterns of the forms, and Aristotle argues that prime matter is drawn into form through the attractive power of the prime mover. In both cases, the divine influence is aggressive and external: something that stands over and against God is brought into order through divine action. There is none of this in Aquinas. Following the church fathers, Thomas speaks of *creatio ex nihilo*, the bringing of the universe in its entirety into being from nothing. Creation in the proper sense is not the shaping of matter (since prime matter is itself a creature); it is not a spatial event (since space is a creature); and it does not take place in time (since time itself is the result of creation). There is, quite literally, nothing "outside" of God that would be ontologically capable of receiving the act of creation. In the third question of the *De potentia*—where Thomas develops this counterintuitive notion most thoroughly—we find a remark that is paradoxical to an almost Zen-like degree: "that which receives the creative act is created by that which it receives."[8] In a word, absolutely everything that exists in the world derives its being completely, and in every aspect, from the creative power of God. This means, on the one hand, that the creature is utterly dependent on God, but it entails, on the other hand, that there is absolutely nothing in the creative act that is violent, aggressive, or invasive. The world in its totality is from God, and God, in the most radical sense, lets the world be. What comes forth from God is utterly of God, yet, as finite and created, it is infinitely other than God, so that the integrity of creation is a function of its absolute dependency upon the Creator. Admittedly, none of this makes sense in the context of our ordinary speech about worldly things. If a person came too close to me, I would accuse him of being domineering and manipulative; if a woman were utterly dependent upon a man (or vice versa), we would properly describe their relationship as dysfunctional. But once more, it is just this sort of over-and-againstness and mutual exclusivity that is being denied in the doctrine of *creation ex nihilo*. It is not despite the divine closeness, but rather precisely because of it, that the creature can be itself.

Correlative to the doctrine of creation from nothing is the doctrine of the *analogia entis*. For Thomas, God cannot be construed, as we have seen, as one being among many; rather, he must be conceived as the act of being that is otherly other than the realm of beings. God and creatures are not—as in Duns Scotus—beings categorized as varying types in the genus "existence." Rather, created things are participants in the primordial act of existence and hence are beings in only a mitigated and analogical sense. None of this implies pantheism of course, but it does mean that all of finite existence, while retaining its creaturely integrity, shares here and now in the to-be of God. Furthermore, the analogical conception of being entails the connectedness of all finite things to one another through God. Since all created realities come into being through a continual act of creation, they are all, despite their enormous differences at the surface level, linked together at the deepest ground of their existence. To be sure, creaturely connections can never be utterly noncompetitive or noncontrastive, but when they are effected at the level of *creatio ex nihilo*, they participate in something of God's way of relating. This is why Augustine could remark that one person loves another more and better when he loves him "in God." Now what does this incarnational ontology have to do with Thomas's understanding of human flourishing? In a word, everything. Like all creatures, human beings are most integrally themselves in the measure that they are totally dependent upon the noncompetitive God. The difference is that human beings can consciously and freely either affirm or deny this ontological paradox; they can cooperate with the noncontrastive transcendence of God, or they can resist it. At the heart of the moral life, for Thomas Aquinas, is the realization of our freedom (our choice for the good) in surrender to the God who not only transcends all earthly values, but whose very goodness consists in a letting-be of the other. Our freedom is properly correlated to the truth of things (organic interconnection) and to the Truth who is God (noncompetitive transcendence).

The Compromise of the Distinction

What we have been describing is the extremely subtle equilibrium that characterizes the Christian worldview. Because the relationships between God and the universe and among created things are so "delicate" in their metaphysical structure, it is quite easy to misconstrue them. It required the graced genius of an Aquinas to articulate them with even relative adequacy. In both Protestantism and its secular counterpart, philosophical modernity, we witness a fudging of *the* distinction and a concomitant misunderstanding of the rapport between the divine and the nondivine, a mistake that has had far-reaching theoretical and practical consequences. Before turning to the writings of Karol Wojtyla, it is necessary at least to sketch the contours of this dissolution, since his humanism is in many ways a response to it.

   It is commonly remarked that Martin Luther placed great stress on the transcendence of God, but it is less often appreciated how his particular interpretation of that transcendence flowed from his reading of the two-natures doctrine of Chalcedon. As we saw, the classical tradition—very much including Aquinas—stressed the noncompetitiveness of the natures joined in the one person of Christ, but Luther construed the natures in a much more contrastive manner, so that the divinity of Jesus threatened to swallow up his humanity. This led to the dichotomization between Creator and creature that can be seen throughout Luther's theology: For God to get all of the glory, humanity and the cosmos as a whole must be stripped of glory. God is placed by Luther in a transcendent realm almost as a gesture of protection, as though any closer contact with the world would compromise him. This distantiation was made possible, furthermore, through the univocal conception of being introduced by Scotus and given fuller expression by Occam and his nominalist successors who in turn helped to shape Luther's philosophical vision.[9]

   This Protestant misinterpretation of the God–world relationship was bequeathed to the secular philosophers of modernity, who in various ways sought to resolve the tension between humanity and a fundamentally competitive God. Descartes, Berkeley, and the Deists rendered God a somewhat distant and diffident justification for the essentially secular projects of politics and science. Spinoza solved the problem by simply dissolving the distinction between God and the world altogether: *Deus sive natura*. And most dramatically, Hobbes, Nietzsche, Feuerbach, Marx, and Sartre saw that a competitive God had to be eliminated if humanity is to reach full political, social, and personal flourishing. Nowhere is this principle more clearly stated than in Sartre's pithy syllogism: "If God exists, I cannot be free; but I am free. Therefore God does not exist."[10] If Luther separated God and humans in order to protect God, the atheists did so in order to protect us. Michael Buckley has shown that as modernity unfolded, the competitive God took on more and more the features of the devil, the ancient "enemy of the human race."[11]

It has been central to the project of Louis Dupré to demonstrate that modernity involved the unweaving of the intertwined tapestry of God, world, and self that classical Christianity had maintained.[12] As we saw, when God is understood as the sheer act of being itself, then cosmos and soul find their integral meaning in relation to the divine. But when God is demonized, world and psyche lose their ontological moorings and hence their connection to God and to one another. The loss of objective meaning is correlative to the characteristically modern positing of the subject as source of meaning. Dupré has shown that it was not subjectivism itself that marks the modern—for a kind of turn to the subject can be found in Plato, Plotinus, Augustine, and Bonaventure—but rather the view that the subject creates value rather than recognizing it. Sartre's existentialism is therefore but the explicitation of what was implicit in modernity from Descartes on.

KAROL WOJTYLA AND THE PROBLEM OF FREEDOM

As a twentieth-century son of Poland, Karol Wojtyla was perhaps uniquely positioned to survey and understand the tension between the systems we have been describing. As a young man, in the twenties and thirties of the last century, Wojtyla took in through every pore a vibrantly Catholic culture. In the liturgy, public devotions, poetry and drama, personal prayer, and the political/social life itself, the young man witnessed a world permeated by the Catholic attitude and spirit. Then, commencing in the late thirties, and continuing through the forties, fifties, and sixties, Wojtyla found himself caught between two ideological systems—Nazism and Communism—that were made possible by the breakdown of the Catholic synthesis.[13] As he wrestled with these especially fierce outgrowths of modernity, both of which claimed to be an authentic humanism, he felt compelled to articulate why the true friend of humanity was precisely the incarnational Christianity that both Nazism and Communism repudiated.

The Catholicism that Wojtyla absorbed viscerally through prayer and aesthetically through drama came to him in a more intellectual form during his studies in Rome. There, under the inspiration of Garrigou-Lagrange and others at the Angelicum, Wojtyla studied the philosophy and theology of Aquinas, as well as the mysticism of John of the Cross. Upon his return to Poland as a priest, he did pastoral work for a brief period and then, at the prompting of the Cardinal Archbishop of Cracow, Adam Sapieha, he began studies for a second, civilly recognized doctorate.[14] The topic he chose for his research was the phenomenological ethics of Max Scheler, one of the most gifted and spiritually alert disciples of Husserl. In the prologue to his major work *The Acting Person*, Wojtyla admitted that, despite his disagreements with him, Scheler has remained perhaps the most profound influence on his own work.[15] Therefore, to understand precisely how he sought to engage modernity philosophically, it is important for us to explore Wojtyla's relationship to the Schelerian project.

What Wojtyla immediately appreciated in phenomenology was what attracted figures such as Dietrich von Hildebrand and Edith Stein to the discipline, namely, its robust objectivism. Over and against the tired Kantianism of his time, Husserl had famously cried *zu den Sachen selbst* (to the things themselves). The Kantian distinction between noumenon and phenomenon Husserl took to be wrong-headed and counterproductive, and he accordingly encouraged his disciples to describe the objectively real as it appeared to a properly intentional consciousness. Max Scheler applied this method to the problems of ethics, arguing that morality flows ultimately from certain basic intuitions of objective value *(Wert)*. The suspicion of Kant that Scheler inherited from Husserl took an even more pointed form in the context of this ethical analysis. Kant had driven a wedge between the interior and purely formal realm of the categorical imperative and the exterior dimension of feeling and inclination, insisting that the former was alone the ground for proper moral deliberation. Scheler reacted strongly against this excessive rationalism and formalism and held that moral intuition is largely affective, embodied in nature, a feeling with the values that show themselves.[16] This Schelerian stress on bodiliness and passion would exert a powerful influence on Wojtyla's moral thinking. Another feature of the Kantian moral system that Scheler found unpalatable was the element of autonomous self-regard. The claim that "the only thing that can be described as unambiguously good is a good will" led, Scheler felt, to a sort of Pharisaism, a fussily introspective obsession with the integrity of the will itself. Better for the moral subject to lose himself in the intuition of objective value.[17]

Wojtyla's analysis of Scheler touched on both of these reactions to Kant. Though he reverenced the importance of the body in moral assessment, Wojtyla held that feelings as such could never ground the ethical life. He was convinced that values had to be apprehended primarily by intellect, lest one devolve into an unstable and relativizing subjectivism. And he thought that the Kantian autonomy, rightly understood, was not Pharisaism but rather a gathering or creation of self that was indispensable to the moral project. As he reflected further, he came to see that Kant and Scheler situated themselves on opposing sides of a whole series of unhealthy dualisms: between duty and inclination, autonomy and passivity, freedom and truth. His own project then took shape as a bridging of these divides, especially the last. As a phenomenologist, Scheler stood, however inadequately, for the great classical value of objective truth, while Kant stood for the central modern value of freedom and self-determination. What they lacked was the integrating Catholic worldview that would allow for the coexistence of both values.

Wojtyla's mature thought came to expression in two texts, *Love and Responsibility*, essentially lectures from his Lublin course on the morality of marriage and sexuality, and *The Acting Person*, an extremely dense philosophical meditation on freedom and action, which he penned while attending the sessions of the Second Vatican Council. The very difficulty of the prose in *The Acting Person*—even seasoned philosophers often found it impenetrable—led some to speculate that Wojtyla was trying to keep his deepest intentions hidden from Communist censors. Then again, perhaps it was simply the result of blending the two quite disparate philosophical systems of Thomism and phenomenology.

The best way to get at Wojtyla's argument in *The Acting Person* is to revisit the classical thomistic distinction between an *actus humanus* (a human act) and an *actus hominis* (an act of a man).[18] The latter, of course, is something that a man happens to do, like sneezing or reacting instinctively upon being startled, whereas the former is an act that proceeds from the deliberation of intellect and the choice of will. An *actus hominis* is accidental to the person, whereas an *actus humanus* is the product of the gathered and responsible self. Against this Thomistic background and in accord with his Schelerian training, Wojtyla endeavors to analyze more precisely the nature of such an act. On the one hand, a properly human act is a response to an objective value that appears in the world, to some good that is consciously appreciated as desirable. Here Wojtyla thinks that Scheler's phenomenology is more correct than Kant's deontology. On the other hand, a truly human act is also supremely subjective in the measure that it contributes to the process of self-creation. And here Kant's characteristically modern stress on autonomy is more correct than Scheler's insistence on passivity before the world of value.

We have to proceed with some care at this point, for it is quite easy to misconstrue Wojtyla's language in an almost Pelagian direction. What he means is that there are two objects—one direct and the other indirect—to every deliberate moral act. First, the good to be sought—food, shelter, fame, friendship—is desired, but second, the good of the self, the excellence of the moral subject as such, is simultaneously sought. In moral choice, one is always desiring a particular end *and* choosing the kind of person one wants to be, so that the subject itself is treated quasi-objectively. Wojtyla goes so far as to say that the person, as efficient cause of his own deliberate action, is at the same time the efficient cause of his own self.[19] The debt to Aristotle's theory of habit and character formation should be clear here, but Wojtyla radicalizes Aristotle in light of modernity's stress on freedom and autonomy. The will's active shaping of character "adds to the world a perfection no one else can add," a new *kind* of value. Borrowing from the Kantian tradition, he speaks of this capacity to stand over and freely shape the moral self as "transcendental." In this emphasis on self-determination, Wojtyla sounds like Kant, Jefferson, and Rousseau and does in fact push beyond the insufficiently dynamic anthropology of Aquinas.[20] What makes all the difference—and here we come to the heart of it—is that this act of self-creation does not proceed from the dynamism of the will itself nor from an arbitrary choice, but from the always concomitantly chosen objective good.

The objective transcendentals—the good, the true, and the beautiful—ground and make possible the subjective "transcendentalism" that Wojtyla describes. And this is the same dovetailing of freedom and truth that stood at the very heart of Aquinas's Christian humanist project.

JESUS CHRIST AS SUBJECTIVE AND OBJECTIVE NORM

To this point, we have seen how Karol Wojtyla has reconciled, through his own version of transcendental anthropology, the modern concern for autonomy and the classical concern for truth, but we haven't yet considered the rapport between freedom and the truth of God, especially as that truth has been made manifest in Jesus Christ. This relationship, which, for reasons both methodological and prudential, was relatively muted in Wojtyla's philosophical writings, came to rich and explicit expression in the encyclical letters that he would write as Pope John Paul II. As many commentators have noted, the passage from Gaudium et Spes, 22—"it is only in the mystery of the Word Incarnate that light is shed on the mystery of man"—has served as a leitmotiv and hermeneutical key for John Paul II.[21] The adoption of this theme has extremely important methodological implications, for it reverses the momentum of so much liberal theological speculation that has tended to read (and hence misread) Christ in light of man instead of vice versa. But for John Paul, it has a more substantive meaning as well, namely, that Jesus Christ is the truth about humanity in both the objective and subjective sense, that is to say, he is the goal which the will seeks and he is the proper structure of the autonomous person. In the last section of this paper, I will sketch the outlines of this Christocentric anthropology.

The opening chapter of John Paul's 1993 encyclical Vertitatis Splendor is an analysis of Matthew's account of the conversation between Jesus and the rich young man. Found in all three of the synoptic Gospels, this scene has been identified by N. T. Wright as a turning point and hinge in the Gospel narrative, and for John Paul as well, it is a key text. For the Pope, to grasp the meaning of this story is to understand the central dynamic of the New Testament, the free response to Jesus' offer of eternal life. Stanley Hauerwas has exulted that this major statement of Catholic moral theology commences, not with philosophical abstractions, but with Jesus. Though it certainly represents a departure from more standard accounts, the Christocentrism of *Veritatis Splendor* should not be surprising to the attentive student of Karol Wojtyla's thought, for what is on explicit display here, I maintain, is the Christianity that had, from the beginning, characterized all of Wojtyla's moral philosophy, even in its most abstruse expressions. The truth to which subjective freedom is oriented has always been ultimately the truth who is the person of Christ.

In Matthew's telling, a young man comes to Jesus and asks, "Teacher, what good must I do to have eternal life?" For the Pope, this honest and searching question symbolizes the universal longing of the human being for moral integrity.[22] As such, it is not primarily a question regarding rules, commandments, and prohibitions, but a quest for "the full meaning of life." Jesus' initial response is the somewhat enigmatic: "Why do you ask me about what is good? There is only one who is good" (Matt. 19:17). In fact, this cuts to the heart of the matter. The greatest mistake that the moral searcher can make is to presume that the goal of his quest can be found in any good or truth other than God. One of the most insistently repeated themes of the Bible is that, since we are made according to God's image, we will not find fulfillment in anything other than God, or in any simulacrum of divinity. And this insight is repeated by practically every major figure in our tradition, most famously and poetically by Augustine ("our hearts are restless until they rest in thee"), more rationally but just as clearly by Thomas Aquinas in the opening questions of the *Prima secundae*.

How is this prime objective value to be sought? Jesus asks the rich young man whether he has followed the commandments—"you shall not murder; you shall not commit adultery; you shall not bear false witness; honor your mother and father . . . love your neighbor as yourself"—and the young man responds affirmatively. Here we are at the first stage of moral development, but the distinctive mark of biblical ethics is already visible. Since the one we seek is himself an act of self-forgetting love, we attain him only to the degree that we become internally conformed to his way of being. Hence all of those egregious violations of love—murder, adultery, hatred of one's neighbor, and so on—must be eliminated in the seeker after God. The Pope cites the clearest New Testament affirmation of this principle: "If anyone says, 'I love God,' and hates his brother, he is a liar; for he who does not love his brother whom he has seen, cannot love the God whom he has not seen" (1 John 4:20). The reaching of the goal presupposes, in a word, a preliminary gathering of the self around the precepts of love.

But the real drama of this story begins precisely at the point where one might be tempted to say that ethical reflection ends. Somewhat plaintively, the young man says, "I have kept all these; what do I still lack?" (Matt. 19:20). Though we may suspect that it is only someone very young who could claim that he has kept all of the commandments, we still notice something of great importance in his intuition and question. Because the human being is made in God's image, his soul has a kind of infinite *capax*, an expansiveness that corresponds, however imperfectly, to the fullness of the divine reality. Therefore the simple keeping of the fundamental commandments—most of which are negative in character—can never be enough to satisfy the spirit. In Mark's version of the story, Jesus then looks at the man with love and says, "Go, sell what you own, and give the money to the poor, and you will have treasure in heaven; then come and follow me" (Mark 10:21). The look of love, of course, is a marvelous detail, for it signals, not only Jesus' encouragement of the young man and an approval of his question, but also the divine grace that is required for the next step in the moral itinerary. Once the soul has been shaped in the direction of love through the discipline of the commandments, it is now ready for a more complete and dramatic self-emptying. It is ready for the *sequela Christi*, the following of Christ on the path of discipleship. And this is a matter, not only of external imitation, but of the deepest inner conformity to Christ, a walking with him in the manner of an apprentice shaping his life in accord with his master's. It goes beyond the commandments, because it involves a total gift of self, even to the point of death, for Christ leads the disciple in one direction, the cross. This "law of the gift," as George Weigel describes it, comes to more explicit expression at the end of *Veritatis Splendor* when the Pope analyzes the limit case of Christian martyrdom.[23] Though he doesn't court death, the disciple of Jesus accepts death when circumstances are such that there is no other way to bear witness to the holiness of God and the dignity of human life.

A first theme to which we should attend in the story of the rich young man is that of freedom. Of his own free will, the man comes up to Jesus and poses his question. Jesus answers him and then stands open to further dialogue; finally, he invites him to the deepest form of life. At no point in this conversation is there a hint of violence or coercion. Even at the end, when the young man walks away sad, unable to respond to Jesus' demand, the Lord lets him go. The true God, as we have seen, does not compete with freedom; rather he awakens it and directs it. Second, we notice a dovetailing of the inner and outer, of the objective and the subjective, that we remarked in Wojtyla's philosophical treatment of the human act. The choice of the proper object for freedom—God—corresponds at every stage to the choice to be conformed unto Christ. The *sequela Christi* is hence freedom's objective and subjective norm. In choosing Christ, the person opts for his proper end (because Jesus *is* the God he seeks), and he creates his proper self (for Jesus *is* the paradigm of a renewed humanity). When Paul says, "it is no longer I who live but Christ who lives in me," he implies that the fully gathered self is the self that is conformed to the point of identity with the thoughts and desires of Jesus. Thomas Aquinas confirms this intuition in saying that Christ is, simultaneously, the Truth and the Way, the former because he is God and the latter because he is human.

Conclusion

It begins and ends with the law of the gift. Thomas Aquinas thought that the Incarnation was *conveniens* because it corresponds so fully with the kind of reality God is, that is to say, one that is *diffisivum sui*. As God gives himself away, humanity is lifted up. By the same token, Thomas thought that full human flourishing was accomplished in the act of surrender to the ultimate good who is God. Karol Wojtyla, speaking in a more modern idiom, said that human freedom is realized in a surrender to the truth of God; and then he announced that that truth is none other than a God who hands over his life to us. For both thinkers, the most authentic humanism, therefore, consists in a meeting of two ec-stasies, divine and human, a dovetailing of two freedoms, a coming-to-gether of an infinite and finite mode of being-for-the-other.

In a word, for both Thomas Aquinas and Karol Wojtyla, authentic humanism *is* Jesus Christ.

Notes

1. Bertrand Russell, *A History of Western Philosophy* (New York: Simon and Schuster, 1972), 462.

2. Thomas Aquinas, *Summa theologiae,* IIIa, q.1, art. 1., in *Summa Theologica,* vol. 5, trans. Fathers of the English Dominican Province (Westminster, Md.: Christian Classics, 1981).

3. Robert Sokolowski, *The God of Faith and Reason* (Washington, D.C.: Catholic University of America Press, 1982), 34–39.

4. Karl Barth, *The Humanity of God* (Atlanta: John Knox Press, 1960), 43.

5. Kathryn Tanner, *Jesus, Humanity, and the Trinity: A Brief Systematic Theology* (Minneapolis: Fortress Press, 2001), 1–8.

6. Anselm of Canterbury, "Proslogium," in *St. Anselm: Basic Writings,* trans. S.N. Deane (LaSalle, Ill.: Open Court, 1974), 7.

7. Sokolowski, *God of Faith and Reason,* 8.

8. Thomas Aquinas, *Quaestio disputata de potentia Dei,* q. 3, art. 3, in *Quaestiones disputatae,* vol. 2 (Turino: Marietti, 1965), 43.

9. Colin Gunton, *The One, the Three, and the Many: God, Creation, and the Culture of Modernity* (Cambridge: Cambridge University Press, 1993), 56–58.

10. Jean-Paul Sartre, *Existentialisme est un humanisme* (Paris: Les Editions de Nagel, 1970), 21.

11. Michael Buckley, "Modernity and the Satanic Face of God," in *Christian Spirituality and the Culture of Modernity: The Thought of Louis Dupré* (Grand Rapids, Mich.: William B. Eerdmans, 1998), 101.

12. Louis Dupré, *Passage to Modernity: An Essay in the Hermeneutics of Nature and Culture* (New Haven: Yale University Press, 1993), 93–105.

13. See George Weigel, *Witness to Hope: The Biography of Pope John Paul II* (New York: Harper Collins, 1999), esp. 44–87.

14. Jaroslaw Kupczak, *Destined for Liberty: The Human Person in the Philosophy of Karol Wojtyla/John Paul II* (Washington, D.C.: Catholic University of America Press, 2000), 6–7.

15. Rocco Buttiglione, *Karol Wojtyla: The Thought of the Man Who Became John Paul II* (Grand Rapids, Mich.: William B. Eerdmanns, 1997), 118.

16. Kupczak, *Destined for Liberty*, 34–36.

17. Ibid., 11–12.

18. Karol Wojtyla, *The Acting Person*, English trans. (Dordrecht/Boston/London: Reidel, 1979), xiii–xiv.

19. Buttliglione, *Karol Wojtyla*, 129–40.

20. Kupczak, *Destined for Liberty*, 57.

21. Weigel, *Witness to Hope*, 169.

22. John Paul II, *Veritatis Splendor*, in *The Encyclicals of John Paul II*, ed. J. Michael Miller, C.S.B. (Huntington, Ind: Our Sunday Visitor, 1996), 679.

23. Weigel, *Witness to Hope*, 136–37.

Chapter Nine

GOD AS ARTIST

THE IDEA OF GOD AS ARTIST HAS PLAYED A VITALLY IMPORTANT role in our tradition and has been, in quite interesting ways, revived by some contemporary theological writers. Following the lead of Hans Urs von Balthasar, I have found that, in so much of the patristic and medieval traditions, God the artist is a sort of master idea, a theological form that sheds light in all directions, illuminating our understanding of Trinity, creation, providence, Incarnation, and the problem of evil. Through post-modern Christian thinkers such as John Milbank and Catherine Pick-stock, I have discovered that this classical idea has important implications for ethics and social theory as well. In the course of this presentation, I shall endeavor to explore these insights and connections—both ancient and contemporary—that radiate forth from the compelling notion of God as the maker of beautiful things.

ART, BEAUTY, AND THE ARTIST

In order to approach our topic, we must first make some conceptual and terminological clarifications: what precisely is art, who is the artist, and how are both related to the beautiful? In his elegant and influential text *Art et Scolastique*, Jacques Maritain rehearses Aquinas's distinction between three modes of intellectual activity: the speculative, the practical, and the artistic.[1] In accord with the first, one contemplates the truth for its own sake, "theorizing" in the literal sense of the Greek term *theorein,* looking intently at the truth in its pure state. This is the intelligence of the philosopher. In accord with the second form of intellectuality, one seeks to know the ethically correct course of action, to have the *recta ratio agibilium* (the right mind in regard to things to be done). This is the intelligence of the prudent or morally alert person. Here the focus is not on the truth in itself but rather the truth inasmuch as it leads to the perfecting of the agent through choice and action. And in accord with the third form of reason, one seeks the truth with regard to things to be made *(recta ratio factibilium).* This is the form of intelligence characteristic of the artisan and the artist, those who shape matter according to intelligible patterns. Here the stress is on truth, not as an end in itself, nor as the guide to action, but as a principle for making. Thus, the philosopher is an intellectual who looks, the moral agent an intellectual who acts, and the artist is, in Maritain's phrase, *un intellectuel qui opère.*[2] This means that the artist's concern is form or objective intelligibility precisely as it shines in, through, and across matter.

With this clarification in mind, we can understand much more readily the perhaps surprisingly objective and rational account of beauty that we find in Aquinas and most of his predecessors. For Thomas, the beautiful is *quod visum placet,* that which having been seen, pleases. This formula—so typical of the scholastics in its laconicism and precision— would be misunderstood if the *visum* were construed in an exclusively visual or sensible way. Maritain eagerly reminds us that, for Aquinas, what is seen in aesthetic perception is the form or intelligibility of an artifact. Yet, lest we devolve into an excessive rationalism, it is equally important to remember the distinction between speculative and aesthetic perception. The philosopher considers form in abstraction from matter, while the artist considers it as it plays in matter. Whereas for the philosopher form is regarded *sub ratione veri* (under the rubric of the true), for the artist or aesthete, it is contemplated *sub ratione delectabilis* (under the rubric of the delightful) and thus awakens the pleasure implied in *placet.*[3]

In order to determine more precisely the nature of this aesthetic form, we must turn to the thirty-ninth question of the first part of the *Summa theologiae,* where Thomas provides his most thorough account of beauty. "For beauty includes three conditions, integrity or perfection, since those things which are impaired are by the very fact ugly; due proportion or harmony; and lastly, brightness or clarity, whence things are called beautiful which have a bright color."[4] Maritain delineates the meaning of these terms when he comments that the intellect delights in *integritas* because it loves being and perfection, *consonantia* because it loves order and unity, and *claritas* because it loves light and intelligibility. But to my mind the best explication of these three ideas is found in James Joyce's autobiographical novel, *A Portrait of the Artist as a Young Man*. Joyce was carefully trained in scholastic philosophy and maintained a lifelong interest in it, commenting once that the only real intellectual choice is between scholasticism or nihilism. Midway through the novel, Joyce's alter ego, Stephen Dedalus, engages his friend Lynch in a lively conversation around the topic of beauty. After citing the quote from the thirty-ninth question of the *Summa*, Stephen offers his commentary, using the visual aid of a "basket which a butcher's boy had slung inverted on his head":

> In order to see that basket, said Stephen, your mind first of all separates the basket from the rest of the visible universe which is not the basket. The first phase of apprehension is a bounding line drawn about the object to be apprehended. . . . You apprehend it as *one* thing. You see it as one whole. . . . That is *integritas*. . . . Then, said Stephen, you pass from point to point, led by its formal lines; you apprehend it as balanced part against part . . . you feel the rhythm of its structure. . . . You apprehend it as complex, multiple, divisible, separable . . . harmonious. That is *consonantia*.[5]

To this point, we seem well within the rational framework of the Scholastic account: The mind has taken in an object as unified, self-contained, and has then appreciated the play of the many that constitute that one. But what do we make of *claritas*, the brightness of color that Thomas spoke of? Stephen Dedalus admits that for a long time the full meaning of that term in Aquinas baffled him. Finally he came to this conclusion:

> When you have apprehended that basket as one thing and have then analysed it according to its form . . . you make the only synthe-

sis which is logically and aesthetically permissible. You see that it is that thing which it is and no other thing. The radiance of which he speaks is the scholastic *quidditas*, the *whatness* of a thing.[6]

Though Stephen's notion of *whatness* sounds a bit closer to Scotist *haecceitas* than to Thomas's *quidditas*, nevertheless it preserves the intellectualism that we have been insisting upon: When the aesthetic mind takes in *claritas*, it is exulting in the *splendor formae* (splendor of the form). After this careful analysis, Stephen describes the effect of the beautiful object upon the contemplator as one of "arrest" and "silent stasis." This too, as we have seen, is in line with scholastic intuitions. When the good is apprehended as good, it awakens in the will a desire to possess; but when the beautiful is appreciated as beautiful, it excites in the mind a desire to look. While the good draws you in, the beautiful stops you in your tracks, establishing thereby the distance required for contemplation.

Joyce gives exquisitely concrete expression to all of this abstract philosophizing in his account of Stephen's encounter with a girl standing in the surf just off Sandymount strand.

> A girl stood before him in midstream, alone and still, gazing out to sea.... Her long slender bare legs were delicate as a crane's.... Her slateblue skirts were kilted boldly about her waist and dovetailed behind her. . . . Her long fair hair was girlish: and girlish and touched with the wonder of mortal beauty her face.[7]

Because she is alone and still, silhouetted by the sea, Stephen can see her as one and perfect, separated from all that might compete for his attention. In a word, *integritas* is on display. Then he carefully follows the "rhythm of her structure," noticing how the various parts of her body and pieces of her clothing relate to one another and to the composite. *Consonantia* emerges. Next, the aesthetic arrest is described: "and when she felt his presence and the worship of his eyes her eyes turned to him in quiet suffrance of his gaze, without shame or wantonness. Long, long she suffered his gaze and then quietly withdrew her eyes from his . . ."[8] Like a medieval maiden sought by a troubadour, she allows him to worship, but at a proper distance, and she feels no shame because she knows that his look is not for the purpose of possession but rather contemplation. Finally, this aesthetic regard and attitude permit the appearance of *claritas:* "Heavenly God! cried Stephen's soul in an outburst of profane joy."[9] This exuberant exclamation is the subjective correlate to the *splendor formae.* When Stephen Dedalus had this encounter, he had just decided not to pursue a vocation as a Jesuit priest. In the wake of his aesthetic ecstasy, he resolved to become a priest of the beautiful, an artist, someone who would report "epiphanies." From that moment forth, he would be *un intellectuel qui opère,* a shaper of matter according to splendid form.

Joyce's justly celebrated account echoes two great loci in the tradition: Dante's encounter with Beatrice and the Diotima speech from Plato's *Symposium.* As a young man, Dante saw the beautiful Beatrice, and this experience awakened in him a desire to produce a poem surpassing in beauty any poem ever written. In a word, it gave him his artist's vocation and, more precisely, set him on the path that led to the writing of the *Divine Comedy.* In her culminating oration in the *Symposium,* Diotima gives voice to the Platonic conviction that the contemplation of beautiful objects and persons leads by a steady progress to a vision of the form of the beautiful itself:

> Starting from individual beauties, the quest for universal beauty must find him ever mounting the heavenly ladder, stepping from rung to rung—that is from one to two, and from two to every lovely body, from bodily beauty to the beauty of institutions, from institutions to learning, and from learning in general to the special lore that pertains to nothing but the beautiful itself—until at last he comes to know what beauty is.[10]

Just as Joyce's encounter with the girl in the surf conduced to an experience of the sacred ("Heavenly God"), so the Platonic aesthete's vision of the lovely body leads, through mystical ascent, to "the open sea" of the beautiful itself. Form seen opens one to the praise and imitation of the ultimate giver of form.

GOD THE ARTIST

These philosophical and literary texts from Plato, Dante, and Joyce serve as a fitting bridge from the clarification of terms to the main topic of this paper: God as artist, the intelligent maker of beautiful things. It is by no means of minor importance that Aquinas offers his definition of beauty in the context of his discussion of the Trinity. Thomas inherits from the tradition stretching back from Albertus Magnus to Augustine and Dionysius the deep conviction that God is, as being itself, the beautiful itself. Question 39 of the first part of the *Summa theologiae* has to do with the relations within the Trinity, and article 8, where the definition is found, considers the problem of the appropriation of specific terms to particular divine persons. Thus, just as *eternal*, though applicable to God as such, is appropriated to the Father because of his unoriginate nature, so, says Aquinas, the term *species* (beautiful or lovely), though correctly applied to all three persons, is appropriated to the Son. *Integritas, consonantia*, and *claritas* are specially attributable to the second person because, first, "he has in himself truly and perfectly the nature of the Father," second, "he is the express image of the Father," and third, "inasmuch as he is the Word which is light and splendor of the understanding."[11] In other words, wholeness belongs to the Logos because he is a complete emanation from the primordial ground of divinity; harmony belongs to him because there is an utter correspondence between him and the one from whom he comes; and radiance is his because, as the divine mind, he is the form of forms. In attributing beauty to the Son, Aquinas echoes Augustine who had claimed "the Word in a certain sense is the art of the almighty God, that through which all things exist."

This Augustinian connection to creation is a vital one. The Father creates the universe precisely through the Son, which is to say, through consulting the divine Logos, much as an artist makes an artifact through consulting the idea of beauty that he holds in his mind. Because the Son is beautiful, everything made through the Son is beautiful. And given the doctrine of *creatio ex nihilo*, the extent of the Son's influence over creation is limitless. Since there is no preexisting matter upon which God works (as for instance in Plato's account of creation through the Demiurge), there is literally nothing that remains untouched by the causal efficacy of the Son. Thus whatever exists, precisely in the measure that it exists, is beautiful. Aquinas states this truth with his customary pith: *ex divina pulchritudine esse omnium derivatur* (the being of all things is derived from the divine beauty).[12]

And we can make this claim even more precise through appeal to the familiar triplet of *integritas, consonantia*, and *claritas*. Whatever exists in the finite realm has wholeness in the measure that it is one, that it is itself and nothing else. And all creatures have consonance inasmuch as they are ordered harmonies, either of form and matter, substance and accident, or, at the very least, of essence and existence. Finally, anything that God makes has radiance because it is possessed of a formal structure that becomes luminous to the contemplative gaze. In the divine artistry, the beauty of the Son produces the beauty of worldly forms that, in turn, become the inspiration for visual and literary artists here below. Maritain comments: "Whether he knows it or not, the artist is consulting God when he looks at things."[13] Another link between heavenly and earthly artistry is found in regard to motivation. Thomas consistently gives voice to the classical conviction that God creates, not out of need, but from a desire to share his goodness. In Dionysian terms, *bonum diffisivum sui*, and so God, the ultimate good, is unsurpassably diffusive of self. In imitation of God, the earthly artist creates, not out of obligation, but because the intensity of the beauty in his imagination spills over into concreteness. Thus, in accord with the medieval dictum concerning the subtle rapport between the orders of being and knowing, divine and human artistry shed light upon one another.

The book of Genesis says that God looked upon each thing that he made and found it good but that he looked upon the ensemble of his creation and found it very good. In his commentary on Genesis, Aquinas says that this distinction shows God's special love for the whole of creation: What God loves above all is not any particular creature but the totality of his creation across space and time. In other words, God makes, not only individual beautiful things, but also and above all, the beauty of the whole, the splendid form which is all of created reality iconically arranged.

At this point in the discussion, it is imperative to address the issue of the dynamic quality of creation in Thomas's theological vision. It is, unfortunately, a commonplace of too many commentators that Aquinas and his medieval colleagues envisioned a fundamentally static cosmos. Nothing could be further from the truth. For Aquinas, God did indeed make the universe good, indeed very good, but not perfect. As the Latin term *perfectum* implies, what is perfect has been thoroughly made, and this making takes place only over time and through the seeking of an end. Everything in creation, from rocks to archangels, is essentially dynamic inasmuch as it moves to fulfillment through desire. Even the inanimate object, resting motionless on the surface of the earth, is, according to Thomas, seeking its end, doing what God made it to do. Each creature and creation as a whole move toward God as to a final cause. Aquinas uses a number of metaphors for the corporate mobility of creation. God's universe is something like a large and bustling household, filled with a variety of people about numerous interrelated tasks, all under the direction of a *paterfamilias*. Or it is like an army on the march, moving into battle in a coordinated way under the supervision of a general. But the master metaphor is that of the artist and his complex work of art. Employing a technically questionable but poetically evocative etymology, the medievals saw a link between *kalos* (beautiful) and *kaleo* (to call). In the measure that it is called into harmony by the final cause, the universe becomes beautiful.

I am fully aware that this insistence upon cosmic purpose and harmony can seem hopelessly naive in light of the myriad horrors of human history, especially those of the last century. Many postmodern thinkers have simply given up on any sort of all explaining metanarrative and have settled for a splintered, ambiguous sense of the whole. But Thomas's understanding of the cosmos, though premodern, was by no means naive, and what is perhaps especially useful in his metaphors is precisely how they shed light on the nature of a complex totality. In any corporate structure, there are various levels of order and understanding. Thus a farmhand on a country estate can be usefully at work on an exceptionally difficult project at the behest of his immediate superior and understand perfectly what he is doing, though he might remain completely unaware of how the performance of his task contributes to the overall design envisioned by the *paterfamilias*. Or a platoon commander in Patton's army might dutifully carry out an order to secure a particular beachhead at great cost to his troops, without for a moment grasping the broadest context for that action.[14] In a corporate and mobile structure, a particular task can seem meaningless when seen from a limited perspective, but can be appreciated as indispensably good when viewed from a more commanding vantage point. Like the author of the book of Job, Aquinas compels us to view the goods and evils of the world, as far as we are able, from the perspective of the divine overseer, to appreciate the cosmos as the gradual and painful arranging of interdependent elements into consonance.

But the trope of art and artist is, with regard to the problem of evil, perhaps the most illuminating. If God is an artist and his canvas is the whole of finitude across space and time, then we are like persons surveying Seurat's pointillist masterpiece *Sunday Afternoon on la Grande Jatte* with our noses pressed against the canvas. That picture reveals its meaning only as one steps back from it, and the colors begin to blend and the lights and darks arrange themselves into patterns. Given our hopelessly limited grasp of space and time, what any of us can see of God's endlessly complex pointillist design are bits and pieces, corners and shadows. Or to shift the metaphor a bit, we are like visitors to a sculptor's studio who see some splendid finished pieces, and amid the inevitable clutter, many sculptures half-completed, some barely begun or only vaguely outlined. And as we puzzle over or delight in this figure or that, we have only the slightest inkling of the massive work of which these many pieces are destined to be part. In accord with the painting metaphor, evils are the shadows in the beautiful composition, and in the sculpture metaphor, they are the inevitable side effects and signs of a work in progress. We find something very similar in Dante. At the very end of the *Divine Comedy*, the pilgrim stares into the beauty of the Trinity and sees "how it contains within its depths / all things bound in a single book by love / of which creation is the scattered leaves."[15] In and through the divine center fully revealed, Dante is able to read all of time and history as a coherent narrative, and he implies that people in any particular age are able to read, at best, individual pages in that book, some luminous, some somber, some meaningless, all frustratingly incomplete. God is a literary artist, and he is very gradually writing, on the pages of time, space, and nature, his tragicomic novel, which we take in in glimpses and snatches. Lest this Dantean image seem naive in regard to real suffering, let us remember that the pilgrim's eschatological vision is had only after a journey through hell and purgatory.

A final clarification: In defending the possibility of the miraculous against the excessive rationalists of his time, Thomas Aquinas says that God is an artist who is not restricted to one "style" of expression. Like Picasso, who changed styles several times each decade, God expresses himself in a surprising and variegated way, according to his reasoned purpose and perhaps even according to his playfulness and exuberance. Are the shifting, unpredictable movements or nature and history perhaps but the result of this divine aesthetic playfulness?

The Breakdown of the Artistic Vision and Its Recovery

I mentioned earlier how the medieval sense of cosmic design and divine artistry seem naive to many postmoderns. But this disenchantment has roots that go back to the period just following the high Middle Ages. Umberto Eco carefully traced the evolution of the medieval understanding of the beautiful and noticed that a major shift occurred in the writings of Duns Scotus and William of Occam. Scotus's metaphysics of *haecceitas* and Occam's explicit nominalism both led to an attenuating of the ontology of beauty that we have been describing. When the individual thing has primacy, the interconnectedness of all creatures, the *consonantia* of the finite realm, is severely understressed. Indeed, Occam can say *praeter illas partes absolutas, nulla res est* (outside of these absolute parts, there is no real thing).[16] And this cosmic disconnectedness is even more fully established when, as in Scotus, a univocal conception of being holds sway. In Thomas's analogical understanding, the many created beings participate most intimately in the divine to-be and are hence, as we saw, joined to one another through the divine center. But when being is taken univocally, God and creatures are instances of a general, overarching principle and hence exist, as it were, side by side, without an essential connection.

It is worth noting that Luther, Calvin, and the other great Reformers were almost all trained in a nominalist philosophical tradition. And hence it is not surprising that they underplayed the theme of cosmic beauty. In accord with Scotist and Occamist assumptions, the Reformers distantiated God from the world and thereby severed the ties that bind creatures to one another in harmonic patterns. Furthermore, Luther's deep suspicion of all forms of mysticism and of a kataphatic theology of glory is congruent with his decidedly non-Thomistic philosophical formation.

Some strands of modernity could be seen as secularized forms of Protestantism. The distantly transcendent God of Luther evolved into the irrelevant or nonexistent God of much modern philosophical speculation from Descartes to Marx. And this even more dramatic marginalization of God conduced toward an even more complete dismantling of the medieval icon of a beautifully made and arranged cosmos. The political implications of this breakdown are no more apparent than in the work of Thomas Hobbes, one of the fathers of modern social theory. Where Aquinas, in line with his participation metaphysics, held society as natural to human beings, Hobbes saw humans in the natural state as simply antagonistic individuals, set violently against one another. Whenever community or socialization comes to be, it emerges artificially through a social contract mutually agreed to by warring individuals for fundamentally self-interested reasons. This view of society, though tempered somewhat by John Locke, came to shape the polities of the liberal democracies of the eighteenth century. Government's purpose became, not the establishment of justice rooted in cosmic harmony, but the defense of rights, which are, according to Locke's telling definition, "that which a person cannot not desire." In short, the protection of self-interested individuals from one another became the raison d'être of the state and its institutions. A "beautiful community," rooted in the harmony of nature and established through the artistry of God, faded quickly from memory.

This particular genealogy of ideas has its roots in the speculation of Hans Urs von Balthasar and has been developed in recent years in the remarkable work of John Milbank and his disciples, the proponents of what has been termed "radical orthodoxy." In his book *Theology and Social Theory*, Milbank urges us simply to resist the modern trajectory and to recover a participation view of both creation and society. He sees a connection between the Hobbesian social ontology underlying modern political arrangements and the essentially violent social ontology that undergirded the politics of ancient Rome.[17] Both modern and Roman society were grounded, ultimately, in faulty metaphysics and false worship, because both denied, in different ways, a participation understanding of the relation between God and the world. While the god of modernity was, at best, distant and uninvolved, the gods of ancient Rome were projections of human antagonism and, concomitantly, guarantors of sacred violence. Milbank finds instructive the strategy employed by St. Augustine in his critique of Roman polity. In the *City of God*, Augustine attempts no rapprochement with Rome; rather, he exposes Roman justice as fraudulent in contrast to the true justice of Christianity. Roman order, he argues, is rooted in the constant threat of violence and an institutionalized unwillingness to forgive, whereas the *ordo* of the Church is founded on the nonviolence and enemy-love urged in the Sermon on the Mount and exemplified utterly on the cross of Jesus.[18]

And then Milbank follows Augustine in effecting a correlation between this compassionate praxis of the Christian church and a metaphysics of creation from nothing. In the mythologies and philosophies of the ancient world, creation was imagined as a violent act, since it involved the victory of one god over another, or at the very least, the aggressive shaping of some primordial substance into order. But when Christians began to reflect on creation in light of the Paschal Mystery, they conceived of it as *creatio ex nihilo*, a sheerly generous and nonviolent act by which God, without mediation, brings the whole of finite reality into being. This implies that peace—and not antagonism—constitutes the primordial truth of things.[19] Further, since on this reading all creatures come forth from and are sustained by the divine source, they are necessarily in relation to one another through God. Thomas's participation account is but a fuller working-out of this Augustinian intuition. In a word, Augustine's sense of the beautiful community is grounded in his metaphysical conviction that the created world is a harmonious product of God the artist.

One of the most intriguing elements in Milbank's recovery of Augustine is his exploration of a little-known text of the master, the *De musica*, a dialogue composed during Augustine's Italian sojourn in the period surrounding his conversion and baptism. The first sections of the dialogue are a technical analysis of harmony, meter, rhythm, and the other formal elements of music, but the last section of the *De musica* is a splendid correlation between music and metaphysics. Just as notes come forth, endure for a time determined by the musician, and fade away, so creatures, made ex nihilo and hence always bearing in themselves the heritage of nonbeing, come forth from God and endure precisely as long as God sees fit. Furthermore, just as particular notes situate themselves in the context of lines, harmonies, and the overall composition in accord with the will of the composer, so individual creatures are, according to the will of the divine musician, similarly arranged in numerous overlapping contexts of harmony and musical order. And perhaps most remarkably, just as notes are not so much "things" or substances as relations, so creatures, coming forth ex nihilo from the divine causality, are most accurately described as relations in reference both to God and to one another. The harmonic and fundamentally nonviolent play of creatures is what Augustine illumines with this musical metaphysics.[20] We find something similar in the *Confessions* when Augustine compares transient human lives to the quickly passing sounds of individual words in a speech. In each case, the rising and falling of particular elements allow for the production of a meaning that depends upon and yet transcends them. Lurking behind both metaphors, of course, is an intense sense of God as artist, here an artist of sound rather than of light and color, but still someone arranging the manifold of creation into a harmonic unity that becomes radiantly intelligible.

Milbank and his disciples use this metaphysical insight to combat various forms of liberation theology, which they take to be grounded in a fundamentally antagonistic social theory. The violent clash of social classes (as in Gutiérrez) or genders (as in much feminist theology), or races and ethnic groups (as in black liberation theology) is predicated upon a nominalist, nonparticipation metaphysics derived from modern assumptions. Though the desire for liberation is surely praiseworthy, the means chosen by these authors to combat oppression are, for Milbank, ethically and metaphysically incongruent with an ontology of nonviolence.[21] One of his followers, Catherine Pickstock, has accordingly urged that the liturgy assume its properly central role in the regulation of the moral and social life of the community.[22] The sign of the cross, the Gloria, the readings and homily, the prayers of the faithful, the presentation of the gifts, the prayer of the angels, the consecration, the Lord's Prayer, the act of communion, the dismissal—all together constitute an iconic display of the *communio*/participation understanding of being. The liturgical act ought therefore to be the interpretive lens through which economic and political life is understood as well as the guide and inspiration for those who would participate in those arenas. In this context, she comments approvingly on the vibrant relationship in the medieval period between the liturgical life of the Church and the social life of the community. What modernity would call the "secular" realm—finance, entertainment, manufacture, and so on—was, for the medievals, permeated by the sacred, ordered by rhythms of the liturgical year. In a word, the ritual beauty of the liturgy, reflective of the primal beauty of the Trinity and the cosmos, led to the cultivation of the beautiful society down to its most ordinary details. What Pickstock urges is an unapologetic recovery of this Augustinian vision in order to counter the ill effects of modernity's invention of secularity.

CONCLUSION

That God is a maker of beautiful things is, as I suggested at the outset, a master idea of Christian revelation. In its light, we understand God himself as a radiant play of wholeness and harmony; we see creation in its entirety across space and time as a rose window or, more dynamically, as a bustling household or a marching army; we perceive good and evil in their endlessly complex mutuality and relativity; and we grasp a new teleology in regard to ethics and politics. In contemplating this idea, we gaze with admiration at the one whose intelligent and artistic gaze is bringing the cosmos into *integritas, consonantia,* and *claritas*.

Notes

1. Jacques Maritain, *Art et Scolastique*, in *Jacques et Raissa Maritain Oeuvres Complètes*, vol. 1 (Fribourg: Editions Universitaires, 1986), 621–39.
2. Ibid., 637.
3. Ibid., 643.
4. "Nam ad pulchritudinem tria requiruntur. Primo quidem integritas sive perfectio; quae enim diminuta sunt hoc ipso turpia sunt. Et debita proportio sive consonantia. Et iterum claritas; unde quae habent colorem nitidum, pulchra esse dicuntur." Thomas Aquinas, *Summa theologiae*, Ia, q. 39, art. 8.
5. James Joyce, *A Portrait of the Artist as a Young Man*, 480.
6. Ibid.
7. Ibid., 433.
8. Ibid., 433–34.
9. Ibid.
10. Plato, *Symposium*, 211 c, in *The Collected Dialogues of Plato*, ed. Edith Hamilton and Huntington Cairns (Princeton, N.J.: Princeton University Press, 1961), 562–63.
11. "Filius habens in se vere et perfecte naturam Patris . . . inquantum est imago expressa Patris . . . inquantum est Verbum quod quidem lux est et splendor intellectus." Aquinas, *Summa theologiae*, 1a, q. 39, art. 8.
12. Aquinas, *De Divinis Nominibus*, lect. 5.
13. Maritain, *Art et Scolastique*, 681.
14. Robert Barron, *The Strangest Way: Walking the Christian Path* (Maryknoll, N.Y.: Orbis Books, 2002), 140–41.
15. Dante Alighieri, *The Divine Comedy: Paradiso Canto XXXIII*.
16. William of Occam, *Ordinatio* 30, 1, cited in Umberto Eco, *Art et beauté dans l'esthétique médiévale* (Paris: Bernard Grasset, 1987), 170.
17. John Milbank, *Theology and Social Theory: Beyond Secular Reason* (Oxford: Blackwell, 1990), 390–91.
18. Ibid., 399–405.
19. Ibid., 423–27.
20. Augustine, *De Musica*, in *Oeuvres de Saint Augustin*, vol. 7, *Dialogue Philosophiques* (Paris: Desclée de Brouwer, 1947), 473–75.
21. Milbank, 249–52.
22. Catherine Pickstock, *After Writing: The Liturgical Consummation of Philosophy* (Oxford: Blackwell, 1998), 135–58.

Chapter Ten

GENESIS AND JOYCE: NARRATIVES OF SIN, GRACE, AND THEONOMY

An Essay in Honor of Andrew Greeley on His Seventieth Birthday

Iᴛ HAS BEEN A CENTRAL CONTENTION OF ANDREW GREELEY, FOR AT least the past twenty years, that Catholicism is borne and expressed most powerfully through narrative. When asked why Catholics stay in the Church, his standard answer is that they like the stories. These tales of grace are written on parchment, placed between the covers of books, painted onto glass, carved into stone, shaped into cathedrals. Whatever their form, their function is the same: to present the drama of God's tireless, relentless love, pushing into human life, in a word, Incarnation. What I would like to reflect on here, in a conscious attempt to honor the life and work of Andrew Greeley, is a reading-together of two great stories, the biblical narrative of the Fall of Adam and Eve and James Joyce's funny, tragic, and finally grace-filled account in *A Portrait of the Artist as a Young Man* of how Stephen Dedalus comes to realize that his life's work

139

is to be a priest of the beautiful. I want to show that each tale displays the awkward oscillation between heteronomy and autonomy and then reveals the dynamics of the right rapport between us and God that can only be called theonomy. For both Joyce and the author of Genesis, we human beings try tragically to manipulate God (autonomy) or to submit to an illusory God who, from the outside, oppresses and moralizes (heteronomy). What we only dimly glimpse is the hope against hope that God is the deepest ground of our own lives, the alluring and unavoidable power that wants nothing more than to make us fully alive (theonomy). It is this third option that both Genesis and *A Portrait of the Artist* hold out to us as a salvific possibility.

BACK TO THE GARDEN

We are all, I trust, well acquainted with the basic structure of the Genesis narrative concerning the creation and fall of Adam and Eve. Let us consider first therefore the general tone and setting of this strange story. We have a God who makes figurines out of the mud, toys in the shapes of animals and human beings; we have a perfect garden, carefully divided by four sparkling rivers and containing two magical trees; we hear of incomprehensible prohibitions and arbitrary threats; we see a naked man and a naked woman living together unselfconsciously, without the complications and ambiguities of sexuality; we overhear a talking snake; and we finally are invited to feel the fierce shame of two people who know they have done wrong. Does this curious tale not have all the marks of a children's story or of a dream? Is it not told, in fact, from the standpoint of a childlike consciousness? Are we not being drawn here into a mode of thinking and seeing typical of someone in preadolescence?

In his *Systematic Theology*, Paul Tillich offers us a reading of the Fall that is characterized by penetrating psychological and spiritual insight. He reminds us that theologians over the centuries have idealized the situation of Adam in paradise, heaping on him every conceivable virtue and presenting him as the paragon of humanity. The difficulty with such an interpretation, for Tillich, is that it makes the Fall incomprehensible (why would such a perfect person succumb to temptation?) and, more important, it overlooks the radically incomplete, immature quality of the first humans in the garden. Adam and Eve are not perfect but rather, as the setting of the story itself suggests, they are like children in a state of what Tillich calls "dreaming innocence."[1] To be in dream consciousness is to be in a world midway between illusion and reality, suspended between what is and what could be. And to be innocent is to be, depending on the context, either inexperienced, nonresponsible, or without moral guilt. In any sense, it is to be in a condition *prior to* or *outside of* the real engagement of the mind and will. Any concrete act, even the most virtuous and praiseworthy, to some degree compromises the innocence of the actor, since it involves the agent, willy-nilly, in the vagaries and conflicts of the moral arena. Innocence, therefore, is the state of soul characteristic of the child, the one who has not yet fully lived, who has not taken the plunge into the roiled sea of action and responsibility. Adam and Eve are perhaps best to be imagined, therefore, not as fully mature adults, but rather as young people just on the cusp of adolescence, teenagers both attracted to and repulsed by the possibility of leaving the garden.

Everyone knows the lure of innocence. In our imaginings, our dreams, our fairy tales and romantic movies (Spielberg!) we routinely return to the world of childhood. With aching nostalgia we recall the beauty of that perfect, untrammeled, and uncomplicated state of affairs, that "garden" in which all was well. Part of what makes that time so idyllic, at least in memory, is the clear and unambiguous relationship between the childlike ego and the various authorities that surrounded it. When we were young, we heard commands, prohibitions, and encouragements from god-like figures—parents, teachers, religious leaders—whose goodness and rectitude we implicitly trusted. Their power—and our unquestioned acquiescence to it—made our lives pure, simple, and successful. The story of Adam and Eve opens, psychologically, in this preadolescent setting, in this Eden watered by four rivers and containing all good things, in this arena of clear and unquestioned limits.

But innocence, precisely in its incompleteness, carries within itself the seeds of its own destruction. With the expansion of his mind, imagination, and will, the child inevitably becomes uncomfortable with the constraints of innocence. He begins to wonder whether the authorities above him might be incorrect, whether the restrictions placed on him might be unreasonable, and most importantly, whether he might be able to make his own responsible decisions in freedom. In short, he stands at the wall of the garden and peers out into the frightening but enticing world around it. As we saw, he will certainly feel the pull to stay within the narrow but safe confines of the garden, but he will almost unavoidably feel with greater urgency the desire to jump the fence. Every adolescent feels the tension produced by this awakened or "aroused" freedom. Part of his psyche longs for the safety of his parents' and his society's strictures and greatly fears what might happen if those barriers are crossed, while another part of his soul fears that his freedom might never be realized if he does not live for himself. For Tillich and others, the divine command not to eat of the tree of knowledge is the voice of that first fear, and the serpent's suggestion to do so is the voice of the second fear. Like anyone on the cusp of adulthood, Adam and Eve find themselves suspended between two anxieties and seduced by two suggestions: stay in the garden—leave the garden; remain a child in safety—become an adult in risky freedom.

Again, it is crucial to approach this story as if for the first time, and without the overlay of the theological interpretive tradition, according to which the serpent is automatically associated with the devil. What Genesis itself has told us is that all of God's creatures are good and that the serpent is the "cleverest" or "shrewdest" of them all. Does this shrewdness necessarily have a nefarious overtone or is it perhaps indicative of special insight? And is the serpent, in its own way, acting as an agent of divine purposes, drawing the childish souls of Adam and Eve into maturity and freedom? Could it be that the Creator placed the snake in the garden, not as an arbitrary tempter or tester, but rather as a catalyst toward maturity, just as he places within all of our psyches the restless quest to transcend the limitation of dreaming innocence? Now this is not to suggest that the snake is an unambiguously positive character or that his successful temptation redounds only to the good. As is so often the case in this story, we are on shifting ground.

Let us look more closely at the positive values that he holds out to them: knowledge of good and evil *and* "being like God." To *know* good and evil, in the biblical sense, is not merely to have theoretical knowledge of two moral states; rather, it is to be concretely and experientially in touch with good and evil in oneself and in the world precisely through one's moral engagement. A person comes to *know* the tensions and ambiguities of finitude—the good and the bad—through the tumble out of dreaming innocence into actual existence. Tillich reminds us that the word *existence* is derived from the Latin term *existere* whose basic meaning is to "stand out from."[2] One begins to "exist" when one stands out from the generality of societal and parental expectations and acts *on one's own*, on the basis of one's own thinking and willing. It is into this "existence" that the serpent lures Adam and Eve, as he lures all adolescents on the brink of maturity. And here, it seems to me, we can see the godliness and positive "shrewdness" of the snake; we can see why God placed him in the garden with his beloved Adam and Eve. In this sense, the *knowledge* of good and evil, an intensity and vividness of experience gained through freedom and decision, is something altogether desirable. It is a characteristic of a consciousness that has emerged from the shadowy realm of dreaming innocence into the clear light of awareness and responsibility. At the prompting of the snake, Adam and Eve finally have *acted* in a properly human sense, and this should be cause for rejoicing. Furthermore, this very tumble into existence does indeed make the first humans "like God." In his supreme freedom and self-actualization, God "knows" good and evil. God's is not a childish consciousness caught in the web of illusion or controlled by the will of another; on the contrary, it is marked by unsurpassed self-possession and freedom. Adam and Eve come to participate in this divine mode of consciousness precisely through their "fall" from the garden of dreamy childish heteronomy. Here again, the "shrewdest" of God's creatures performs an indispensable task of mystagogia, leading awakening human consciousness into a more godlike state.

This perhaps surprising interpretation of the positive role of the snake might take on greater plausibility when we recall the "children's story" context for this narrative. God has told his human creatures that they could eat of any tree in the magic garden except for the tree of the knowledge of good and evil, a plant of particular beauty and lusciousness. Then, without in any way sealing off the tree or blocking access to it, the lawgiver conveniently leaves the scene. Is the scenario not similar to that of a parent who expressly and dramatically forbids a child to open the refrigerator door and then, without locking the door or sequestering the child, departs? In such a case, hasn't the parent planted in the mind of the child an almost irresistible fascination with what might be in the refrigerator and hasn't she, consequently, almost guaranteed that the child will violate her command? Is the prohibition itself not a kind of lure to thought and action, a prompt to the expansion of consciousness and responsibility? If, in the Genesis account, there were nothing good about the eating of the fruit of the tree, then God appears as, at best, an arbitrary legalist and, at worst, a cruel seducer, purposely arousing freedom and then ruthlessly punishing the exercise of that freedom. Is it not more plausible to suggest that God, through the agency of the serpent, is, almost playfully, cajoling his rational creatures in the direction of a broader mind and a deeper responsibility?

Now none of the above is to suggest that the snake is unambiguously positive and that the Fall is the best thing ever to happen to us. Adam and Eve are indeed lured into freedom and maturity, but they are lured awkwardly, errantly, and dangerously. To find the point, the edge, where the seduction to existence slides into the seduction to egotism is to put one's finger on the essence of the originating sin. We have seen the positive dimension of the snake's temptation to know good and evil and to be like God, but there is a decidedly negative side to this suggestion, precisely in the way that it is framed. The serpent's opening gambit is intriguing: he asks the woman, "did God say 'you shall not eat of any tree of the garden'?" One can almost imagine the feigned look of shock on the serpent's face as he formulates this question. He seems to insinuate that God must be a strange and difficult lawgiver, desirous of keeping his rational creatures under strict control. Is his question not subtly planting in the mind of Eve the beginnings of resentment toward God, of rivalry with him and, above all, *fear* of him? How could God have imposed prohibitions on his children and what must his reasons be? Though undoubtedly troubled by the question, Eve, childlike innocence still intact, answers directly: "We may eat of the fruit of the trees of the garden, but God said, 'You shall not eat of the fruit of the tree which is in the midst of the garden, neither shall you touch it, lest you die.'" Specifying the nature and limited range of the divine prohibition, she, for the moment, holds off the general fear of God that the serpent had tried to awaken, but the snake is not so easily put off. He assures her that she will not die if she eats of the tree and that, in point of fact, it is God's fear and jealousy of *her* that prompted this arbitrary commandment: "for God knows that when you eat of it your eyes will be opened and you will be like God, knowing good and evil." At the root of the snake's temptation is the assumption that God and human beings are essentially rivals, involved in a desperate zero-sum game of competition and mutual antagonism. We ought to be fearful of God because he crushes us with his commands, and God ought to be afraid of us because we might supplant him with our knowledge; God doesn't want us to be like him because his majesty would then be compromised, and we don't want to remain in ignorance because our existence would then be threatened. To be at the expense of another, to be over and against, to be through clinging, these are all the marks of the sinful stance of soul. Fear of the other is the cause and the consequence of sin.

Eve is awakened to self-consciousness through the words of the serpent and through her action, but to a warped and illusory self-consciousness, to an awareness of herself as an isolated ego threatened by an imposing and overbearing divinity. She has become "like" God in order to protect herself from God; she has changed herself into the "supreme" being in order to hold her own against the other highest reality. So she eats of the fruit proffered to her by the serpent and, with remarkable ease, convinces her husband to do the same.[3] "And immediately their eyes were opened and they realized they were naked." Ingeniously, the author of Genesis identifies the first and most devastating result of the fearful clinging which is sin: shameful self-consciousness. Having turned to themselves out of fear, Adam and Eve "know" their nakedness and vulnerability. They have left the garden of dreaming innocence and they have come to self-possession (which is all to the good), but they have come to know themselves as open to the attacks of the other, as exposed, as susceptible to verbal assault and insinuation. Shamed and frightened, they "make aprons so as to cover themselves." Covering, defending, making armor, hiding—all are characteristics of the beleaguered ego now precariously at the center of the universe. From the standpoint of the ego fortress produced by fear, the other can be seen only as an enemy or potential enemy, and one's own life can be appreciated only as something vulnerable to invasion and hence as something that must be covered up, concealed, defended. Once more, it is entirely appropriate that the author of Genesis keeps us in the symbolic field of sexuality here. Our first parents cover up their genitals immediately after they have eaten of the tree, that is to say, they hide what is most intimate and personal, what is, in fact, the mode of deepest union with the other. Once the ego reigns at the center, the very act which should be a celebration of self-forgetfulness becomes frightening and dangerous and shame-producing. From the perspective of fear, sexual intimacy—and all of its attendant emotional engagement—is the single most dangerous human act, the one most fraught with perils, since it puts the ego at greatest risk.

Now when the first sinners sense the presence of God making his way through the foliage of the garden, they instinctively hide themselves, thus playing out the fear that the snake had placed in the mind of Eve. To their now unconditioned and centralized egos, the divine must appear as a threat and a rival, one from whom escape is the proper strategy. It is incorrect, I think, to interpret their action as simply the childish avoidance of the arbitrary punishment that they know will follow the transgression of the divine command. There is something much more subtly "adult" at work here, namely, the conscious and willful desire to establish independence from God, to find a place where the press of God will not be felt.

The great insight of the author of Genesis, of course, is that there is no place to hide from God. The Creator effortlessly foils his creatures' pathetic attempt to conceal themselves and he confronts them: "Where are you?" Adam's answer is of enormous spiritual moment: "I heard the sound of thee in the garden, and I was afraid because I was naked; and I hid myself." The first human being, the original sinner, witnesses to the basic dynamic of egotism: In clinging to myself, he implies, I realized how terribly vulnerable I am (nakedness) and how much of a threat you are to me (and so I hid). Covering up and hiding are the principal consequences of the fearful enthronement of the ego, and the spiritual moral desert in which all of us human beings live is the result of those simple but devastating "original" moves. Our entire social, economic, political, and military establishment can be seen as the frantic and finally self-defeating attempt to cover up our nakedness, to protect our egos. We surround ourselves with objects, gadgets, toys, condominiums, VCRs, designer clothes, Pentium computers, insured bank accounts, political parties, and atomic weapons—all of them descendents of the loincloths sewn together by Adam and Eve. All of these are, to the sinful soul, defense mechanisms, armor plating, means of concealing the very capacity for love that is the one thing that will authentically save us from our fear. And the ranginess and creativity of our sinfulness, our violence, our betrayal, our blasphemy, our prejudice, our butchery, our quiet resentment, our refusal to forgive—all of those are the offspring of our first parents' concealment in the shrubbery and underbrush of Eden. All of our perversion of soul is the consequence of a desire to escape from God, to make ourselves isolated sovereigns in the garden.

One way to read the magnificent 139th psalm is as a lament of the sinful ego:

Where can I run from your love?
If I climb the heavens you are there
If I sink into the grave, you are there.
If I take the wings of the dawn and dwell at the sea's furthest end, even
there your right hand holds me up.

Could the psalmist be giving voice to the sinful *desire* to flee from the press of the divine, to find *someplace* where God is not, some ground where he can stand without the threat of God's intervention? Could this not be another version of Adam's desperate and finally futile attempt to conceal himself from the sight of God? On this reading, the psalm itself is an ironic, almost playful, acknowledgment that this hiding game of the self-elevating ego is hopeless, that there is, in the end, no place to run, and that, just perhaps, the proper attitude is one of laughing surrender to this hound of heaven who will not be put off the trail.

147

As the story of the Fall unfolds, the author of Genesis displays the consequences that follow from this fearful grasp of the ego and the concomitant dread of God. When God challenges Adam, "have you eaten of the tree of which I commanded you not to eat?" the man blames his wife and, by implication, the God who brought her into being: "the woman whom thou gavest to be with me, she gave me of the fruit of the tree and I ate." And when the woman is confronted, she conveniently passes the buck to the snake: "the serpent beguiled me, and I ate." The sovereign ego cannot accept blame or responsibility; it must defend itself at all costs, holing up in its protective fortress. In fact, it deflects attacks by objectifying the other and then projecting its own guilt onto the now dispensable scapegoat. Thus the man demonizes the woman and the woman demonizes nature, and both indirectly demonize the divine author of finitude. Each actor in the story has, by the end, been effectively boxed in, isolated from the others, set apart. The Zen scholar D. T. Suzuki famously commented on the Judeo-Christian system: "God against man/man against God; man against woman/woman against man; humans against nature/nature against humans—funny religion!" His observation, of course, has its roots in the Genesis account we have just been studying, but it seems to me that he has missed its tragic irony. This universe of conflict and mutual antagonism is the *consequence of sin* and by no means the intention of the Creator. We do in fact live in a world characterized by these wearying battles between objectified humanity, nature, and divinity, but such a world is the construct of the fallen consciousness, an illusion created by the fearful egos of men and women. The metaphysical reality hiding behind the veil of illusion is the realm of unity, of God in the world and the world in God. Mutuality, interpenetration, love is the true ground of being that has been obscured by the objectifying tendency of the self-elevating ego. And the purpose of the Judeo-Christian religion is to shift consciousness so as to recover an authentic vision of the universe in accord with God's intentions. *Pace* Suzuki, our religion is not content with or tolerant of this awful tension between God, humanity, and nature, but it does force us to see the fallen mind that has produced such a state of affairs—hence the iconic value of this strange story of the garden.

After the dialogue between God and his sinful creatures comes to a close, there follows a brief divine soliloquy that G. W. F. Hegel called one of the most significant yet unremarked upon elements of the account of the Fall.[4] God effectively admits that the serpent was right: "Behold, the man has become like one of us, knowing good and evil." Over the centuries, the few commentators who have dared to address themselves to this strange remark have opined that God is being ironic or sarcastic here, implying that the "equality" with God is illusory. But Hegel takes the narrative at face value and sees in this remark God's own affirmation of the positive value of the tumble out of dreaming innocence. Yes, they have become like the divine in their greater self-consciousness and self-possession; they have abandoned the narrowness and naiveté of the garden, and this condition is straightforwardly acknowledged by God. Again however, as we have seen, this fall into existence and responsibility takes place through fear and results in the self-enthronement of the ego. Therefore, the beauty of the awakening to maturity is marred by the onset of egotistic antagonism. God *sees* both dimensions of the Fall (they have become like us, *and* they are riven by dissension and terror), and the icon of the garden is meant to lure us into a similar breadth of vision.

The danger to be avoided here is obvious. On the one hand, one might see the Fall as one-sidedly negative and hence wish to restore the descendents of Adam and Eve to the innocence of the garden. On this reading, the great crime of the first parents is disobedience, breaking the law of God, and the recovery of the garden involves the uncomplicated acquiescence to the demands of the divine law, reasonable or not. As we have already suggested, such a strategy is spiritually debilitating because it implies a sort of return to the womb, a retrieval of a childishly naive consciousness. It is intriguing to note in this context that God places cherubim and the wheeling sword of flame at the entrance of Eden in order to prevent the first couple from ever returning there. Having climbed successfully over the wall of childish innocence and legalism, having become like God in depth and maturity of consciousness, the human animal must *not return to Eden*, since such a regression would amount to surrender. And this temptation to read the account of the first sin in a legalistic and entirely negative way is by no means of merely academic interest. Whenever spiritual strategies and ecclesial policies revolve essentially around the issue of obedience, we are in the grip of such an interpretation. On a somewhat grander cultural plane, whenever we hear calls for an uncritical acceptance of authority, a return to a premodern sensibility, we have the repudiation of the consciousness expansion and maturation of the race that took place at the Enlightenment. To refrain from raising the hard questions, to settle into the easy acceptance of what has always been said and done, to bask in the glow of "parental" approval, is basically to return to the infantilizing security of the garden.

On the other hand, to give the account of the Fall a basically positive reading is to tumble into the Promethean trap. Prometheus disobeyed the divine prohibition and stole fire from the gods thus incomparably benefiting the human race. In punishment for his transgression, he was bound to a rock for all eternity and an eagle was sent to devour the sinner's liver each day. This is the newly mature and conscious human being as the defiant hero, the one who sets himself willfully and gladly in opposition to the divine, accepting all of the dire consequences of his heroic choice. Read in this romantic fashion, the story of Adam and Eve is the account of the human race come of age and claiming its rights and prerogatives in the face of a reluctant divinity. But the assumption of such a reading is, once more, that the divine and the human are basically rivals and that one is glorified only at the expense of the other.

What stands at the heart of the Genesis account of the Fall is the presentation of these two errant and incomplete perspectives: the naiveté of dreaming innocence and the antagonism and violence of Promethean egotism. What we do not see is the proper point of view, the stance of independence and responsibility (beyond the innocence of the garden) coupled with a joyful union with God envisioned not as a rival but as the ground and source of one's own being (beyond the negativity of the Fall). It is this middle or third state, this barely glimpsed possibility, which functions as the usually unstated *telos* of the entire biblical narrative. To find this condition of consciousness beyond the garden but free of sin is the opening of the third eye, the realization of the Kingdom of God, the experience of the New Being. It is this transformed *nous* or mind that appears with compelling power in Jesus Christ and that conditions, as I have argued, all of Christian life.

In his *Systematic Theology*, Paul Tillich names these three states of consciousness as heteronomy, autonomy, and theonomy. In the heteronomous state of mind, so thoroughly critiqued by the Enlightenment, one is uncritically beholden to the demands of the "other," the authority that stands outside oneself and that is usually given concrete form in the government, in family structures, and in the Church. At the other extreme from heteronomy is autonomy, the self-ruling ideal of the eighteenth century. Here one awakens and relies upon the inner voice of reason and becomes one's own *nomos* or law. For Tillich, autonomy is a positive evolution from the childishness of pure heteronomy, but it is far from ideal, since it inevitably leads to a sort of inflation of the ego, a puffing up of oneself and one's individual goals and ideals. And in turn it can result in a confrontational and antagonistic stance toward other autonomous agents and authorities. In short, it can take on the characteristics of what we have been calling the promethean attitude. The final evolution, says Tillich, is toward theonomous consciousness. This is a surrender to the authority of God—not a God imagined as an external lawgiver, but rather the God who dwells within one as one's own deepest ground and source. Theonomous consciousness is a mind filled up with the authority of the God who is "closer to us than we are to ourselves," the "other" who is nearer to us than our own minds and wills. As such, theonomous mind stands beyond the split between heteronomy and autonomy, pushing past yet containing the perfections of both. It is this mind that we do not see in the Genesis story; it is this mind that is the elusive lure of the whole tradition.

Theonomy in Joyce's *Portrait of the Artist*

A twentieth-century author who explores the dynamics of the account of the Fall with startling and often disturbing insight is the Irish Catholic writer, James Joyce. Though he claimed to have repudiated the Church of his birth and baptism, Joyce remained, almost despite himself, irredeemably

Catholic, and the imagery, doctrine, narratives, and liturgical rituals of Catholicism can be seen as the structuring elements in his fiction. In his *Portrait of the Artist as a Young Man*, we have a subtle and vivid account of the progress from dreaming innocence, through Promethean rebellion to something at least bordering on *metanoia*, a mature and responsible relationship with the God who gives meaning and savor to life.

Joyce's quasi-autobiography begins, famously, with an evocation of childhood in the language of childhood: "Once upon a time and a very good time it was there was a moocow coming down along the road and this moocow that was coming down along the road met a nicens little boy named baby tuckoo." It is easy to imagine the young child curled up in his father's lap listening with rapt attention to this narrative concerning the moocow and himself, the "nicens little boy," living in that "very good time." Psychologically we are on the same ground here as in the beginning of the account of the Fall: dreaming innocence. Just as Adam and Eve moved at first in easy and uncomplicated union with the law-giving God, so the young Stephen Dedalus rests comfortably in his father's arms and attends, unquestioningly, to his story. The entire first half of *A Portrait of the Artist* is a psychologically detailed narrative of the transition out of this state into something like rebellion and independence.

The process of consciousness transformation begins in the rough and tumble of Stephen's boarding school. Away from home at a very young age, the boy is making his confused way through the maze of older bullies, dull peers, and the priests endowed with an absolute and incomprehensible authority. One day Stephen breaks his glasses while playing and, since he is practically blind without them, he is formally excused from his schoolwork. Into the boy's classroom strides the prefect of studies, a sort of chief disciplinarian, whose task it is to frighten the students into doing their assignments. After insulting and severely beating one boy, the prefect turns his attention to young Stephen whose heart "jumps suddenly" when the older man addresses him: "Why are you not writing like the others?" Even when Stephen's teacher explains, the prefect is less than satisfied. He insinuates that the perfectly innocent boy has been "scheming" to get out of his work and he orders him to hold out his hands for the discipline. Stephen is practically overcome by the physical pain of the beating, but what unnerves him even more is the shame and humiliation of the ordeal: "The scalding water burst forth from his eyes and, burning with shame and agony and fear, he drew back his shaking arm in terror and burst out into a whine of pain." But what is most devastating of all is the dawning realization that this outrage had been perpetrated by a priest, by the representative of God, by one whom Stephen considered the absolute moral authority: "The prefect of studies was a priest but that was cruel and unfair." In that moment of insight, Stephen Dedalus begins the tumble out of the garden of dreaming innocence and into a sense of his own moral authority. Sometimes, he comes to see, the voice of divine authority is without substance, and its threats are nothing but the aggressive shouts of bullies.

Mustering enormous courage, the little boy, still without his glasses, makes his way after supper into the inner sanctum of the Jesuit fathers in order to confront the rector himself and explain the injustice that had been visited upon him. Joyce beautifully evokes the mythic power of authority in the mind of a child as he describes Stephen's approach to the office of the rector: "It was dark and silent and his eyes were weak and tired with tears so that he could not see. But he thought they were the portraits of saints and great men of the order who were looking down on him silently as he passed." The boy is in the holy of holies, the very seat of authority, and he is being judged by the worthies of the past who look down on him reproachfully. Yet he continues his courageous march, coming at last to the rector's room. Despite his fear and through his tears, Stephen lays out the injustice of what had happened to him, and the rector kindly agrees to speak to the prefect of studies. A sense of triumph growing in his heart, the boy makes his way back down the long corridor, gradually gaining speed, until he emerges into the daylight. He races past the cinder path and comes to the playground where his peers form a circle around him and beg to know what had transpired in the rector's office. When he tells them of his dramatic confrontation, they cheer him and then lift him up as a hero.

What we see in this beautifully narrated account is the first inkling of aroused freedom, the sense of independence and integrity. It comes, Joyce sees, in the moment when one realizes that the authorities—even when they bear impressive titles and carry instruments of discipline and are enshrined in formal portraits—can be wrong. It happens when one, for the first time, judges the external authority against the demands of the internal authority of one's own mind and conscience and "falls" from naive acquiescence. In Tillich's language, the move from pure heteronomy to autonomy has begun. Stephen's heroic enthronement at the end of this first section of A Portrait of the Artist is entirely appropriate because his rebellion has effectively stirred his soul to life and started him on the long hero's journey to authenticity and transformation of consciousness.

If the first section of A Portrait deals with the first vague stirrings of autonomy, the peering over the wall into freedom, the second section recounts the dramatic and soul-wrenching tumble out of the garden. Young Stephen has moved into adolescence and finds himself torn between the simple world of religion, study, and moral discipline and the chaotic universe of freedom, strange new ideas, and, above all, sexual experience. Vainly he tried to keep the forces of life and novelty at bay, building around himself a "breakwater of order and elegance against the sordid tide of life without him," and damming up "the powerful recurrence of the tides within him." He is carefully tending to the walls of the garden, hoping that they might keep out the freedom that both terrifies and beckons him. But as he himself admits, such an effort is "useless," for "from without as from within the water had flowed over his barriers." This is a wonderful psychological portrait of a person whose freedom is fully "aroused" though not quite actualized. The barriers that protect dreaming innocence have been fully breached, and it is now only a matter of time before the dreamer rides the waves to freedom. But as we saw in the Genesis story, the transition out of innocence almost inevitably entails a "fall," a break, a rupture—and usually of a sexual nature. For an Irishman of James Joyce's generation, there was something almost uniquely thrilling and terrifying about the experimentation with forbidden sexuality, and we can practically taste Joyce's own feelings of dreadful ambiguity through his account of his alter ego's fall.

Stephen Dedalus, the pious and studious teenager, the model young man, finds himself wandering by night in the lurid brothel section of Dublin. "He wandered up and down the dark slimy streets peering into the gloom of lanes and doorways. . . . He wanted to sin with another of his kind, to force another being to sin with him and exult with her in sin." Is this not what Eve must have felt when she heard the words of the serpent? Did sin itself—precisely in its forbiddenness and freedom—not captivate and lure her childlike soul out of the garden? Did she not, like Stephen Dedalus, "exult" in sin in an altogether legitimate sense, and did she not want to share this exultation with another? Let us listen to Joyce as he describes the very moment of passage from dreaming innocence. Stephen has come finally to the door of the brothel: "Before the doors and in the lighted halls groups were gathered arrayed as for some rite. He was in another world: he had awakened from the *slumber* of centuries" (emphasis mine). First, he sees the gathered prostitutes as priests presiding over a sacred rite because there is indeed something holy about the transition from the garden to responsibility; there is something divinely sanctioned about this expansion of consciousness and thus the agents of it are appropriately described as bearers of the Mystery. Then he clearly understands what this encounter entails: the passage to another world, that is to say, to another dimension of psychological and spiritual experience. In sinning with the prostitutes, he does indeed awaken from the dream state of his childlike awareness, from the "slumber of centuries," and tumble, with exhilaration and, as we shall see, enormous pain into autonomy. Am I implying that this transition from childish awareness to freedom is altogether good? By no means. Like his mythic forebears, Adam and Eve, the fallen Stephen will feel the terrible burning pain of his egotism and self-absorption. Like them he has fallen, awkwardly, into a stance of arrogance and aggressivity. Engaging in impersonal and abusive sex with near strangers is hardly a sign of a well-integrated soul, and it is precisely this negative aspect of his sin that Stephen is forced to *see* in the next section of the book.

This dreadful and wonderful ambiguity of sin is described with particular delicacy in the well-known third section of the *Portrait* at the center of which is Joyce's harrowing and unforgettable account of a hellfire sermon. As this central section of the book opens, young Stephen is still making his way through the means streets of Dublin by night, still desperately in love with the freedom and daring of sin itself. But soon he runs headfirst into a crusading Jesuit missionary who functions beautifully as a symbol of his newly awakened sense of guilt and moral responsibility.

With his many classmates, Stephen takes his place in chapel on the Wednesday preceding the feast of St. Francis Xavier to hear the annual retreat talks. Following the precepts of the spiritual exercises of Ignatius Loyola, the Jesuit retreat master moves the boys through a sort of guided meditation on the four "last things": death, judgment, heaven, and hell. Stephen is only mildly interested in the first two presentations, but his entire soul is engaged when the speaker begins to paint his horribly vivid picture of hell. Purposely appealing to the imaginations of his young hearers, the priest describes the horrors that will beset the senses in hell. First the sense of sight is overwhelmed: "It is a never-ending storm of darkness, dark flames and dark smoke of burning brimstone, amid which the bodies are heaped one upon another without even a glimpse of air." Then the sense of smell is infinitely offended: "All the filth of the world, all the offal and scum of the world . . . shall run there as to a vast reeking sewer when the terrible conflagration of the last day has purged the world." And the sense of touch is tormented: "the sulphurous brimstone which burns in hell is a substance which is specially designed to burn for ever and forever with unspeakable fury. . . . The blood seethes and boils in the veins, the brains are boiling in the skull, the bowels a redhot mass of burning pulp, the tender eyes flaming like molten balls." But then he reminds them that these sensual pains are as nothing compared to the moral and psychological suffering of the condemned: "The damned howl and scream at one another, their torture and rage intensified by the presence of beings tortured and raging like themselves. . . . The mouths of the damned are full of blasphemies against God and of hatred for their fellow sufferers."

On and on he goes, continually intensifying the terrible experience, painting the picture in ever more colorful and vivid hues. Even reading the text of the sermon as it appears in the pages of the *Portrait* is shocking; one can only imagine the effect that it had on a young, intelligent, and impressionable boy, especially one who knew that he had climbed the wall of the garden and was in full flight of mortal sin. The description of

Stephen's reaction to this horrible sermon is arguably the most arresting in the book: "Could it be that he, Stephen Dedalus, had done those things? His conscience sighed in answer. Yes, he had done them, secretly, filthily, time after time, and hardened in sinful impenitence, he had dared to wear the mask of holiness before the tabernacle itself while his soul within was a living mass of corruption."

The sermon convinces Stephen that he is destined for this everlasting hellfire. It throws back at him the terrible and largely repressed feelings of guilt that he had cultivated since beginning his sexual career. The intensity of his reaction shows that the authorities of society and church, which he had to some degree challenged and overcome, are by no means powerless in his soul. Like Adam and Eve after the Fall, Stephen Dedalus, upon hearing the reproachful voice of moral authority, becomes ashamed and endeavors to cover himself. Literally fearing for his spiritual life, Stephen heads to the confessional and, overcoming all of his embarrassment and humiliation, pours out his long list of sins to a somewhat stupefied elderly priest. Receiving absolution, Stephen emerges from the darkness of the confessional into the bright light of moral renewal: "The muddy streets were gay. . . . In spite of all he had done it. He had confessed and God had pardoned him. His soul was made fair and holy once more, holy and happy." Now at this stage of the story, it appears as though all we have said about the positive value of the tumble from dreaming innocence is trumped. It appears as though we are dealing with a standard story of the movement from moral purity through a fall from grace to a renewal of purity through confession. This young man has, it seems, been effectively frightened back into the garden whence he came and where he properly belongs.

But such an interpretation would be valid only if the story ended at this point. In fact, it unfolds as a sort of comic lampoon of Stephen's attempt to return to the garden, to sequester himself behind the high walls of piety and repression. Section four of the *Portrait* opens with Stephen's almost obsessive consecration of time: "Sunday was dedicated to the mystery of the Holy Trinity, Monday to the Holy Ghost, Tuesday to the Guardian Angels, Wednesday to Saint Joseph, Thursday to the Most Blessed Sacrament of the Altar, Friday to the Suffering Jesus, Saturday to the Blessed Virgin Mary." He has himself surrounded; there is literally no time for anything but the most sublime spiritual pursuits; every moment is defended. Stephen attends daily Mass, prays for the intentions of the Pope, mortifies his spirit and his senses, recites the rosary even while walking down the sidewalk, becomes the president of the Sodality of the Blessed Virgin, and finally, in the climactic turning point of section four, he entertains the possibility of becoming a Jesuit priest. He imagines his name, "the Reverend Stephen Dedalus, S.J." and he exults in the power and prestige that title will give him. In short, he hurls himself with reckless abandon back into the safety and moral certitude of dreaming innocence, even to the point of considering becoming one of the guardians of the garden whose hypocrisy he had already seen through as a child.

We know that this cannot last. Once one has left the confines of dreaming innocence, one cannot ever really go back. As we saw, this is symbolized in the angelic defense of Eden: God does not want his rational creatures to return to a childish state of consciousness. He wants them rather to move forward with their newfound freedom and responsibility *and to purge it of its egotism.* So the young Stephen Dedalus cannot remain in his fantastic spiritual castle; in accordance with a basic law of the spirit, he must move forward. "The wisdom of the priest's appeal," he finally realizes, "did not touch him to the quick. He was destined to learn his own wisdom apart from others or to learn the wisdom of others himself wandering among the snares of the world. The snares of the world were its ways of sin." This last line is extremely rich. What Joyce is implying here is that the way to spiritual maturity lies outside the garden of dreaming innocence, along the thorny path of fallen freedom. As we have often seen, this is not to glorify egotism or to underestimate its destructive power, but it is to say that regression to a more primitive form of consciousness is never a viable route to awakening. It is only in the "wild heart of life" that authenticity is to be found.

Soon after his rejection of priesthood and the garden, Stephen has the chief epiphanic experience of the book. While standing on Sandymount strand outside of Dublin and gazing out at the sea and the assembled crowd of people, he spies a girl. She is so still and serene and beautiful that Stephen is caught up in aesthetic arrest, simply captivated: "She was alone and still, gazing out to sea; and when she felt his presence and the worship of his eyes her eyes turned to him in quiet suffrance of his gaze. . . . Long, long she suffered his gaze and then quietly withdrew her eyes from his." When young Dante first saw Beatrice, he was caught up out of himself into a rapture of contemplation; something similar is happening here. In the wake of his vision on the shore, Stephen cries out, "Heavenly God." In the beauty of the girl, a beauty so sublime that he does not want to have it or possess it but only bask in it, he senses something of the transcendent beauty that creates and sustains the universe. In this moment of rapture, he comes into contact for the first time in his life with the God who is not an overbearing lawgiver, or a demanding "outsider," but rather the ground and source of all that is, the Beauty that is reflected in the beauties of creation. In this ecstatic encounter, Stephen sees the path that will lead from egotism to surrender; God is no longer a rival to be avoided or desperately placated, but is rather a nurturing power in whom Stephen can find himself.

It would be terribly wrong to see the hellfire sermon and Stephen's reaction to it simply as unfortunate setbacks on the road to integration. In point of fact, it was essential for Stephen to *see* the darkness into which he had fallen, the possessive and self-absorbed egotism. Though the encounter with prostitutes was legitimately described as a sacred event from one angle, from another perspective, it was mortally wrong, and the guilt that Stephen felt over it was justified. Sex with a prostitute is a desperate perversion of the unitive nature of the sexual act and a heartless exploitation of another human being. Amounting in the end to the use and abuse of another, it is a peculiarly appropriate expression of rampant egotism. At the end of this remarkable fourth section of the *Portrait*, we glimpse the beginnings of Stephen's vocation: not to the formal priesthood of the Catholic Church, but to the artistic priesthood, the priesthood of the soul. He is to become a servant of beauty and a reporter of epiphanies, manifestations of the divine through earthly radiance. The artist's task and privilege—which Stephen claims as his own—is to scout out and describe moments of beauty, times when the harmony and essentiality of a thing or event shines with revelatory brightness. He is to notice, isolate, and describe the radiant harmonies that speak of the ultimate harmony which is God, and in this enterprise he finds his deepest raison d'être. For the sake of this vocation, all else is forsaken. In an often-cited speech to his friend Cranly, Stephen defends the integrity of the sacred path he has chosen: "I will not serve that in which I no longer believe whether it call itself my home, my fatherland or my church: and I will try to express my-self in some mode of life or art as freely as I can and as wholly as I can, using for my defence the only arms I allow myself to use—silence, exile and cunning." Intriguingly, Joyce borrows these last words from a me-dieval book of monastic discipline. Like the monk, the artist must conse-crate himself to the task of mediating the divine presence, even when that responsibility places him at odds with all that society and church deem worthy of respect. There must be no returning to the garden of heteron-omy, nor must there be the self-destructiveness of egotism. Rather, the self must surrender to the deeper and richer demands of the divine as they press upon him, and in that surrender it will be transformed. Joyce is naming here the moment when the third eye opens up. Having de-scribed Stephen's journey from heteronomy through cocky manipulative autonomy, Joyce hints at the beginnings of theonomy in the psyche of his young protagonist. Through the intervention of grace (and no other word seems appropriate), Stephen was seized by a vision of the divine and found the courage to surrender to its power, thereby finding his life and vocation. This is the mirror of the Genesis account in which our first par-ents pass from innocent acquiescence to divisive egotism to a graced openness to salvation.

And then finally, at the very end of the book, Stephen is ready to fly. He resolves to leave his homeland of Ireland and seek his spiritual for-tune in Europe. All that has preceded has been a preparation for this as-cent and escape. He has jumped the wall of the garden and has, through the grace of beauty, at least begun to purify himself of the stain of self-absorption. The wings that he dons are those of the Holy Spirit.

NOTES

1. Paul Tillich, *Systematic Theology*, vol. 2 (Chicago: University of Chicago Press, 1967), 33.

2. Ibid., 20.

3. It is interesting to note that in traditional theology the woman is approached by the serpent first due to her ignorance and weakness. In some contemporary feminist theologies, a different rationale is provided: The snake tempts Eve first because he must use all of his subtlety and wiles in order to persuade the stronger and more clever woman. Having lured her into eating of the fruit, the temptation of the man is a matter of course!

4. G. W. F. Hegel, *Lectures on the Philosophy of Religion*, ed. Peter C. Hodgson (Berkeley: University of California Press, 1988), 444.

Part IV

PREACHING THE MESSAGE

Chapter Eleven

"I'm Waiting; I'm Waiting": An Advent Meditation

ADVENT IS THE LITURGICAL SEASON OF VIGILANCE, OR TO PUT IT more mundanely, of waiting. During the four weeks prior to Christmas, we light the candles of our Advent wreaths and put ourselves in the spiritual space of the Israelite people who, through many long centuries, waited for the coming of the Messiah (How long, O Lord?).

There is a wonderful avant-garde German movie called *Run, Lola, Run*. Its main character is a young woman who finds herself in a terrible bind: she needs to gather an enormous amount of money in a ridiculously short period of time. And so, throughout the movie, she runs and runs, desperately trying through her own frantic efforts to make things right, but nothing works. Finally, at the moment when she finds herself at the absolute limit of her powers, she slows to a trot (she had been, of course, running), looks up to heaven and says, "Ich warte, Ich warte" (I'm waiting, I'm waiting). Though she does not explicitly address God and though there has been no hint throughout the movie that Lola is the least bit religious, this is undoubtedly a prayer. And in the immediate wake of her edgy statement/request, a rather improbable solution to her problem presents itself. Lola's prayer has always reminded me of Simone Weil—another restless contemporary European woman—whose entire spirituality is predicated upon the power of waiting, or in her language, of expectation. In prayer, Weil taught, we open our souls, expecting God to act, even when the content of that expectation remains unclear. In their curious vigilance and hoping against hope, both Lola and Simone are beautiful Advent figures.

BIBLICAL ANTECEDENTS

Their attitude is, of course, deeply rooted in biblical revelation. From beginning to end of Scripture, we discover stories of people who are compelled to wait. The patriarch Abraham received the promise that he would, despite his old age, become the father of a son, and through that son, the father of descendants more numerous than the stars in the night sky. But the fulfillment of that promise was a long time in coming. Through many years, as he and his wife grew older and older, as the likelihood of their parenthood became increasingly remote, Abraham waited. Did he doubt? Did he wonder whether he had misconstrued the divine promise? Did he waver in his faith? Did he endure the taunts of his enemies and the pitying glances of his friends? Probably. But he waited, and in time, the promise came true. Abraham's great-grandson Joseph, the wearer of the multicolored coat, saw in a dream that he would be a powerful man and that his brothers would one day bow down to him in homage. But the realization of that dream came only after a long and terrible wait. He was sold into slavery by those very brothers, falsely accused of sexual misconduct, humiliated, and finally sent to prison for seven years. Just imagine what it must have been like to endure years in an ancient prison—the discomfort, the total lack of privacy, the terrible food in small amounts, sleeplessness, torture, and above all hopelessness. This is what Joseph had to wait through before his dream came true in a most unexpected way. The people of Israel were miraculously delivered from slavery in Egypt, led across the Red Sea by the mighty hand of Moses— and then they waited. A journey that would normally have taken only a few weeks stretched to forty years, as they wandered rather aimlessly through the desert. The book of Exodus frequently gives us indications of what this time of vigil was like: "The people grumbled against Moses, 'we are disgusted with this wretched food . . . why did you lead us out into this desert to die; were there not graves enough in Egypt?" They were hardly models of patience! Even poor Noah had to wait, cooped up in the ark with his irritable family and restless animals, while the waters slowly retreated.

And in the course of the Christian tradition, there is much evidence of this spirituality of waiting. Relatively late in life, Ignatius of Loyola realized that he was being called by God to do great things. But before he found his path, he passed, in the course of many years, through a wide variety of experiences: a time of stark asceticism and prayer at Manresa; wandering to the Holy Land and back while living hand-to-mouth and sleeping in doorways; taking elementary courses in Paris, sitting alongside young kids; gathering a small band of followers and leading them through the Spiritual Exercises. Only at the end of this long sojourn— with the founding of the Company of Jesus—did he realize the great thing that God called him to do. In Dante's *Purgatorio*, the theme of waiting is on prominent display. Dante and Virgil encounter a number of souls who slouch at the foot of the mountain of Purgatory, destined to make the climb to heaven, but compelled, for the time being, to wait. How long? As long as God determines.

A Little Theology

All of this, I submit, is very, very hard for most of us. I suppose we human beings have always been in a hurry, but modern people especially seem to want what they want when they want it. We are driven, determined, goal oriented, fast moving. I, for one, can't stand waiting. As a Chicagoan, I find myself, unavoidably, in a lot of traffic jams, and nothing infuriates me more. You are stuck in place, usually behind a massive truck, and you have no idea when you will get where you want to be, and there is nothing you can do about it. I hate waiting at doctors' offices; I hate waiting in lines at the bank; I hate waiting for the lights to come back on when the electricity fails. So when I'm told that waiting seems to belong to the heart of the spiritual life, I'm not pleased, for here too, I want answers, direction, clarity, and I want them pronto. I desire to feel happy and to know what God is up to; I need my life to make sense— now. I'm pleased to live a spiritual life, but I want to be in charge of it and to make it unfold according to my schedule: "Run, Barron, Run." All of this is profoundly antipathetic to the mood and spirit of Advent.

So what sense can we make of the countercultural and counterintuitive spirituality of vigilance? The first thing we have to realize is that we and God are, quite simply, on different timetables. The first letter of Peter states this truth with admirable directness: "To you, O Lord, a thousand years are like a day." To the God who stands outside of space and time and who orders the whole of creation, our hours, days, years, aeons have a radically different valence and meaning. What is a long time to us is an instant for God, and hence what seems like delay to us is no delay at all to him. What seems to us like dumb and pointless waiting can be the way that God, in his unique and finally mysterious manner, is working his purposes out. Richard Rohr has summed up the spiritual life in the phrase "your life is not about you," and this insight is particularly important in terms of the present question. "Why isn't God acting how I want and when I want?" Perhaps because your life is part of a complex whole, the fullness of which only God can properly grasp and fittingly order.

But we can make things even more specific. Is it possible that we are made to wait because the track we are on is not the one God wants for us? Chesterton said that if you are on the wrong road, the very worst thing you can do is to move quickly. And there is that old joke about the pilot who comes on the intercom and says, "I have good news and bad news for you, folks; the bad news is that we're totally lost, but the good news is that we're making excellent time!" Maybe we're forced to wait because God wants us seriously to reconsider the course that we've charted, to stop hurtling down a dangerous road.

Or perhaps we are made to wait because we are not yet adequately prepared to receive what God wants to give us. In his remarkable letter to Proba, St. Augustine argued that the purpose of unanswered prayer is to force the expansion of the heart. When we don't get what we want, we begin to want it more and more, with ever greater insistency, until our souls are on fire with the desire for it. Sometimes, it is only a sufficiently expanded and enflamed heart that can take in what God intends to give. What would happen to us if we received, immediately and on our own terms, everything we wanted? We might be satisfied in a superficial way, but we wouldn't begin to appreciate the preciousness of the gifts. After all, the Israelite people had to wait thousands of years before they were ready to receive God's greatest gift.

Or else, even if we are on the right track, and even if we desire with sufficient intensity what God wants to give, we might still not be ready to integrate a particular grace into our lives or to handle the implications of it. Joseph the dreamer clearly wanted to be a great man, but if he had been given political power and authority when he was an arrogant kid, the results would have been disastrous both for himself and those under his control. His many years of suffering—his terrible wait—made him, when the moment arrived, a ruler of both wisdom and deep compassion. And so, when his brothers did indeed finally bow down to him, as he foresaw in his dream, he was able to react, not in vengeance, but in love: "I am Joseph, your brother."

Some Practical Suggestions

What practically can we do during the season of waiting and vigil keeping? What are some practices that might incarnate for us the spirituality I've been describing? Might I suggest first the classically Catholic discipline of eucharistic adoration? To spend a half hour or an hour in the presence of the Lord is not to accomplish or achieve very much; it is not really "getting" anywhere; but it is a particularly rich form of spiritual waiting. As you keep vigil before the Blessed Sacrament, bring to Christ some problem or dilemma that you have been fretting over, and then pray Lola's prayer: "Ich warte; Ich warte." Say, "Lord, I'm waiting for you to solve this, to show me the way out, the way forward. I've been running, planning, worrying; but now I'm going to let you work." Then, throughout Advent, watch attentively for signs. Also, when you pray before the Eucharist, allow your desire for the things of God to intensify; allow your heart and soul to expand. Pray, "Lord, make me ready to receive the gifts you want to give," or even, "Lord Jesus, surprise me."

A second—and more offbeat—suggestion: do a jigsaw puzzle. Find one of those big, complex puzzles with thousands of small pieces, one that requires lots of time and plenty of patience, and make of it an Advent project. As you assemble the puzzle, think of each piece as some aspect of your life: a relationship, a loss, a failure, a great joy, an adventure, a place where you lived, something you shouldn't have said, an act of generosity, etc. So often the events of our lives seem like the thousand pieces of a jigsaw, lying incoherently and disconnectedly before us. As you patiently put the puzzle together, meditate on the fact that God is slowly, patiently, according to his own plan and purpose, ordering the seemingly unrelated and incongruous events of our lives into a picture of great beauty.

Thirdly and finally, take advantage of traffic jams and annoying lines—really anything that makes you wait. And let the truth of what Jean-Pierre de Caussade said sink in: "Whatever happens to you in the course of a day, for good or ill, is an expression of God's will." Then, instead of cursing your luck, banging on the steering wheel, or rolling your eyes in frustration, see the wait as a spiritual invitation. During the time when you are forced to slow down, pray one of the great repetitive, vigil prayers of the Church, such as the rosary or the Jesus prayer ("Lord Jesus Christ, Son of God, have mercy on me a sinner"). In fact, with this resolution in mind, hang a rosary around your rearview mirror at the beginning of Advent. Consider the possibility that God wants you at that moment to wait and then sanctify the time through one of those savoring prayers.

CONCLUSION

The entire Bible ends on a note, not so much of triumph and completion, as longing and expectation: "Come, Lord Jesus." From the very beginning of the Christian dispensation, followers of the risen Jesus have been waiting. Paul, Augustine, Chrysostom, Agnes, Thomas Aquinas, Clare, Francis, John Henry Newman, and Simone Weil have all waited for the second coming and have hence all been Advent people. During this season, let us join them, turning our eyes and hearts upward and praying, "Ich warte, Ich warte."

Chapter Twelve

THREE PATHS OF HOLINESS

In June of 1997, I visited St. John's Abbey in Collegeville, Minnesota, for a retreat. While there I had an opportunity to talk at some length with Fr. Godfrey Diekmann, one of the giants of the liturgical movement in this country and a major player in the shaping of Vatican II's document on the reform of the liturgy. Godfrey was in his upper eighties, but his mind, wit, and tongue were as sharp as ever. Caught up in the enthusiasm of his conversation and the excitement of his reminiscences, I asked him, "Godfrey, if you were young again and you could mount the barricades, what would you speak out for today in the Church?" The old warrior hit me on the knee with his cane and said, without hesitation, "Deification!" What Godfrey Diekmann was referring to, of course, is a central doctrine in so many of the church fathers whom he loves: We human beings are, in Christ, drawn into the very life of God, transfigured into divinity. Waving his cane like an orchestra conductor, he continued, "In the thirties, I went from Rome to Germany to hear the lectures of Karl Adam, and I'll never forget what he said. He told us that we start at the top, that we start as children of God. The essence of the spiritual life is not trying to make ourselves worthy of God, because God has already made us worthy. The essence of the spiritual life is to live out the implications of our dignity as deified children of the Father." He paused for a few moments and then he said quietly, "That's what I'd fight for. That's what I'd tell the people."

At the center of Christian faith is the dizzying truth that God has broken open his own heart in order to allow us to share his life. The Father sent the Son into godforsakenness, into marginalization, physical suffering, psychological agony, even into death itself, and then in the Spirit, he called him back. But in the return to the Father, the Son carried with him all of us whom he had embraced, showing us that nothing can finally separate us from the heartbroken love of God. When we, through Baptism, enter into the drama of Christ's mission, we are deified, made children of God, rendered holy. The holy life is not primarily about moral excellence or spiritual athleticism or any sort of human achievement; it is about being drawn, by grace, into a dignity infinitely beyond our merits or expectations. Godfrey was right: it is about deification.

Now the holy life "shines," it radiates, it appears. In saints, poets, fools, and friends of God, deification takes on flesh and assumes a form. As the wild diversity of the communion of saints testifies, there is nothing uniform about holiness, but there are certain basic patterns and styles that emerge in the community of the deified. What I would like to do in the course of this chapter is to "walk around" holiness, seeing its various angles and profiles and faces, hoping to catch facets of it as the light plays on them. In the spirit of Avery Dulles, I will present three "models" or paradigms of holiness, various paths of being holy that have emerged in the Christian tradition and become incarnate in those that realize they begin at the top.

First Path: Finding the Center

The massive rose windows of the medieval Gothic cathedrals were not only marvels of engineering and artistry; they were also symbols of the well-ordered soul. The pilgrim coming to the cathedral for spiritual enlightenment would be encouraged to meditate upon the rose of light and color in order to be drawn into mystical conformity with it. What would he or she see? At the center of every rose window is a depiction of Christ (even when Mary seems to be the focus, she is carrying the Christ child on her lap), and then wheeling around him in lyrical and harmonious patterns are the hundreds of "medallions," each depicting a saint or a scene from the Scriptures. The message of the window is clear: When one's life is centered on Christ, all the energies, aspirations and powers of the soul fall into a beautiful and satisfying pattern. And by implication, whenever something other than Christ—money, sex, success, adulation—fills the center, the soul falls into disharmony. Jesus expressed this same idea when he said, "Seek ye first the Kingdom of God and his righteousness and the rest will be given unto you." When the divine is consciously acknowledged as the ground and organizing center of one's existence, something like wholeness or holiness is the result.

This same truth is indicated frequently through "soul" language. Soul is not, for Christians, some spiritual entity alongside of the body; instead, it is the deepest center and source of all that we are: body, emotions, passions, and mind. It is what the Bible calls "the heart," that place—sometimes soft and pliable, other times hard as a rock—that God most often addresses and in which he longs to dwell. It is that deepest wellspring that Teresa of Jesus calls the "interior castle" and Meister Eckhart refers to as the "inner wine cellar" and Thomas Merton knows as the *point vièrge*, the "virginal point" where we stand unsullied in the presence of God. When we live in the interior castle, we are safe; when we are at home in the inner wine cellar, we are regularly intoxicated with the spirit; when we identify with the virginal point, we are one with God. When we live in this space, we are, in a word, holy.

Perhaps the most powerful New Testament evocation of holiness as centeredness is the account of Jesus' calming of the storm at sea. As Jesus and his disciples make their way to the other side of the Sea of Galilee, storms blow up and the apostles panic, fearing for their lives. All this time, despite the roaring of the waves and the tumult of the screaming men, Jesus remains, improbably, asleep. The sleeping Christ stands for that place in us where we are rooted in the divine power, that soul-space where we are, despite all of the vagaries and dangers of life, one with the God who governs the whole cosmos and whose intentions toward us are loving. Even when every aspect of my person is agitated and afraid, that central place is peaceful, at rest. Of course, we see that Christ, once awakened by the disciples, rebukes the winds and calms the waves. This means that the source of peacefulness in the whole of one's person, the spiritual power that can restore calm to the stormiest life, is the inner Christ, the ground of the soul.

Another artistic evocation of the center is the "wheel of fortune" that can be found on so many of the medieval cathedrals. At the top of the wheel is a portrait of a king and over his head is the inscription *regno*, I am reigning; clockwise on the wheel, to the king's left, is a figure shown plummeting down and next to him is the motto *regnavi*, I have reigned; at the bottom is a pauper and accompanying him the saying *sum sine regno*, I am without power; and finally, still moving clockwise, we find a well-dressed man ascending toward the king and next to him is the hopeful inscription, *regnabo*, I will reign. But at the center of the wheel, at that unchanging point where the spokes come together, there is a depiction of Christ. The point is simple and powerful: This wheel of fortune turns and turns throughout one's life, moving one from power and privilege to weakness and penury and then back again. There is really only one guarantee that we have: Whatever state we are in is not our permanent state, for the wheel inevitably spins. But despite the myriad changes, whether one is king or pauper, there is a still-point, a reliably fixed center, where one can find peace and stability. This is Christ; this is the divine power that holds us whether we are great or small, whether we are popular or despised, whether we are king of the world or a beggar on the street. What the symbol of the wheel tells us is this: Don't live your life on the rim of the circle, but rather at the center—and you will find holiness.

Why have so many of the friends of God had that odd insouciance, that almost comical indifference to death? Why could Ignatius of Antioch encourage the beasts to devour him? Why could St. Lawrence, frying on the gridiron, tell his tormentors to turn him over because he was already done on that side? Why can Brother Bill Tomes stand in the crossfire of Chicago street gangs in order to force a cease-fire? Because all of these people live in the center, in that place of peace that no storm can shake, in that holy ground opened up for us by God's broken heart.

Second Path: Knowing You Are a Sinner

G. K. Chesterton once said that the saint is the one who knows he's a sinner. Another way to state the same thing: The holy person has no illusions about herself. It is an extraordinary and surprising phenomenon that the saints seem to be those who are *most conscious* of their sinfulness. Even a cursory reading of Teresa of Avila, John of the Cross, Augustine, Therese of Lisieux reveals that these undoubtedly holy people were painfully aware of how much they fall short of sanctity. At times we are tempted to think that this is a form of attention-getting false humility, but then we realize that it is proximity to the light that reveals the smudges and imperfections that otherwise go undetected. A windshield that appears perfectly clean and transparent in the early morning can become opaque when the sun shines directly on it. Standing close to the luminosity of God, the holy person is more intensely exposed, his beauty *and* his ugliness more thoroughly unveiled. But there is nothing fearsome in this self-revelation, just the contrary, for only what we know and see about ourselves through the graceful light of God can be controlled, changed, or rendered powerless. Hence we find that wonderful conflation of the two senses of *confessio* in our tradition: the confession of sin which is tantamount to a profession of the goodness of God. Nowhere is this clearer than in the appropriately entitled *Confessions* of Augustine, a sustained and psychologically detailed admission of sin dovetailing with a hymn of praise to the God of forgiving light.

I realize that this emphasis on confession has become problematic in recent years. Does it not lead to an obsessive or neurotic self-absorption or even to a dangerously low self-image, and does it not reinforce a view of God as prying and judgmental? In truly holy people, knowledge of sin is not denigrating but liberating because it enables them to break through the subtle illusions and self-deceptions that finally stand in the way of joy. And the most dangerous of these lies that we tell to ourselves is that everything is just fine: "I'm OK; you're OK." I like Anthony de Mello's Gospel-inspired comeback: "I'm an Ass and you're an Ass." Christianity is a salvation religion, and thus its basic assumption is that there is something wrong with us, indeed something so wrong that we could never in principle fix it ourselves. We are members of the dysfunctional family of humanity, and egotism, fear, violence, and pride have crept into all of our institutions and into our blood and bones. And therefore any attempt of ours to lift ourselves out of the problem, any schema of perfectibility, be it political, psychological, or religious, any conviction that we can make it right, is illusory and dangerous. Just as a child is "saved" from a dysfunctional family only when, as a kind of grace, he sees that there is another way of being family, so we are saved from the dysfunction of sin only when Jesus' way of nonviolence and love, a path not *of* the world, appeared *in* our world. To push this analogy just a bit further, just as the child living in a household under the fear of violence *did not fully grasp that there was something wrong until he had seen a saner household*, so we human beings did not fully grasp the extent and danger of our sin *until Jesus' way appeared* as a sharp contrast. His grace was (and is) a sort of searchlight that reveals the dark recesses of our own egotism. As many Protestant theologians have indicated, the cross of Jesus remains a constant and potent sign of judgment, a calling to mind of sin. When God's own heart was revealed in the mission of Jesus, we human beings responded, not with grateful acceptance, but with violent rejection. Therefore the horror of the crucifixion—God's own Son pinned by us to an instrument of torture and left to die—discloses that most painful truth that we would like to keep secret even from ourselves: We prefer our egos to God.

It is for this reason, I think, that so many of the spiritual masters can strike us as a bit sharp and overbearing, out of step with the psychological etiquette of our times. Whether it is Thomas à Kempis on every page of the *Imitation of Christ* reminding us that we are flawed, or the desert fathers harshly calling us to repentance, or Martin Luther insisting that salvation is not a prize that the grasping ego can claim, or Jesus himself laying bare the self-deception of the Pharisees, the spiritual teachers concur in forcing us to see the truth. Bob Dylan said, "The enemy I see wears the cloak of decency," and an essential part of the spiritual program involves the removing of that cloak.

Dante's *Divine Comedy* is a mystagogic itinerary, a holy journey of the soul. It ends with the ecstatic vision of the white rose of angels and saints surrounding the blinding light of the trinitarian God, but it begins in the dark but liberating insight that something is wrong: "Midway upon the journey of our life / I found myself within a forest dark / For the straightforward pathway had been lost." Before he can find the right path, Dante is compelled to make a side trip through hell, witnessing firsthand the suffering of the damned. What he is really seeing, of course, is his own sinfulness, and the vision is harsh and relentless. When Dante swoons from the horror of a particular view, Virgil, his mystic guide, kicks him, forcing him to be aware. He leaves hell finally by the only possible route: climbing down the hairy sides of Satan himself. The message of the poem is clear: no way up but down; no real holiness without awareness; at least part of being a saint is knowing you're a sinner.

Third Path: Realizing That Your Life Is Not about You

When we live wrapped up around our own egos and their pathetic fears and aspirations, we inhabit the narrow space of the *pusilla anima* (the little soul), but when we forget our awful seriousness, when we live in a risky freedom, when we leap ecstatically beyond what we can know and control, we inhabit the infinite expanse of the *magna anima* (the great soul). The title given to Mohandas Gandhi, the *Mahatma*, is etymologically close to this Latin phrase, and it means the same thing. Holy people are those who realize that they participate in something and Someone infinitely greater than themselves, that they are but a fragment of Reality. Far from crushing them, this awareness makes them great, capacious, whole. Richard Rohr says that the initiation rites of young men in various primal cultures have precisely this purpose: to convince the adolescent, through fear, scarification, separation from family, and confrontation with nature and its powers, that he is not in control and that his life has meaning and savor only in relation to a greater Whole. Without these experiences, the young person will convince himself that *he* creates the pattern of his life and that *he* has to figure it all out. The result of this sort of calculating and egotistic rationalism is imprisonment in the *pusilla anima*.

In a hundred ways, our theological and spiritual tradition attempts to cultivate the great soul, to lure us into that wonderful conviction that

It is not about us. At the very end of John's Gospel, the risen Jesus confronts Peter and, after moving him from confession to mission, tells him a secret: "When you were young you put on your own belt and walked where you liked; but when you grow old you will stretch out your hands and somebody else . . . will take you where you would rather not go." In his youth, Peter labored under the illusion that he could control his life: He walked where he liked and he tied his own belt. But in his old age— the time of wisdom—he will realize that his life has all along been under the direction of a Power that his ego cannot begin to understand or manipulate. In taking him where he does not want to go, this Power will introduce him to the *magna anima*.

The Swiss theologian Hans Urs von Balthasar speaks often of the "Theodrama." This is the drama written and directed by God and involving every creature in the cosmos, including those sometimes-reluctant actors, human beings. On the great stage which is the created universe and according to the prototype which is Christ, we are invited to "act," to find and play our role in God's theater. The problem is that the vast majority of us think that we are the directors, writers, and above all, stars of our own dramas, with the cosmos providing the pleasing backdrop and other people functioning as either our supporting players or the villians in contrast to whom we shine all the brighter. Of course, our dramas, scripted and acted from the narrow standpoint of the small soul, are always uninteresting, even if we are playing the lead role. The key is finding the role that God has designed for us, even if it looks like a bit part. Sometimes, in a lengthy and complex novel, a character who has seemed minor throughout the story emerges, by the end, as the fulcrum around which the entire narrative has been turning, the player in comparison with whom the "main characters" fade into relative insignificance. There is a wonderful scene in Robert Bolt's *A Man for All Seasons* in which Richard Rich, a promising and ambitious young man, petitions the saintly Thomas More for a position among the glitterati at the court of Henry VIII. More tells Rich that he can offer him a position, not as a courtier, but as a simple teacher. The young man is crestfallen, and More tries to cheer him up, "You'd be a good teacher." Rich fires back: "And if I were, who would know it?" The patient More explains: "Yourself, your friends, your pupils, God; pretty good public that!" What More assumes is the profoundly spiritual truth that the only audience worth playing for is the divine audience, and the only drama worth acting in—even in the smallest role—is God's. Rich wants a starring role, but More reminds him that it profits him nothing to play even the biggest part in the ego's drama if he misses his role in the Theodrama. When you find the pearl of great price, you must sell *everything else* and buy it.

Now all the doctors of the spirit tell us that when we make the painful transition from the small soul to the great soul we experience liberation and exaltation. We're out of the prison of the ego and its incessant demands, and we are opened to the adventure of discerning and responding to God's will. In his *Abandonment to Divine Providence*, the seventeenth-century Jesuit Jean-Pierre de Caussade encourages us to see every event in our lives—good and bad, fortunate and unfortunate—as expressive of the gracious will of God. When, through faith, we see every moment and every creature as an ingredient in the divine plan, when we know that there is a gracious providence at work in the universe, we live in joyful surrender and with a sense of wonder. What is God doing for me now? What path is opening up to me? Why did God send that person, that trial, that pleasure to me just now? One of the most popular spiritual books of the decade is the *Celestine Prophecy*. What struck me when I read this text—and one reason, I think, for its success—is the enormous emphasis placed on what we would call "providence." The various characters meet under surprising and unexpected circumstances, and these meetings turn out to be precisely what each person needed for his or her next step in the spiritual life. The book teaches us to regard the events and conversations of our lives, not as mere coincidences, but as expressions of a "desire" for spiritual advancement that suffuses the cosmos. When one strips away some of the "new-agey" language of the *Celestine Prophecy* and situates this idea in the context of a belief in a personal and providential God, we are not that far from Jean-Pierre de Caussade. The Christian spiritual teachers would hold that God's loving care for the world is not occasional and interventionist, but rather constant and all-embracing. And therefore we can and should abandon our lives, even in the smallest details, to this divine love, trusting that God will show us the way. In the recent film, *The Apostle*, Robert Duvall's character, having been stripped of money, reputation, and status, rededicates himself to the service of the Lord, trusting that God will show him the path to walk. He enters a town he does not know and when he comes to a crossroad he asks, with disarming naiveté, "Alright, Lord, which way should I go, left or right?" At just that moment, he comes upon the person who will eventually open his life in a new direction. "I will lead the blind on their journey; by paths unknown I will guide them," says the Lord through the prophet Isaiah. And Jesus tells his disciples, "That is why I am telling you not to worry about your life and what you are to eat, nor about your body and how you are to clothe it.... It is the pagans who set their hearts on all these things. Your Father well knows you need them." Is this just pious boilerplate or do we believe it, even to the point of basing our lives upon it? Part of what it means to live in the great soul is to de-center the ego and live in exciting and unpredictable relationship to the Mystery, realizing that our lives are not about us.

CONCLUSION

We start at the top. We have been drawn into the broken heart of God. We are a holy people. This means that we can find the centered place of peace, that "virginal point" where it is no longer we who live but Christ who lives in us. This means that we can see through all of our self-deceptions and illusions, that we can stand in the blinding but finally exhilarating light of Truth. And this means that we can fly, we can break the bars of the prison, we can leave behind the *pusilla anima* and surrender to the delicious Mystery.

Yes, it's about deification. Thanks be to God, it's not about us.

Chapter Thirteen

THE GRANDFATHER AND THE VOICE FROM THE WHIRLWIND: A MEDITATION ON PREACHING THE PROBLEM OF SUFFERING

ABOUT FIVE YEARS AGO, I DELIVERED A HOMILY ON THE SUBJECT OF God's benevolent and providential direction of the cosmos. I felt that the sermon had been inspiring and informative, and the numerous people who complimented me afterward confirmed my own assessment. But after everyone else had streamed past me, an older man approached and, eyeing me warily, said, "Father, I'm on a quest, and your homily didn't help." "Oh, really," I responded, "what do you mean?" He then proceeded to tell me a terrible story. He had two granddaughters, ages five and seven, both of whom were suffering from a terminal disease that the doctors could neither control nor understand. All that they knew for sure was that both girls would die and that, before death, both would go blind. He told me that the elder child had just lost her sight and that the younger was lying awake at night, crying in terror as she contemplated her future. "Father," he continued, "my quest is to find out why God is doing this to my granddaughters. I've been to priests, ministers, rabbis, and gurus, and I've never gotten a very good answer—and frankly, your homily shed very little light." I was flabbergasted, stunned. Never had the "problem of evil"—reconciling the goodness of God with the presence of suffering—appeared to me so concretely and in such a challenging way. All I could muster by way of response was, "I don't know why God is allowing such an awful thing, but I believe that your quest is a holy one."

Obviously, my preaching that day had not proved very helpful to that grandfather. And I must confess that, in the wake of his devastating story, I was tempted simply to avoid the issue in the future. But proclaimers of the Gospel cannot duck the question, for the declaration of God's love will become rather quickly unconvincing if powerful evidence to the contrary is not somehow addressed. So what do we say, and how do we say it?

SOME THEOLOGICAL CLARIFICATIONS

I certainly labor under no illusion that a classroom lecture and a homily are identical, but at the same time I resist the temptation to divorce the two. For the greatest masters of our tradition—Augustine, Aquinas, Bonaventure, Teresa of Avila, Newman, Dorothy Day—there is no substantial divide between theology and spirituality. They knew that speech about God (theology) was meant to be not only informative but transformative and that, therefore, a homily—that uniquely important form of spiritual rhetoric—ought to be thoroughly informed by a theological vision. I think that, especially in regard to the preaching of the issue under consideration here, clear thinking is indispensable. So first, some theology.

Thomas Aquinas said that our knowledge of God is largely negative in character inasmuch as we know much more surely what God is not than what God is. Thus in reference to the problem of God's relationship to evil and suffering, we are perhaps best advised to employ a sort of via negativa, determining as far as we can how not to think about it. First, in our enthusiasm to find a solution to this dilemma we ought not to compromise what Karl Barth called "the godliness of God," thereby turning the divine into something creaturely. In the nineteenth century, the British philosopher John Stuart Mill gave explicit and elegant expression to an intuition shared by many people across the centuries: that the traditional understanding of God is irreconcilable with the terrible fact of evil. Here is the way that Mill formulated his argument: If evil exists (and it surely does), then God cannot be, simultaneously, omniscient, omnipotent, and omnibenevolent. For if he were all-knowing, he would be aware of evil, and if he were all-powerful, he could do something about it, and if he were all-loving, he would want to do something about it—and if all of these obtained at the same time, evil would not exist. Six centuries prior to Mill, Thomas Aquinas—in one of the objections to his article on the existence of God—gave even pithier expression to this intuition that the fact of evil rules out the traditional understanding of God. He said that if one of two contraries were infinite, the other would be altogether destroyed; but God is described as the infinite good; therefore it seems to follow that if evil exists (and it surely does), then the all-good God cannot be.

These are, it has to be admitted, powerful arguments, and the intuition that informs them has compelled people across the centuries to dispense with the classical biblical notion of God. A recent and very influential case in point is Rabbi Harold Kushner who expressed his philosophy of God's relation to evil in his book *When Bad Things Happen to Good People*. Like Mill, Kushner could find no way to square the traditional idea of God with the fact of evil, and he accordingly affirmed that God, though indeed all-knowing and all-loving, is nevertheless not all-powerful. Though God sees all that happens and wishes well to the universe, he is powerless to undo certain evils. A philosophy that similarly denies the omnipotence of God is Manichaeism, the view that the good God who reigns over the spiritual realm is caught in a terrible conflict with the evil God who presides over the material universe. Precisely because it expresses a rather common-sense view of things (good and evil do seem to be in conflict with each other), Manichaeism has proved to be a remarkably durable perspective, appearing most recently in the *Star Wars* movies—where forces of light and darkness do battle for mastery of the cosmos—and in much Jungian and New Age speculation. These denials of the divine omnipotence effectively dissolve the problem of evil and would allow one to give a rather clear theoretical answer to the question of the grandfather. One could tell him that his granddaughters are suffering because, at least in their case, the powers of evil are triumphing

183

over God or that God, though deeply sympathetic to the plight of the girls, is powerless to rearrange the material forces that have produced their pain.

The problem is that the dilemma has been resolved at far too high a price, namely, the loss of the divinity of God. In the biblical perspective, God cannot be thought of as one being among many, precisely because he is the creator of all things. Since God creates the totality of finitude out of nothing, he himself cannot be caught in limitations of space and time, nor implicated in the nexus of contingent relations. He is in no sense dependent upon or conditioned by the world that he himself brings into being in its entirety. Therefore, it is nonsensical to speak of God, in relation to his creation, as anything less than omnipotent (what would limit his power?), anything less than omniscient (what of his world couldn't he know?), anything less than omnibenevolent (how could he hate anything he has made?). More to it, in the biblical vision of things, God not only creates the universe but also continually sustains and governs it. In the book of Wisdom, we find this claim: "God's wisdom stretches from end to end mightily and orders all things sweetly." The implication is that nothing escapes God's vision *and* God's active direction. We see the same assumption in the accounts of Israel's history: whether Israel flourishes or languishes, whether it wins battles or loses them, whether Solomon is ruling it wisely or Ahab wickedly, God is operative, active. Isaiah the prophet states this principle most dramatically when, speaking in the person of God, he writes: "I am the Lord; I create weal and I create woe, I create light and I create darkness." The biblical question is never whether God is involved in the affairs of earth, but rather *how*. Thus the scriptural authors would have considered John Stuart Mill's dilemma a phony problem: for them, the full godliness of God and the existence of evil not only can but must be reconciled.

But does this strong biblical position not back us into another corner? Does it not compel us to say that the good God somehow produces evil, coming thereby into conflict with himself? Such an admission would be a second dysfunctional "solution" to the problem of evil. God cannot be seen as the cause of evil for two reasons: first, because God is thoroughly good, and second, because evil, as such, is not a thing to be caused.

Augustine and Aquinas both maintain that evil is not so much a thing as a lack or a privation of a good that ought to be present, a *privatio boni*. Thus, cancer is bad in the measure that it conduces to the corruption of organs and tissue; and blindness is evil because it is the absence of vision; and sin is a bending or malformation of the will—in Henri de Lubac's phrase, "this mysterious limp." Evil is like a cavity or decay and "exists" therefore only inasmuch as it is parasitic upon some good. God, who is Being itself and the creative ground of whatever is, cannot possibly cause what is not, and this is why our tradition speaks of God's "permitting" evil to come into his creation. But, one might still ask, doesn't this simply push the question back one step? Why would God permit something as monstrously evil as the suffering of the two granddaughters?

Augustine held—and he has been followed by numberless theologians—that God does so in order to bring about some greater good. Can we see this relationship between the permission of evil and the emergence of a good that would not otherwise obtain? Sometimes. In regard to moral evil, it is relatively easy to see that God might allow even terrible sins—Hitler's holocaust or the terrorist attacks of September 11—so that the greater value of human freedom might be preserved. And in regard to physical evil—earthquakes that devastate cities or the disease that was threatening the lives of the granddaughters—we notice something similar. Anglican priest and quantum physicist John Polkinghorne has argued that a "free-process" defense of God's ways could be mounted. On his reading, God permits the physical universe to have its own integrity and independence, so that it unfolds according to its natural rhythms. But this means that there are times that the universe comes into conflict with itself: the thriving of the lion depends upon the demise of the antelope; the crash of a primeval meteor (simply following its natural trajectory) results in a catastrophe for countless living things on this planet; the creativity and novelty that allows for evolution also allows for the emergence of cancer cells; and so on.

Where has our largely negative theologizing about this issue brought us? We know that we cannot preach that God is less than God or that God is the cause of evil. And these negations have, in turn, led us to Augustine's principle that evil is permitted for the sake of a greater good. Now, in speculating as to the nature of that greater good, we ventured onto more positive ground, and in that measure, we have put ourselves in danger. Though there is undoubtedly something right about the "free-will" and the "free-process" defenses, we would, I imagine, be fairly reluctant to share those particular insights with the grandfather. What precisely the all-good God intends when he permits evil in his cosmos remains a mystery, and the deepest "solution" to our problem is had in the surrender to that mystery.

THE ANSWER TO JOB

There is a logical fallacy that runs as follows: Because all explanations for a given phenomenon are inadequate, all are equally good (or bad). This fallacy has led us down some of the blind alleys that we have already explored, and it is important to see that we are especially susceptible to it in regard to our notoriously thorny problem. I have just said that the deepest resolution of this dilemma involves a surrender to mystery, but that does not entail an embrace of lazy thinking. The book of Job—the Old Testament's deepest engagement of the problem of evil—also brings us to the threshold of mystery, but it assumes, at every turn, the principles that we have already highlighted. The author of the book of Job never doubts for a moment that God is fully God, nor does he ever assert that God is the direct cause of suffering. And the undergirding assumption of God's great speech to Job is that something like the permission of evil for the sake of a greater good is the case. What is decisive is Job's willingness to accept the fact of this permission without grasping the details of it.

We know the central moves of the narrative well. Job, an upright man, is, with God's permission, tested by Satan. In the course of a single day, he loses his wealth, his family, and his health and is invited by his wife (in one of the great biblical cameos) to curse God and die. He refuses to do so, sitting in abject misery on a dung heap, accepting God's will but utterly consternated at the injustice of it. For seven days and nights, his friends sit in compassionate silence with him, but eventually they feel compelled to speak, theologizing that Job's suffering must be rationally explained as a response to Job's own iniquity. Disgusted finally with their idle speculations and in the anguish of his own righteousness, Job—like the grandfather—calls God out.

The Lord of the universe then speaks out of the desert whirlwind— obscuring Job's vision, reminding him of how little he actually sees: "Who is this that darkens counsel by words without knowledge? Gird up your loins like a man, I will question you and you shall declare to me. Where were you when I laid the foundation of the earth?" (Job 38:1–4). Then God takes Job on a tour of the cosmos, compelling him to acknowledge mystery after mystery: the movements of the sea, the expanse of the earth, the origin of the rain and the snow, the arrangements of the constellations, the number of the clouds, the behavior patterns of animals, and so forth. God's speech reaches its culmination with the evocation of two of his strangest and mightiest creatures: "Look at Behemoth, which I made just as I made you ... it is the first of the great acts of God—only its maker can approach it with the sword" (Job 40:15, 19) "Can you draw out Leviathan with a fishhook ... will it make many supplications to you? Will you play with it as with a bird, or will you put it on leash for your girls?" (Job 41:1–5). Scholars have speculated that Behemoth might be a crocodile and Leviathan a great whale; the point is that these are two creatures that probably rarely figure in Job's calculations concerning the meaning of the universe, and yet they are, as much as he, part of God's creation and ingredient in God's providential plans. This frightening and awesome oration of God is meant, not to humiliate Job, but to expand the horizons of his mind, to show him that he is surrounded on all sides by mysteries beyond his ken. In the measure that he takes this in, Job will be able to appreciate that his suffering must be situated in an infinitely complex nexus of cause, effect, influence, and action, which only God can properly grasp and control. At the conclusion of the speech, Job knows that God is God, that God has permitted him to suffer, and that the deepest ground of that permission remains utterly beyond his capacity to understand.

Some Images Inspired by Job

Can we say more? In a purely theoretical sense, the answer to that question is probably negative. But we can, I think, move closer to the abstract truths, inhabiting them a bit more thoroughly, through appeal to imagery. These illustrations, which I will cull from many different parts of the tradition, might prove especially helpful to those who seek to preach to this problem.

One of Thomas Aquinas's favorite images for God is that of the artist. It can be found throughout his writings and it serves to illumine a variety of theological themes from creation to providence to the Trinity. But it is particularly clarifying in regard to the mystery of suffering. God is like an artist because he externalizes in a materially objective way a beautiful form that he has raised in his mind. Each individual creature is an object of God's artistic efforts, but it is the universe as a whole that is the primary and proper end of his aesthetic endeavor. On Thomas's reading, Genesis expresses this truth when it says that God found particular creatures good but that he found the whole of his work *very* good. Thus God's artistic work is the whole of creation across space and time, involving every finite thing that has existed, that exists, and that will exist. Is it finished? Obviously not. It would be much nearer to the truth to call it a work in progress. And therefore to move through this life is something like walking through an artist's studio: We see some finished pieces, glorious in their perfection, but we see others that are half-completed, still others barely begun—and all of it a bit of a mess, the overall coherency of the project to be achieved only at the eschaton.

To pursue the artistic image a bit further, looking at the painting that God is working on is something like surveying Georges Seurat's pointillist masterpiece *Sunday Afternoon on La Grande Jatte* with one's nose pressed against the canvas. It is only when one backs away from the Seurat that the millions of points of light and color blend sufficiently to allow the forms and overall pattern to emerge. Seeing it up close, focusing his attention on only a tiny fraction of the painting, a viewer would be, at best, confused. So even the most perceptive and intelligent surveyor of God's work sees the tiniest fraction of its total design and, naturally enough, has a tendency to pronounce it meaningless, or at least confusing.

At the conclusion of *The Divine Comedy*, the pilgrim Dante, having made his way through hell, purgatory, and heaven, stares into the beauty of the Trinity. As he looks he sees, "how it contains within its depths / all things bound in a single book by love / of which creation is the scattered leaves." This tragedy, that friendship, this battle, that victory, all the events of history—these are imagined by Dante as individual leaves from a great book, whose author is God and whose meaning is buried in the mystery of the trinitarian love. Only at the conclusion of time, only when we stare into the divine face, will we see the pattern. Here below, we pick up a page now and again—perhaps an uplifting part of the story, perhaps one of its darker moments, perhaps something that makes not a bit of sense.

In a lecture that he gave toward the end of his life, the American philosopher William James compared us human beings to a dog that wanders into a library. The canine takes in the colors, shapes, and patterns around him; he sees all of the books, the tables, the globe, the inkwells—but he grasps none of it, for those objects belong to a world of meaning that his mind is incapable of perceiving. So we see everything that is going on around us, but we *get* very little of it, precisely because all the events that surround us are part of a theodrama, a divinely scripted play, the plot, movement, and resolution of which remain beyond our ken. To say, therefore, that the world makes no ultimate sense is a bit like James's dog (if he could speak) pronouncing on the uselessness and incoherence of a library.

When I was doing full-time parish work, a young father shared this story with me. His three-year-old son had undergone surgery for a fairly serious malady. In the wake of the successful operation, the young child was in terrible discomfort and looked to his father for reassurance. The father told me that what especially unnerved him was the look in his son's eyes. The boy knew that he was in terrible pain and that, somehow, inexplicably, his father was doing next to nothing to help him. "The problem," the father told me, "was that I couldn't explain to him what surgery was and why he had to go through this pain because he was just too young to understand. All I could do was ask him to trust me that it would work out." This story struck me as a metaphor for God's relation to us in our suffering. Is there a final "meaning" to our suffering? The Bible and tradition, I have been arguing, compel us to answer that question in the affirmative. But are we, in our present condition and with our severe epistemic limitations, capable of taking that full meaning in? Obviously not. And do we not, like that little child, look at our Father God, when we suffer, with a mix of puzzlement and anger? And does God not pledge to us his solidarity and love, even as he remains incapable of "explaining" what is happening to us?

Conclusion

I lost track of the grandfather who posed that awful question after my homily. I don't know what happened to his granddaughters. But I have prayed for all of them over the years. And that man's face and question have stayed in my mind in a nagging way. Would he be any more satisfied with this reflection than he was with my sermon? I doubt it. But I would reiterate what I said to him that day: that his quest was a holy one. Even in the midst of his terrible anguish, he sought for God. Though no clear answers were coming his way, he kept looking, and his perseverance was a sign that, even in the darkness, grace was operative in him.

That grandfather had all of the intelligence and dignity of Job; I can only hope that he has found some comfort in the awful voice that comes from the whirlwind.

Chapter Fourteen

A SERMON FOR CHILDREN
OF THE SEVENTIES

I REMEMBER THE DAY WELL. I STOOD WITH MY CLASSMATES IN THE St. John of the Cross gymnasium, and I was dressed in the height of early seventies fashion: blue blazer, big maroon tie, extremely groovy white pants, and, bringing the outfit to completeness, orange round-toed platform shoes. As we waited to receive our eighth-grade diplomas from the hands of Fr. Bennett, our pastor, cultural forces were swirling around us that would, willy-nilly, shape our consciousness and affect the way we would see the world and relate to our faith. We graduates of the class of '73 were not the children of the serene and prosperous fifties, nor of the idealistic and revolutionary sixties; no, we were to come of age in the riven and ambiguous seventies.

Just a few months before our graduation, American military involvement in Vietnam came to an end, only to be followed two years later by the collapse of the Saigon government that we had striven so mightily and for so long to defend, even at the cost of 58,000 lives. Whether viewed from the left, center, or right, this public policy came to be judged as a colossal failure, and its shadow was to fall across the whole of the decade. The summer after graduation, I sat on an ottoman in our family room watching, with a combination of fascination and incomprehension, the Watergate hearings that seemed to play every day on every channel. My earliest political memories and experiences center around the names

John Dean, H. R. Haldeman, John Ehrlichman, Jeb Stuart Magruder, and Charles Colson. As my parents endeavored to explain to me the contours of the Watergate phenomenon that summer, many of my convictions concerning politicians, public institutions, and political rhetoric were being subtly shaped. And, of course, those convictions were only solidified when, the following August, the president, having lost the support of his own party, resigned his office amidst scandal and disgrace.

During our eighth-grade year, we were each obliged to present an autobiography. I told my life story, such as it was, and at the end of my reflections I shared with the class my vocational aspiration: to be president of the United States. My teacher, Sister Lorraine, told me that that was an admirable career goal, and then she posed the question: "Bob, who are your political heroes today?" I had nothing to say; I was stumped. This was surely due in part to youthful naiveté, but it was also a sign that the seventies was not an era of heroes. If one surveys the popular culture of that period, one notices the early films of Scorsese and Coppola, movies like *Mean Streets* and *The Godfather* and *The Conversation*, explorations of the seamy underside of American life. And the main players in these films were not the morally upright protagonists of an earlier era; they were antiheroes, played by the likes of Gene Hackman, Dustin Hoffman, and especially Jack Nicholson. They were characters divided against themselves, morally ambiguous, noble precisely in their most nefarious moments. If we wanted to find clear heroes and clear villains, we had to go to a "galaxy far, far away." *Star Wars* came out when we were seniors in high school.

The first presidential election in which my classmates and I voted was that of 1980. What was the political climate at that time? The nation was just recovering from the oil embargoes and gas shortages of the mid-seventies, inflation was out of control, unemployment was skyrocketing. Responsible people were speaking of the breakdown of the American economy, and President Jimmy Carter was alluding to a malaise settling over our society. Not a time of optimism and confidence.

And what was our experience of the Church? Those of us who graduated from grade school in 1973 began our Catholic education in 1965, the year the Vatican Council ended. What we moved into, accordingly, was not the confident Church of the fifties or the heady revolutionary Church of the conciliar period, but the confused and confusing Church of the postconciliar era. I have often referred to mine as a lost generation with regard to things Catholic. Quite frankly, our teachers didn't know what to tell us. They knew that the old had been placed into question but the new had not yet arrived, and thus instead of biblical narratives or church doctrine we were treated to banners and collages and political slogans. I remember once in sixth grade, our religion teacher, a nun, invited us to listen to James Taylor's "You've Got a Friend" and then, with our eyes closed, to draw the feelings that the song evoked. In seventh grade, we all labored mightily to make a banner featuring outlines of our hands and the superscript, "We are building the Kingdom of God." We were, of course, oblivious to the sheer Pelagianism of the motto. A telling detail: Our performance in courses such as math, science, history, and English were evaluated with a traditional letter grade, while our progress in less "serious" disciplines such as art, music, and P.E. was traced with "checks," a kind of pass/fail designation. We received checks, not grades, in religion. That the faith could be studied as a serious academic enterprise obviously struck our teachers as unlikely. Sermons in the seventies revealed the inner struggles and questions of the preacher far more than the saving grace of God. When writers from an older generation speak of the fire and brimstone Catholic preachers and missionaries who imposed a clear-cut doctrine and brooked no opposition, I can only smile. Amidst all of the agonized self-searching of the preachers of my generation, I would have appreciated a little fire and brimstone if only for the sake of novelty.

As a result of all this, most of my classmates are a bit at sea when it comes to a Catholic sense of Scripture, dogma, liturgy, and church history; and many of them have, today, drifted into other expressions of Christianity or into a vague secularism. There developed in many of us a conviction—for the most part unconscious—that the Church, tentative, vacillating, often simply an echo of the culture, had little to tell us. And if one looked honestly at church life in the seventies, one saw priests and nuns leaving active ministry in droves, Mass attendance plummeting, and a sort of ecclesial "malaise" that mirrored the cultural one Jimmy Carter spoke of.

Now what did all of this mean for the graduates of the class of 1973? It meant that we grew up canny, wary, skeptical, even a bit cynical. The grand cultural institutions that had supported and given meaning to our parents' lives seemed to rest on shaky foundations, and we were reluctant to entrust ourselves to them. We developed, to use the current academic jargon, a strong hermeneutic of suspicion. And this skepticism, this suspicion of the world, has also opened us, I would argue, to the surprising, discontinuous narratives of the Bible. Oddly, the Scripture is a book especially well suited to children of the seventies.

If we survey the Bible from Genesis to Revelation, we find story after story about the disaster that follows from an over-reliance upon human ideas, leaders, and institutions. The pattern is set in the story of rebellion in the Garden of Eden and in the still disturbing account of the building of the Tower of Babel. When we through our efforts and achievements hope to storm heaven and claim for ourselves a share of divinity, we inevitably fall. And if we peruse the books of the prophets Isaiah, Ezekiel, Jeremiah, Amos, and Daniel, we find repeated condemnations of kings who put themselves above the law, of political policies based on greed and violence, and of cultural institutions that rest on the oppression of the poor. And if we look to these same prophetic figures, we encounter some of the bitterest critiques of ineffectual religion ever written. Isaiah, for example, gives voice to the passionate anger of God at a religion that has lost its soul: "What are your endless sacrifices to me? I am sick of holocausts of rams and the fat of calves. . . . Bring me your worthless offerings no more, the smoke of them fills me with disgust." And the vitriol of the Old Testament prophets seems as nothing when compared to the fire of Jesus' own words against the political and religious establishment of his time: "You scribes and Pharisees, you frauds. . . . You are whitewashed sepulchres, all impressive on the outside but on the inside full of filth and dead men's bones." Something tells me that those of us who came of age in the post-Vietnam and post-Watergate period understand the spiritual import of these stories and sayings only too well. We who grew up in the era of "malaise," both social and religious, can comfortably inhabit the space opened up by these texts.

And there is little, in the Scripture, of the mythological tendency to glorify or idealize human beings. The main characters of the biblical narratives are, for the most part, antiheroes, figures as riven and ambiguous as any Jack Nicholson character. We find Moses the liberator of his people, and the one who was petrified to speak before Pharoah; we have Jacob, who bore the promise, and who also stole his birthright from his brother and then had to wrestle with God; we read of David, the great king, and the contemptible murderer of Uriah the Hittite; we hear of Jeremiah who was summoned by God and who was overwhelmed by a sense of his own unworthiness; we meet Peter, the rock upon whom Christ would build his Church, and the scoundrel who denied his master in his moment of greatest need. And which Scorcese character speaks this line: "I cannot understand my own behavior. I fail to carry out the things I want to do, and I find myself doing the very things I hate. . . . What a wretched man am I! Who will rescue me from this body doomed to death?" It is, of course, the Apostle Paul speaking to the tiny Christian community gathered in Rome. The biblical authors labor under no illusions about human beings. In fact, there is probably no document in Western literature that describes humans with more brutal honesty than the Scriptures. Our clay feet, our ambiguous motives, our split consciousness, the debilitating anxiety that shadows even our most confident projects—all of it is laid bare by the great revelation texts.

And the reason for this is once again clear. The biblical authors insist, in season and out, that as long as we rest our lives on our own egos, we will never find joy. Only when we can say with Paul, "it is no longer I who live, but Christ who lives in me," can we experience liberation. Only when we know in our bones that our lives are not about us, only when we acknowledge that there is a "power at work in us that can do infinitely more than we can ask or imagine," can we be saved. And what the Bible proposes over and again as a means to this realization is the spiritual exercise of coming to terms with our own weakness, debility, insufficiency. This is designed, of course, not to depress us, but to de-center us and thus to free us. When we rest on ourselves and our own ego accomplishments, we live in what the spirit masters call the *pusilla anima*, the little soul, the soul precisely as wide as the contours of the ego, but when we are rooted, not in ourselves, but in the divine power that animates the cosmos, we live in the *magna anima*, the great soul, whose breadth is measureless. The problem with heroes is that they get lured so easily into the "little soul"; the advantage that antiheroes enjoy as they stand amidst the ruins of their egos is that they are opened to the "great soul." Maybe we children of the seventies, so skeptical of our "heroes," are particularly apt to get this message.

Does all of this mean that the biblical authors have given up on the human race, have become simply pessimistic about human institutions and achievements? Not really. It just means that they refuse to put their *faith* in them. Faith, in a scriptural context, means ultimate trust. To pose the question about faith is to wonder where we finally anchor our lives; where we, in the last analysis, "stand"; where we, at the end of the day, orient our lives. When the ego's works are shaken, turned upside down, we tend to lose "faith" in them, and this, from a biblical standpoint, is all to the good, for we are not designed to root ourselves in something as vacillating and tiny as the ego. We are meant to put our final trust in that strange, awesome, and enticing power that infinitely transcends who we are and what we can do. In Luke's Gospel, Jesus says, "Get yourselves purses that do not wear out, treasure that will not fail you, in heaven where no thief can reach it and no moth destroy it." Any "purse" or treasure of this world—any ideal, movement, insitution, or person here below—will wear out, will prove unworthy of our final confidence. "Isn't it the truth?" exclaim the children of the seventies, and "so be it" say the authors of Scripture.

And so classmates of the class of 1973, fellow inheritors of so many broken promises, rejoice that in God's providence you are not liable to succumb to the subtlest of temptations: faith in this world. And then don't despair; rather, join your soulmates Moses, Isaiah, Jacob, David, Peter, and Paul in the journey of authentic faith, the road to the great soul.

Part V

THE WAY OF
NONVIOLENCE

Chapter Fifteen

Thomas' Merton's
Metaphysics of Peace

I HAVE NEVER BEEN COMFORTABLE WITH INTERPRETATIONS— proposed either gleefully from the left or regretfully from the right—that claim that a huge gap yawns between the early Thomas Merton of the *Seven Storey Mountain* and the older Merton of, say, *Conjectures of a Guilty Bystander* or *Faith and Violence*. There is, to be sure, a rather remarkable development from one to the other, but, as Newman knew, authentic development is always marked by a continuity of principles and stability of form. It will be my contention in this chapter that the young Merton's conversion to Catholicism (described so vividly in his autobiography and attendant writings in the forties and fifties) involved an immersion into an entire worldview, a significant dimension of which is a metaphysics of peace, and that this conviction found full expression in his later writings on war and nonviolence. Obviously, the explicitation of this implicit belief came only after long years of prayer, study, conversation, and the discipline of the monastic life. But there is, I will argue, no reason to suppose that Merton's commitment to nonviolence in the 1960s involved the slightest betrayal of the worldview that he adopted in the 1930s, just the contrary. I will try to show that the latter is, in fact, nothing but a practical consequence of the former rightly understood.

MERTON AND AQUINAS

In a particularly lively section of *The Seven Storey Mountain*, Merton speaks of his discovery of Etienne Gilson's *The Spirit of Medieval Philosophy* at the Scribner's bookstore on Fifth Avenue and how that book revolutionized his life. He bought the text because he was enrolled in a course in medieval French literature and "had five or ten loose dollars burning a hole" in his pocket.[1] But he was mortified when he noticed the *nihil obstat* and the *imprimatur* on the frontispiece. So disgusted was he by this association with Catholic dogma that he was sorely tempted to hurl the book out the window. By "a real grace," he didn't throw it away; in fact, he actually read it.

The "big concept" that he took from Gilson's study was "contained in one of those dry, outlandish technical compounds that the scholastic philosophers were so prone to use: the word '*aseitas*.'"[2] This term designates the fact that God exists through himself or by himself (*a se*), that he is, in Aquinas's language *ipsum esse subsistens*, the sheer act of to-be itself. This pithy but profound description convinced him that what Catholics mean by God is not some "vague and rather superstitious hangover from an unscientific age," but rather something "deep, simple, and accurate."[3] A child of his skeptical age, Merton had assumed that the God in whom Christians believed was nothing but a projection of their desires and "subjective ideals," a Feuerbachian fantasy or Freudian wish fulfillment. There is a parallel between this awakening and one described in Evelyn Waugh's *Brideshead Revisited*. The novel's narrator, Charles Ryder, from his postconversion perspective, remembers that during his own period as a convinced agnostic it never occurred to him that religious dogma could ever constitute a serious worldview or be anything but the consequence of "complexes."

What are the implications of this revolutionary idea that so galvanized the young Thomas Merton? A first is this: God is not *a* being, not one existent among many, not a thing above or alongside of the world. Rather, *ipsum esse*, while remaining radically other than any finite existent, is the ground of finite existence and therefore must be, as Aquinas put it, "in all things by essence, presence, and power."[4] Augustine expressed the paradox in an elegant formulation: God is *superior summo meo et intimior intimo meo*, both higher than my highest thought and closer to me than I am to myself. But this divine intimacy entails, furthermore, the connectedness of all created realities through God. The deepest center of any one creature's existence coincides with the deepest center of any other creature's, since that center is none other than the divine power of being. As fellow participants in God's act of to-be, all things are related to one another in the most intimate way possible, for they are all ontological siblings. Thus, when he wrote of "brother sun and sister moon," Francis of Assisi was employing, not simply evocative poetry, but rather accurate Christian metaphysics. And when Meister Eckhart—who sat in the Dominican chair of theology at Paris just a generation after Aquinas— spoke of a shared "sinking" into God, he too was but drawing out the implications of this radical metaphysics of divine to-be.[5]

When the young Merton explored the town of St. Antonin in southern France, he found this understanding of reality reflected in the very structure and layout of the place. All of the roads and alleyways conduced to the Church reigning splendidly in the center, and it was therefore impossible, he found, to move around the city without being drawn, eventually, to the liturgy, to the Eucharist, to the sacred.[6] We hear an overtone of this when, later in the *Seven Storey Mountain*, Merton speaks of the monastery of Gethsemane as "the real capital of the country in which we are living . . . the center of vitality that is in America . . . the cause and the reason that the nation is holding together."[7] At the conclusion of the *Divine Comedy*, a work that Merton specially reverenced, Dante sees the heavenly empyrean as a white rose, an ordered harmony gathered around a luminous center, and he envisions the saints and angels as bees carrying grace from that flower to the far corners of creation. Obviously, both Dante and the town planners of St. Antonin knew full well that the world is a dangerous and violent place, but they also knew, through their Christian convictions, that the deepest reality of things is peace—and this they expressed in their art.

The notion of the divine *aseitas* has implications, as well, for the way we understand the very act of creation. If God is *ipsum esse subsistens*, then whatever else comes to existence must be created ex nihilo, literally from nothing. There can be nothing outside of the sheerly subsistent God from which or on which he works, no preexisting matter or substrate with which he creates. Though God is like an artist in his creative imagination and intelligence, he is not like a sculptor who works with marble or a painter who assembles a picture from canvas and oil. But this implies that the act of creation is thoroughly noninvasive, nonmanipulative.[8] God's creative act is one of utter generosity (since he needs nothing outside of himself) and utterly nonviolent (since he shapes nothing outside of himself). And this, in turn, signals the radical disjunction between the Christian account of the world's beginning and most philosophical or mythological versions of the same. In many of the primal myths, creation takes place through some sort of violence: either the conquest of one god by another, or the successful battle against chaos or recalcitrant matter. Even in the philosophical doctrines of Plato and Aristotle, we find that matter—coexisting with the divine from the beginning—is shaped and molded into order. The implication of the Christian doctrine of *creatio ex nihilo* is that nonviolence is the deepest truth of things, noncompetitiveness the ground of being. And thus to live nonviolently is not simply to be ethically upright; it is to be cosmically correct, to go with the grain of creation.

What Thomas Merton took in when he absorbed the medieval philosophy of Aquinas mediated to him by Etienne Gilson was thus a view of the real as the realm of co-inherence, participation, and nonviolence. At the truest and most metaphysically dense level, the universe, he saw, is a reflection of the peaceful and sheerly generous act by which the *ipsum esse subsistens* brings it into being.

THE DISSOLUTION OF THE PARTICIPATION VISION

One of the great ironies of *The Seven Storey Mountain* is that Merton discovered this brilliant medieval vision at a moment when his literary and philosophical culture had largely forgotten or repudiated it. The tired modernity of Merton's youth—expressed aesthetically in some of his favorite writers, such as D. H. Lawrence and Ernest Hemingway, and politically in the Communism with which he flirted—was the consequence of the collapse of a participation metaphysics. One of the first causes of this collapse was, oddly enough, a Franciscan friar, John Duns Scotus. When Scotus insisted that there is a univocal concept of being, he situated God and creation under the same great ontological canopy, effectively setting God alongside of the world, one being (however great) among many.[9] But the juxtaposing of God and creatures amounts to a negation of the participation metaphysics that Aquinas advocated. On the Scotist reading, the world is comparable to God, but it doesn't share in the to-be of God. And when this participation is denied, the essential connectedness of all creatures to one another is also undone.

Scotus' univocal conception of being was carried further and deepened by William of Occam and the nominalists inspired by him, and they in turn had a decisive influence on Martin Luther and the other reformers. The Scotist–Occamist strain can be discerned in Luther's embrace of a radical *theologia crucis* and his effective distantiation of God from the world. Though these theological and metaphysical moves were born of Luther's legitimate concern to guard God's transcendence and sovereignty, they would have been inconceivable within the framework of Aquinas's participation theory. What commenced as an aberrant strain within Christianity reached its full flowering, however, in the philosophy of secular modernity. In the writings of Thomas Hobbes, for instance, we see that once God has been effectively removed from the scene, the world becomes a place of disconnected atoms in motion. This view informs Hobbes's cosmology as well as his famous take on the prepolitical state of nature as a realm where life is "solitary, poor, nasty, brutish, and short." In a complete reversal of Aquinas's nonviolent social ontology, here we see that the "natural" condition of things is individualistic and antagonistic, the war of all against all. Political cohesiveness is not, for Hobbes, a reflection of nature, just the contrary; it is an artificial construct based upon the fundamentally selfish agreement of the social contract. Though they express it a bit more delicately, both Locke and Rousseau share the Hobbesian assumption of a fundamentally violent social ontology, and that assumption shapes their view of the purpose of government as the protection of individual rights rather than the fostering of a community of justice. This tradition is clearly reflected in the language of Jefferson's Declaration of Independence: Governments come to be in order to preserve and protect individuals from one another, and among the fundamental rights of human beings is the freedom to pursue happiness (left completely undefined) as they see fit.

In all of this we see the political consequences of the unraveling of the medieval Catholic vision of participation. Whereas in the medieval view violence and antagonism were seen as sinful aberrations, departures from the natural order of things, on the modern reading, they are reflections of the way the universe is.

THE EPIPHANY AT FOURTH AND WALNUT

The awakening that Thomas Merton experienced through his exposure to medieval Catholic metaphysics triggered a process that eventually led him, in 1941, to enter religious life as a Cistercian of the Strict Observance. Immersing himself in the rhythms and routines of Trappist life, Merton was able, throughout the forties and fifties, to explore the implications of his faith, and this exploration gave rise, not only to his great autobiography, but also to the monastic journal *The Sign of Jonas*, the study of prayer *Seeds of Contemplation*, and many other texts on spirituality and theology. But, as I suggested at the outset of this chapter, a major transition seemed to occur in the early sixties, as Merton shifted to a concentrated focus on issues of war and peace and the praxis of nonviolent resistance. To some degree, this change was prompted by the tenor of the times (the intensification of the Cold War, the beginning of American involvement in Vietnam), but it was also the unfolding of the creation/participation theology that he learned from Etienne Gilson. Before turning to the texts on war and peace, I would like to explore what amounts to a bridge between the earlier and later phases of Merton's development, that is, the moving and popular account of his experience at the corner of Fourth and Walnut in Louisville.

In interpreting this well-loved passage from the *Conjectures of a Guilty Bystander*, we are enormously helped by the recent publication of the complete journals of Merton. On February 28, 1958, just three weeks before Fourth and Walnut, Merton reported a dream: "On the porch at Douglaston, I am embraced with determined and virginal passion by a young Jewish girl. She clings to me and will not let go, and I get to like the idea. I see that she is a nice kid in a plain, sincere sort of way. I reflect 'she belongs to the same race as St. Anne.' I ask her her name and she says her name is Proverb. I tell here that it is a beautiful and significant name, but she does not appear to like it—perhaps others have mocked her for it."[10] On March 4, Merton inscribes in his journal a sort of love letter to this dream figure, expressing his gratitude to her for awakening in him something he had lost and praising her for her "virginal solitude" and the beauty of her name. Now this character of Proverb has been interpreted as Merton's feminine side, as his "anima" in the Jungian sense, as a memory of his childhood—and these readings all probably have validity. But I believe that the key to understanding her is the name that Merton finds so powerful and moving. One of the most important presentations of creation in the Old Testament is found in the eighth chapter of the book of Proverbs, where the wisdom of Yahweh is personified as a girlish figure who plays at the feet of the Creator as he brings forth the world: "The Lord created me at the beginning of his work, the first of his acts of long ago. When there were no depths I was brought forth, when there were no springs abounding with water.... When he established the heavens, I was there ... when he assigned to the sea its limit ... when he marked out the foundations of the earth, then I was beside him like a master worker, rejoicing before him always, delighting in the human race" (Prov. 8:22–31). Given the playful, associative, and fecund quality of Merton's mind (not to mention of his unconscious psyche), is it possible to say that what embraces Merton in his dream, this young girl called Proverb, is a reawakened sense of the purity and innocence of God's creative act?

What gives weight to this interpretation is the proximity of the Proverb dream and the experience at Fourth and Walnut. I will follow the evocative account he gives of this powerful spiritual event in the *Conjectures of a Guilty Bystander*. While in town for a medical appointment, Merton found himself standing at a street corner in a busy section of Louisville's shopping district, crowds of people hurrying by him. He comments: "I was suddenly overwhelmed with the realization that I loved all those people, that they were mine and I theirs, that we could not be alien to one another even though we were total strangers."[11] A dream of separateness that he had cultivated during his monastic years was suddenly over: "We monks belong to God. Yet so does everybody else belong to God."[12] What dissolved for Merton during this encounter is the common modern view that the universe is composed of isolated and mutually antagonistic atoms, divorced from each other because of their common divorce from God. As Merton develops this insight, his language becomes more metaphysically exact: "Then it was as if I suddenly saw the secret beauty of their hearts, the depths of their hearts where neither sin nor desire nor self-knowledge can reach, the core of their reality. . . . If only they could all see themselves as they really *are*."[13]

He could love all of these perfect strangers precisely because they were, at the "core" of their being, his own ontological siblings. Only a metaphysics of creation and participation could ground this mystical experience of union. In one of his texts on prayer, Merton described contemplation as finding that place in you where you are here and now being created by God, discovering, in a word, the core of your being and thus the point of contact with everything else in the universe. In his description of Fourth and Walnut, Merton gives this center a new name: "Again that expression *le point vièrge* comes in here. At the center of our being is a point of nothingness which is untouched by sin and by illusion, a point of pure truth, a point or spark which belongs entirely to God. . . . This little point of nothingness . . . is the pure glory of God in us."[14] The deepest ground of the soul, the virginal point, is best described as "nothingness" precisely because creation takes place, as we saw, ex nihilo, which in turn implies that the most elementary truth about ourselves and the rest of creation is peace and nonviolence. If only we realized this truth, we could live with the grain of the cosmos, and the only practical conclusion would be a life of nonviolence: "It is like a pure diamond, blazing with the invisible light of heaven. It is in everybody, and if we could see it we would see these billions of points of light coming together in the face and blaze of a sun that would make all the darkness and cruelty of life vanish completely."[15] One of the qualities of Proverb that Merton found so attractive was her "virginal purity," and we can see it in this account of the *point vièrge*, the place in all things of unsullied and undisturbed contact with God. Were we to live out of that space and be illumined by that light, sin would, almost automatically, wither away. From a correct understanding of creation (orthdoxy) would come nonviolence and compassion (orthopraxis).

THE WAY OF NONVIOLENCE

Thomas Merton's writings on nonviolence are among the most passionate and controversial in his oeuvre. It is impossible to read, say, *A Chant to Be Used Around a Site With Furnaces*, or *Original Child Bomb*, or *A Devout Meditation in Memory of Adolph Eichmann* without being stirred to either anger or righteous indignation, or perhaps both at the same time. As every biographer has reminded us—and as becomes eminently clear in the journals—Merton had a difficult time getting many of these writings past the censors in his own order. And those that did find their way into print were met with either bewilderment or outright opposition on the part of those who wondered what had become of the pious and socially conservative convert of *The Seven Storey Mountain*. For though he consistently denied that he was a pacifist, Merton, in these texts from the sixties, clearly departed from the straitlaced just-war theorizing of the Cold War–era Catholic Church and ventured into more radical territory. Moreover, he associated, either directly or by correspondence, with some of the better-known peace activists of the time, including Dorothy Day, Daniel Berrigan, James Forest, and Joan Baez. It is my conviction that Merton did not so much depart from a conservative metaphysics and embrace a radical social theory as he uncovered the behavioral implications of what was in fact a radical and countercultural metaphysics.

The most thorough and sustained presentation of Merton's views on the praxis of nonviolence can be found in an article entitled "The Christian in World Crisis" published in June 1964, just one year after the appearance of Pope John XXIII's peace encyclical *Pacem in terris*.[16] What Merton tries to argue in this essay is that nonviolence is a practice deeply

rooted in the truth of things and not the quirky conviction of a few fa-
natics, "maladjusted creatures lost in impractical ideals, sentimentally
hoping that prayer and demonstrations can convert men to the ways of
peace."[17]

At the center of his analysis is a survey of Christian views on war
and peace in the patristic era, beginning with Origen of Alexandria. Expressing a fairly common view in the ancient world, Celsus, Origen's feisty
and stubborn interlocutor, had maintained that Christians, with their
commitment to nonviolence, could not possibly be loyal citizens of the
Roman Empire. Origen responds by admitting, rather blandly, that Christians could not support the emperor through arms, though they could certainly support his legitimate purposes through prayer. What the
contemporary reader finds surprising is, first, the matter-of-fact quality of
this rejoinder (of course disciples of Jesus don't take up arms) and second,
the frank acknowledgment of the power of prayer in the context of the political life. But the heart of Origen's response to Celsus is not practical but
theological. What Christians challenge most vociferously is the Roman
assumption (shared by political powers up and down the centuries) that
wars are necessary, given the basically antagonistic quality of human relationships. In light of the Incarnation of the divine Logos, Christians maintain a hope that the original unity of creation can and will be restored, and
they therefore have the courage to live in nonviolence and forgiveness. Origen argues: "No longer do we take the sword against any nations nor do
we learn war any more since we have become the sons of peace through Jesus who is our author instead of following the traditional customs by
which we were strangers to the covenant."[18] In brief, the arrival of God's
creative power (the Logos) in the midst of human history has effected a
radical shift at both the ontological and epistemological levels: Now the
world is in fact being restored to its original interconnectedness and now
we can begin to see the deepest truth of things, our eyes undimmed by sin.
The violent and antagonistic universe—assumed by both ancient Rome
and modern Europe—is revealed to be, in light of the coming of Christ, a
sort of illusion. Merton summarizes Origen's position as follows: "The
presence in the world of the Risen Savior, in and through his Church, has
destroyed the seeming validity of all that was in reality arbitrary, tyranni-

cal or absurd in the fictions of social life."[19] Therefore, Christians should live stubbornly in the truth (incarnating the end times now) in the hopes that they will thereby dispel the clouds of illusion that surround them.

Merton then turns his attention to another Christian theologian who, 200 years after Origen's *Contra Celsum*, wrestled, on the grandest possible scale, with questions of war and peace. In the *City of God*, Augustine of Hippo offered a theology of history, at the heart of which is an articulation of the relationship between two fundamentally divergent conceptions of human community, one deceitful and the other truthful. Augustine's *civitas terrena* is that collectivity which, predicated upon love of self, is inherently unstable and violent.[20] Turned in on themselves, the members of this society cannot sustain true *communio*, and their being together is therefore accidental and essentially antagonistic. The driving force of this earthly city is what Augustine magnificently calls the *libido dominandi*, the lust to dominate, and this quality is no more fully displayed than in that paragon of earthly justice, the Roman Empire. Rome has indeed established a kind of stability, but, says Augustine, it is phony and dangerous because it is predicated upon the ruthless threat and exercise of violence. Furthermore, the dysfunction of the Roman polity is a reflection and function of the false theology of the empire. The gods and goddesses of Rome—whom Augustine consistently characterizes as demons—are themselves venal, vain, self-absorbed, and violent.[21]

What the Bishop of Hippo proposes as a counterforce is the *civitas Dei*, that community grounded in love for the true God. Given to the Creator, rooted in their common center, the members of this collectivity can find true communion in and with one another. In this context, antagonism is recognized as a lie, a distortion of the truth of things, and thus compassion, forgiveness, and nonviolence can readily surface and flourish. Just as the *civitas terrena* flows from false worship, so the *civitas Dei* is a consequence of right praise. The true God is not a self-obsessed potentate but rather is himself a *communio* of persons ordered hierarchically but noncompetitively; and in the measure that they honor this God, the citizens of the *civitas Dei* become his peaceful icon and reflection.

Merton finds compelling Augustine's insight that in the mythology of Rome, the great city was founded in the wake of the murder of Remus by his brother Romulus, and that this is precisely echoed in the biblical account of the fratricidal Cain as the founder of cities.[22] Whether the fact is viewed positively or negatively, violence conditions the *civitas terrena* from the beginning. And on Augustine's reading, the great representatives of the peaceful *civitas Dei*—Noah, Abraham, Jacob, Joseph, Jeremiah, Jesus, Paul, and others—are, necessarily, pilgrims and wanderers, resident aliens in and among the earthly cities. The peaceful order of the trinitarian community and the peaceful order of creation are the deeply countercultural truths preached by and embodied in the peacefulness of the *civitas Dei*. To be sure, Augustine famously departs from Origen's total commitment to nonviolence and allows for some limited use of coercive punishment and warfare. But this is, as he repeatedly insisted, nothing but a concession to sin—the tragic acknowledgment that sometimes goods have to be protected through the use of force—and certainly not the acceptance of the false theology and metaphysics of the earthly city. It seems to me that this Augustinian resolution is quite close to Merton's own: a fundamental, clear, theologically informed acceptance of the way of peace, without an absolutist embrace of pacifism.

After his consideration of the patristic period, Merton casts a glance at modern political thought as exemplified by Hobbes and Machiavelli and notes—as we did earlier—their effective unraveling of the Christian vision.[23] Then he turns his attention to an analysis of Pope John's *Pacem in terris*, a text that he interprets as a ringing reaffirmation of the integral Christian metaphysics of peace. Though the encyclical treats of individual rights, the need for an international authority, and the tensions of the Cold War, its primary focus and organizing principle is the order of God's creation: Whatever we say about the rapport between peoples and nations must be predicated upon the undergirding truth of the world. Merton says that Pope John's fundamental optimism about the social life flows from Paul's cosmic optimism as expressed in his letter to the Colossians: "All things have been created through and unto him, and he is before all creatures, and in him all things hold together" (Col. 1:16–17). Because the world has been made and redeemed through the divine Logos, things and people, despite all relatively superficial obstacles, "hold together" at the center.

The Christian call for peace is, therefore, not whistling in the dark, but an evocation of the deepest grain of the universe. Merton explicitly links this Pauline vision to the Thomistic metaphysics that so galvanized him as a young man: "Saint Thomas dared . . . to demonstrate the natural goodness of the world as something that could not be fully understood and vindicated except in the light of the revealed doctrine of creation."[24] And then he makes the connection between this intuition and the Pope's argument for peace: "As Pieper said of Saint Thomas, so we can say of Pope John: 'to his mind it would be utterly ridiculous for man to undertake to defend the creation. Creation needs no justification. The order of creation is, on the contrary, precisely the standard which must govern every man's judgment of things and of himself.'"[25] But what is this order—whether expressed by Paul, Origen, Augustine, or Thomas—but the order of participation, connection, nonviolence, and love?

Having invoked so many of the greatest theological thinkers of the tradition, Merton draws his meditations to a close, not with a theologian, but with a saint and poet. Toward the end of his life, St. Francis sent one of his friars to Assisi in order to mediate a dispute between the mayor and bishop of the town. He told him to sing, in their presence, "The Canticle of the Sun," Francis's praise of God in his creatures, for he was convinced that the best way to turn people's minds to peace "was to remind them of the goodness of life and of the world."[26] After the friar sang his hymn, the mayor broke into tears and the bishop confessed his own haughtiness and there was peace between them. As I contended earlier in this chapter, "brother sun, sister moon" can be coherently uttered only by someone who has understood an ontology of participation and connection, a metaphysics of peace.

Conclusion

It has been the central argument in this chapter that the proclamation of creation is the condition for the possibility of real peace, for creation implies both nonviolence and deep interconnection. I have tried to show that Thomas Merton, throughout his career, knew this. He learned it first from the participation ontology of Aquinas that seeped into his mind through Gilson; it was renewed in the virginal embrace of Proverb the dream figure and in the *point vièrge* mysticism of Fourth and Walnut; and it surfaced again in the creation-based summons to peace in his 1960s writings on nonviolence.

I am persuaded, as well, that Merton's meditations on this rapport might indicate a way forward for Catholic and Christian social teaching. Believers in *creatio ex nihilo* have no need to import a social theory from secular or pagan sources, either from Aristotle, Cicero, Adam Smith, or Karl Marx. For a participation metaphysics is itself a distinctive and compelling social theory—one of forgiveness and nonviolence.

Notes

1. Thomas Merton, *The Seven Storey Mountain* (New York: Harcourt Brace Jovanovich, 1948), 189.

2. Ibid., 191.

3. Ibid.

4. Thomas Aquinas, *Summa theologiae*, Ia, q. 8, art. 3.

5. Meister Eckhart, *The Book of "Benedictus": Of the Nobleman*, in *Meister Eckhart: The Essential Sermons, Commentaries, Treatises, and Defense* (New York: Paulist Press, 1981), 240–47.

6. Merton, *The Seven Storey Mountain*, 40–41.

7. Ibid., 363.

8. John Milbank, *Theology and Social Theory: Beyond Secular Reason* (Cambridge: Blackwell, 1990), 424–27.

9. Ibid., 302–6.

10. Thomas Merton, *A Search for Solitude: The Journals of Thomas Merton*, vol. 3, *1952–1960* (San Francisco: Harper Collins, 1996), 176.

11. Thomas Merton, *Conjectures of a Guilty Bystander* (New York: Doubleday/ Image, 1989), 156.

12. Ibid., 157.

13. Ibid., 158.

14. Ibid.

15. Ibid.

16. Thomas Merton, "The Christian in World Crisis: Reflections on the Moral Climate of the 1960s," in *The Non-Violent Alternative* (New York: Farrar, Straus, and Giroux, 1980), 20–62.

17. Ibid., 32.

18. Origen of Alexandria, *Contra Celsum* V, 33, quoted in "The Christian in World Crisis," 41.

19. Merton, "The Christian in World Crisis," 41.

20. Ibid., 43.

21. See Milbank, *Theology and Social Theory*, 390–91.

22. Merton, "The Christian in World Crisis," 43.

23. Ibid., 47–51.

24. Ibid., 59.

25. Ibid.

26. Ibid., 62.

CREATION, TRANSUBSTANTIATION, AND THE GRAIN OF THE UNIVERSE: A CONTRIBUTION TO STANLEY HAUERWAS'S EKKLESIA PROJECT

STANLEY HAUERWAS HAS ISSUED TO US AN EXTREMELY CHALLENG-
ing invitation: to determine whether Christians who share a set of moral,
spiritual, and theological convictions can work together effectively if they
are barred from worshipping together around the eucharistic table.
When I shared this question with Michael Baxter some months ago and
asked his advice as to what to say, he responded, "Tell the non-Catholics
that they can all convert." Knowing Baxter as I do, I realize that this comment was meant both playfully and seriously. Obviously, the Catholic
conviction that common participation in the Eucharist is contingent
upon a common understanding of the nature of Christ's presence in the
sacrament goes a long way toward establishing the tension that Hauerwas puts his finger on. I could take the relatively easy way out and say
(truthfully enough) that a lack of consensus on the real presence does not
preclude all sorts of shared ethical and even liturgical practices among
Catholics and non-Catholics, but such sidestepping would be finally un-
helpful and even a bit patronizing. What I should like to do, therefore,
in this very brief presentation, is to lay out the essentials of the Catholic

understanding of transubstantiation and real presence and to show why an acceptance of this theology is of great importance precisely in regard to the ethical and political convictions of the Ekklesia project.

Lest a discussion of transubstantiation devolve into misunderstanding, two basic metaphysical facts have to be made manifest: first, the distinctiveness of the divine way of being and, second, the distinctiveness of the act of creation. From the Incarnation (involving the noncompetitive juxtaposition of the divine and human natures in Christ), we know that God is not a being in, above, or alongside of the world. Were he so, he could not enter into intimate union with a finite nature. Therefore, God is radically other than the world, but his otherness is a noncontrastive transcendence. Anselm expressed this divine distinctiveness when he said that God is that than which no greater can be thought, implying that God plus the world is not greater than God alone. And Thomas Aquinas gave voice to it by insisting that God is not the *ens summum* (a supreme being among many) but rather *esse ipsum subsistens*, the sheer act of to-be itself. What follows from this paradoxical description is that God can involve himself in creation in a supremely noninvasive, uninterruptive manner. And an implication of this notion of God is that creation is an utterly nonviolent act since it is the event by which God brings the whole of finitude into being ex nihilo. In any sort of this-worldly transition, an external agent effects some sort of change in another, imposing itself on the other, marking it with its energy. But creation is, as Aquinas specifies, not any sort of change, either substantial or accidental, not something that makes a difference in the world, not an "external" imposition on anything at all. The noncompetitive God speaks himself in what is other through a supremely nonviolent act. This distinctive metaphysic of God and the world informs the Catholic doctrine of transubstantiation at every turn.

In one of its formularies on the Eucharist, the Council of Trent maintains that Christ is present *vere, realiter, et substantialiter* (truly, really, and substantially) in the consecrated elements. There are two basic ways to misinterpret this claim, both tending to read the eucharistic change as a this-worldly phenomenon. According to the first (a typical caricature of the Catholic position) transubstantiation entails either some sort of clandestine chemical change in the bread and wine or a metaphysical sleight of hand whereby one set of substances is whisked away and, under cover of the accidents, replaced by another. According to the second (used by numerous contemporary theologians), Christ becomes really present in the measure that the significance of the bread and wine radically changes given the context of a believing assembly and a symbolically charged religious ritual. Here the substantial change amounts to a projection of the meaning-creating capacity of the community. On the first reading, the eucharistic change is, despite certain distinctive elements, not essentially different than a natural substantial change; and on the second reading, it is but an intense exemplification of ordinary entry into a symbolic world. According to the Catholic doctrine, something much stranger is going on.

To help us grasp this, I will turn to the remarkable set of questions in the third part of the *Summa theologiae* where Thomas Aquinas discusses sacraments in general and the *transsubstantiatio* involved in the eucharistic mystery in particular. For Thomas, all sacraments are to be understood under the rubric of signs: A sacrament, he says, is *signum rei sacrae inquantum est sanctificans homines* (a sign of a holy thing inasmuch as it is sanctifying human beings). The "holy thing" in question can be analyzed in terms of the three dimensions of time: In terms of the past, it is the passion of Christ; in terms of the present, it is sanctifying grace; in terms of the future, it is eternal life. In any case, it is Jesus Christ himself precisely in his power to make holy. Because we are humans and not angels, this invisible reality is properly communicated to us through sensible signs, and these visible bearers of grace are the sacraments. Since they are the means by which grace is infused in us, they are said to cause grace, not in a proper sense (that applies to Christ alone), but in an instrumental sense: "Truly an instrumental cause does not act through the power of its own form, but only through the motion by which it is moved by the principal agent." The same noncompetitiveness that enabled God to speak himself through a human nature in Christ allows him both to create the world as a whole and to use humble sensible things as the instruments of his purposes. For Aquinas, the Eucharist is not an exception to this general rule, but rather its fullest exemplification, for in it the signs of bread and wine become the bearers, not only of the power of Christ to sanctify, but of the sanctifying Christ himself in person.

How, more precisely, is this embodiment possible? I would like at this point to make a connection between Aquinas and Wittgenstein. In the *Philosophical Investigations*, Wittgenstein famously compared words to tools in a toolbox. We can't possibly know what a word means apart from the way it is actually used in concrete games of language, just as we can't know what a screwdriver "means" until we see what a worker does with it. The word that Thomas uses to describe the derivatively causal nature of sacramental signs—*instrumentum*—could be very validly rendered in English as "tool." Now there is a whole bevy of words and gestures used in the context of liturgy and prayer, and their meaning is determined, as Wittgenstein saw, by their employment in an entire linguistic system. They are tools that mean in the measure and the way they are worked with. But in all of the sacraments, there is a moment when the minister speaks in the divine first person: "I baptize you; I absolve you; be sealed with the Holy Spirit," and so forth. In these instances, he is speaking in the very person of Christ, signaling that Christ is the one who is using these human words as his tools. In the most dramatic instance of this instrumental causality, the priest at the Eucharist speaks the words of Jesus at the Last Supper: "Take this all of you and eat it, this is my body; take this all of you and drink from it; this is the cup of my blood." Here Christ is seizing certain *instrumenta*, in this case, words pronounced over bread and wine in the context of a religious ritual, and he is using them to speak, not only his power, but his personal presence. He is taking elements that belong already to an intricate game of language and hoisting them into a higher, properly supernatural context, so that they now become his language, his grammar, the bearers of his meaning.

But to speak of divine language and divine meaning is to speak of being, since what God says, is, what God means, comes to be. Long before Austin clarified it for us, God knew how to do things with words. In the Bible, God's words are never merely descriptive but creative: "Let there be light, and there was light; my word never goes forth from me in vain, without achieving the end for which it was sent." Since Jesus is the divine Logos incarnate, his words similarly affect being ("Lazarus, come out; and the dead man came out"); in changing the way things mean, they change the way things are. Hence when the priest speaks the words of Christ over the bread and wine an already humanly meaningful ritual becomes assimilated to the divine language game. And since God's speech affects what it says, it is appropriate to describe *this* transsignification of the bread and wine as ontologically transformative, a change at the level of being. When Aquinas insists that this "change" be referred to as *transsubstantiatio*, he is not recommending that Aristotelian metaphysics is the only or even best conceptual framework for understanding this mystery; rather, he is insisting that we are dealing with a phenomenon so unique that it can only be compared to creation, that properly supernatural act which only God can in principle perform. Aristotle knew of two basic types of natural change—substantial (a living body becoming a corpse) and accidental (a projectile undergoing local motion)—but Aquinas says that the conversion of the total substance of bread into the body of Christ and the total substance of wine into the blood of Christ "is not contained in the species of natural change" and hence is properly called *transsubstantiatio*. In using such a term (and thinking such a thought), Thomas is, of course, speaking Aristotelian nonsense, but he is doing the same when he speaks of creation from nothing. In fact, in question 75, article 8, he makes explicit the connection between the two events, arguing that in both cases there is a transition from one state to another, with no enduring substrate undergirding the process. As we hinted earlier, this lifting up of bread and wine to be the *instrumenta* of God's linguistic purposes has nothing to do with disguised forms of substantial change or with human projections of deeper significance. Both of those would be *species motus naturalis* (types of natural change). It is the noncompetitively transcendent God, capable of affecting being at the most fundamental level, who alone is capable of both creation and transubstantiation. In both cases, the deepest grain of reality—God's sheerly generous and nonviolent gift—is made manifest.

By way of conclusion, I would like to make just one further link between these two ideas. We have seen that creation is a nonviolent act, since it involves no dominance or manipulation of one thing by another. Transubstantiation is the act by which Christ becomes really present—

not simply as static metaphysical stuff, but in the event of his death on the cross. Balthasar argues that in the New Testament person and mission are always related, so that one's deepest personal identity is a function of one's accepting of a commission from God. Jesus' personhood is therefore defined by his taking on the mission to carry the divine love to the limits of godforsakenness and in the face of terrible opposition. What becomes really present in the Eucharist—Jesus' body and blood—is precisely this deepest identity of Jesus, a nonviolent love unto death. It is therefore, like creation itself, a densely objective manifestation of the structure of being, of what Stanley Hauerwas has called "the grain of the universe." Were the eucharistic transformation a this-worldly change, it would never function as an adequate representation of God's nonviolent love. And this is why the worship that flows from and leads to a robustly ontological account of the eucharistic presence is key to the practical work of the Ekklesia project.

Chapter Seventeen

"Comes a Warrior":
A Christmas Meditation

God's world—the universe that came forth good and splendid from the hand of the Creator—is in the grip of dark powers. Isaiah the prophet tells us that we live in "a land of gloom" and that we are "burdened by the yoke of a taskmaster" (Isa. 9:2, 4). We know all too well the texture of that gloom and the weight of that yoke: guns in the hands of teenagers, the hungry and homeless who roam the streets of affluent cities, families riven by the stubborn inability to forgive, depressions and anxieties that haunt us like ghosts, ambitions that succeed only in breaking hearts and wrecking lives, the million acts of violence against bodies and souls, nations baring their teeth and rattling their swords. And as we gaze back on the bloody century that has just come to a close, we see all too much of the darkness of which the prophet speaks: Auschwitz, Hiroshima, Rwanda, Vietnam, Flanders Field, Normandy Beach, Columbine, and the killing fields of Cambodia. Yes, God's world is good, but we seem to live, as C. S. Lewis put it, in enemy-occupied territory, a place where the "powers" in myriad forms hold sway. And all of our attempts to ameliorate the situation—economic reforms, political rearrangements, psychological adjustments—just seem to make matters worse. And so the believer sings his mournful song from the loneliness of his prison: "O come, O come Emmanuel and ransom captive Israel."

The good news of Christmas is that the rightful King has returned to reclaim what is his and to let the prisoners go free. The God announced by all the prophets and patriarchs—by Abraham, Jeremiah, Ezekiel, Amos, and Isaiah—is a God of justice, and this means that he burns to set things right. God hates the sin and violence and injustice that have rendered gloomy his beautiful world, and therefore he comes into that world as a warrior, ready to fight. But he arrives (and here is the delicious irony of Christmas) stealthily, clandestinely, sneaking, as it were, unnoticed behind enemy lines. The King comes as a helpless infant, born of insignificant parents in a small town of a distant outpost of the Roman Empire; and there wasn't even room for him in a common inn.

Stealthily he comes, but powerfully and dangerously. Caesar and Quirinius—potentates who think they are controlling the world with their census—are actually working according to God's plan, paving the way for the King who will dethrone them. When Herod hears of his arrival, he trembles, as well he might, for he knows in his bones that his days are numbered. The sad Jerusalem that he rules through fear and violence is meant to be a holy city, governed according to God's designs, and the new Ruler has just arrived. Herod senses what the shepherds see directly: "and suddenly there appeared with the angel a multitude of the heavenly host" (Luke 2:13). Let us not be naive or sentimental about the angels: A "host" is an army, and this is the army of the infant warrior come to root out the power of the enemy.

There is, of course, another reason for the simplicity and poverty of his arrival: He is to be a soldier, but he will not fight with the violent weapons of the Herods, Caesars, and other kings of this dysfunctional world. Rather, he will wield the sword of nonviolence and the spear of forgiveness; and he will wear the helmet of righteousness and the breastplate of compassion. He will conquer through the finally irresistible power of love, the same power with which he made the universe. In the ancient mythological accounts of creation, God or the gods make the world through a primordial act of violence; they conquer, control, divide, order through force. But the true God makes the universe, not by wrestling an opposing power into submission, not by dominating and destroying a rival, but rather through a sheerly generous and nonviolent act of love. In the language of the philosophers, God creates ex nihilo, from nothing. And so when the Son of God enters his disordered world in order to recreate it, he acts with a similar gentleness and nonviolence. Pharoah, Caesar, Quirinius, Herod—and their like down through the ages to the present day—seek to throw off all constraints, but the Son of God, the creator of the stars and planets, allows himself to be wrapped in swaddling clothes, to be tied up, bound, beholden to the other. The rulers of this world endeavor at all costs to have their own needs met, but the Ruler of the age to come is placed in a manger, for he is to be food for the hungry. The powers seek control, but the Power allows himself to become, in Chesterton's words, "a child too weak to raise his own head."

In all of this, of course, he anticipates the drama of the cross. Over the crucified, Pilate will place a placard announcing "Jesus of Nazareth, King of the Jews," but Caesar's representative will have no idea of the irony of this statement. Roman authority was expressed and maintained through the violent overthrow of opposing powers, through the crucifixion—real and symbolic—of rival kings. Augustine summed up the Roman way with devastating laconicism: *libido dominandi*, the lust to dominate. But the true King, the ruler of cosmos, breaks that power precisely by meeting it with forgiveness, nonviolence, and compassion: Nailed to the cross, powerless, he says, "Forgive them Father, they know not what they do." And in those words, the Roman way (the way of the world) is undone. Every playground bully and every canny politician knows that the *libido dominandi* is always stirred to greater ardor when it is opposed by a similar force: an eye for an eye, making the whole world blind, as Gandhi said. When it is met by harsh and dreadful love, a love willing to give itself utterly away, it dries up.

Now listen again to Isaiah's victory cry, read at the Christmas Midnight Mass: "For the yoke that burdened them, the pole on their shoulder, the rod of their taskmaster you have smashed as on the day of Midian; For every boot that tramped in battle, every cloak rolled in blood, will be burned as fuel for flames" (Isa. 9:4). The yoke, the rod, the boot trampled, the cloak rolled in blood—all the dark works of a fallen world—will be thrown by this newborn king into the fire. Indeed, when he bursts on the public scene, he will make plain his purpose, "I have come, not for peace, but for the sword" and "I have come to light a fire on the earth." Precisely because he carries a sword of compassion and illumines the flame of love, Jesus is the first truly dangerous warrior, the first enemy the powers have really feared.

So for us the followers of this soldier, Christmas is not a sentimental feast, not a harmless festival of cards and gifts and twinkling lights; it is a call to arms, a summons to start a blaze.

We are in prison, but the liberator is here; we are in the gloom, but the torchbearer has presented himself; we are pinned down by the enemy, but the Warrior has come. And therefore we can sing our triumphant song: "Rejoice, rejoice, Emmanuel has come to thee O Israel."

Part VI

PRIESTHOOD
AND MINISTRY

Chapter Eighteen

PRIEST AS BEARER
OF THE MYSTERY

THIS IS AN EXTREMELY DIFFICULT TIME FOR PRIESTS. IN THE LAST several years there have been numerous revelations about the sexual misconduct of the clergy, especially with children and adolescents. Prominent bishops—both in our country and in Europe—have been forced to resign because of the scandal caused by their violation of the vow of celibacy. In my diocese of Chicago, the charges of sexual misconduct by priests have become so commonplace that one is beyond the point of shock and surprise; one is simply numb. Many priests wonder whether permanent damage has been done to the priesthood, whether we will ever recover the trust and confidence that have been lost. Many speculate that numbers of vocations—already low—will simply plummet. Some even opine that this crisis represents the beginning of the end of the priesthood as we know it, the push that will prompt the collapse of an outmoded, indeed dying, institution.

I might suggest, at the outset, that the problems outlined above are, at least in part, symptomatic of a much more fundamental loss of confidence in the priesthood. As many commentators have indicated, too many priests feel at sea, without focus and orientation, without spiritual moorings, unable to articulate for themselves who they are and why they remain faithful to their commitments. In the postconciliar period, myriad new ministers and "pastors" have appeared on the Church scene, and there has been much enthusiastic definition and clarification of their roles; the laity have been enabled and commissioned and brought to much greater involvement—and all of this change has been healthy and revitalizing for the Church. But, I would suggest, many priests feel that, in this reimagination of the life of the Church, their role has been diminished and their unique contribution undervalued. This has, at least in part, led to the general malaise that is so much in evidence today.

I write this chapter out of the conviction that this crisis of confidence should lead, not to speculations about the collapse of the priesthood, but to a renewed commitment to the priesthood and to a deeper understanding of its nature, purpose, and spirituality. This is a time, not for hand-wringing, but for renewed thinking and imagining. We must return to the "sources," to the heart and soul of priesthood, if we are to recover a sense of its meaning and power in the life of the Church.

Let me propose a model, or better, an image that, I believe, captures something of the unique and indispensable quality of the priesthood. The priest of Jesus Christ is, first and foremost, a mystagogue, one who bears the Mystery and initiates others into it.

At the heart of the Christian faith is a confrontation with the all-grounding and all-encompassing mystery of Being itself which is God. The believer is grasped, shaken, overwhelmed by that force which, in Jesus Christ, is revealed as passionate, unconditional love. Without a sense of that ever fascinating and uncontrollable power, the Church becomes, at best, a social welfare organization or a self-help society.

The priest is the one who bears that strange power and who leads the people of God into an ever more intimate contact with it. It is in the carrying out of this task that one is most authentically *priest*, that is to say, the one who performs a sacrifice, linking heaven and earth, mediating between the Mystery and those who have been grasped by it. Christ is the High Priest because, in his own person, he is the reconciliation of creation and Creator, the mediation between Lover and beloved. The mystagogue is, in the depths of his being, conformed to Christ the Priest, shaped according to the icon of Christ, because his whole existence is to become transparent to the Mystery.

The primary "function" of the bearer of Mystery is to hold up to the people of God the great images, stories, and pictures of salvation that are at the heart of the Christian tradition. The mystagogue is the one who has been entrusted with the sacred symbols and given the responsibility of making them speak. He is the artist whose task it is to make the liturgy a great dance expressive of God's grace, a saga whose heart is the drama of God's embrace of all aspects of our fallen humanity. Through his manipulation of color, line, and texture, the painter unveils some truth about nature or about the human condition, and he invites the one who views the painting to enter into that truth. In a similar way, the mystagogical artist, in image, symbol, and story, presents the truth which is God's love in Christ and seduces, draws the worshiping community to share in it.

This artistic or iconic role presupposes that the priest is deeply in touch with the genius of the Catholic imagination. The Catholic vision is based, philosophically, on the *analogia entis*, the analogy or continuity between the being of the world and the Being which is God. Theologically, it is rooted in the Incarnation, God's radical union with Jesus of Nazareth and his entry, by implication, into the whole of the cosmos. According to this view of things, God is present everywhere in the universe, hints and traces of divine love are "spread out on the earth" for those who have the eyes to see them. Bernanos's country priest was seized by the Catholic imagination when he announced, in the face of his enormous suffering and disappointment: "Everything is grace."

If he is to mediate the Mystery, the priest must be gifted with this Catholic imagination and must be a lifelong apprentice of those, throughout the centuries, who have been in the grip of the Catholic sensibility. He must develop an eye that can see the incarnate God in the dome of Hagia Sophia, in the spires at Chartres Cathedral, in the athletes and prophets on the ceiling of the Sistine Chapel, in the light that illumines Caravagio's figures, in Giotto's frescoes of St. Francis, in the stained glass of the Sainte Chapelle. The mystagogue must be an artist filled with the light and energy of the Incarnation, and his vision must be contagious. G. K. Chesterton said that to see the world properly one must stand on one's head. In this way, he sees everything as hanging upside down, as literally dependent on the creator God. The mystagogue is the one who dedicates his life to standing upside down in order to share his peculiar vision with the Church.

Second, the one who bears the Mystery must be teacher and especially preacher. In Christ, God has spoken his definitive word of love. Conformed personally and existentially to that word, the priest speaks of and from the experience of being grasped by God. Paul Tillich says that one cannot help but speak about what concerns one ultimately. The priest is the seer and poet who cannot help but speak the ultimate concern that is God's unreasonable and excessive love. Like Isaiah, his lips have been seared by the fire of God's mind, and like Ezekiel, he has tasted the word, taken it into his flesh and bones, and has found it at once sweet and overwhelming. Study after study has shown that the people in the pews want, above all, good preaching from their priests. It seems to me that this altogether reasonable demand reflects the hunger and thirst for mystagogy, the desire to be told of the Mystery, to be drawn into it.

The preacher of the word must be conformed to the Word that is Jesus Christ and must therefore be a lifelong student, not only of the Scripture, but of the great literary expressions of the Catholic sensibility. He must be able to appreciate the incarnational spirituality in the autobiographies of Augustine, Merton, and Teresa of Avila; he must feel with the otherworld journey of Dante and with the bawdy worldliness of the *Canterbury Tales*; he must be able to share the anguish in the verse of Gerard Manley Hopkins and T. S. Eliot; he should enter into the vision of Peguy and Claudel; he should climb the mountains which are Dostoyevsky and Joyce.

Furthermore, if the priest is to be a mediator between heaven and earth, if he is to speak symbolically of the all-embracing and ever elusive mystery of Being itself, he must be in habitual contact with the Mystery, he must stand stubbornly in the presence of God. He must take with utmost seriousness the command of St. Paul to pray continually, to orient the whole of his being to the love of God. In short, the priest must be a mystic, a contemplative, a person of prayer. This is not the unique vocation of a monk; it is the parish priest, the privileged mystagogue, who must be, in every fiber of his being, formed by prayer.

To put it simply, the priest must be an authentically *religious* leader for his people; he must be, in the richest sense possible, spiritual director, mystical guide, shaman. I think that one of the greatest of the postconciliar mistakes was to turn the priest into psychologist, sociologist, social worker, counselor—anything but a uniquely religious leader. The authentic task of the mystagogue, as I've outlined it, is incomparably rich, constantly challenging; it is the career of the prophet, poet, and visionary. Why would we want to abandon such a role for that of second-rate psychologist or amateur social worker?

Now, someone might object that I am proposing a view of the priesthood that is elitist, intellectualistic, perhaps rather monkish. One might argue that all this literary and artistic refinement is fine for the seminary or university professor but that it is unrealistic for the parish priest. In my view, nothing could be further from the truth. It is precisely the parish priest who has most contact with, and influence upon, the people of God, and it is therefore precisely the parish priest who should be best equipped to know, mediate, and express the Mystery. Sophistication of mind, heart, and sensibility is not a luxury for the parish priest; rather, it belongs to the very essence of who he is and what he does.

In the preconciliar period, the official theology of the Church spoke of an ontological change that occurs at ordination. The priest does not simply receive the commission to perform specific tasks, he *becomes* someone different. This language, understood as elitist and exclusionary, has, unfortunately, fallen into desuetude in the postconciliar Church. Though one can misunderstand the terminology of ontological change as clericalism, one should by no means dismiss the truth enshrined in that rather peculiar formulation. The mystagogue, as I've described him, is not primarily a functionary, not someone entrusted with tasks to perform. First and foremost, he is priest, someone who, in his very being, is the mediator between heaven and earth. Called and formed by God for the service of the community, the mystagogue *is* separate, unique, set apart—in the language of Scripture, holy. Priesthood affects one in one's very being— or it is a sham. Understood primarily as a job or a "ministry," priesthood becomes a shadow of itself and loses its fascination and appeal.

It seems to me that Andrew Greeley is perfectly correct when he says that priests are irresistibly fascinating and that the fascination flows from the uniqueness and peculiarity of their *being*. Those who want to demythologize the language of ontological change and conceive of the priest as only one minister among many are flying in the face of something which is in the blood and bones of the race, something in the deepest religious instincts of human beings. Transculturally and transhistorically, people have always designated certain of their number as "holy," as mediators of the Mystery. And it has always been precisely that separateness, that uniqueness of existence, which has enabled the "holy one" to be transparent to God or to the gods. One of the shortest routes to the desacralization of the Catholic community is, therefore, the "functionalization" of the priesthood. The great Protestant preacher and hymn writer John Wesley once described his preaching style: "I set myself on fire and people come out and watch me burn." To my mind, that could be a description of the "ontological" nature of the priesthood. The priest is not, primarily, someone who works, preaches, ministers, counsels; rather, he is someone who has been set on fire by God, to the core of his being, and who invites others to catch the flame.

It is, I believe, only against the background of the sort of vision of priesthood that I've outlined that the celibacy of the priest can be properly grasped and appreciated. When one tries to justify celibacy on functional grounds, the arguments seem, to me, tinny and unconvincing. For example, it is suggested that celibacy frees one for a greater range of ministry. This might be true in some cases, but it could be just as persuasively argued that the support of wife, children, and home life enables the noncelibate minister to do his job much more effectively than his celibate counterpart. In the same way, some have claimed that the celibate can love more universally and disinterestedly than the noncelibate. Again, this might be true for some, but one could also argue that the especially rich love of the noncelibate for his family serves to intensify and augment the love he has for his congregation. By comparison, the pastoral affection of the celibate for his people could seem superficial.

I rehearse this conversation only to demonstrate that the issue of celibacy can never be decided in terms of practical or even "pastoral" considerations. Indeed, it is only when celibacy is seen as altogether impractical and absurd that we can begin adequately to understand it. Paul Tillich offers a fascinating reading of the scriptural account of the woman who breaks open the jar of perfume in order to anoint the feet of Jesus, in the face of the altogether legitimate objections of the disciples. He says that the woman represents the unreasonable or excessive element that must be part of the response to one's ultimate concern. Kant's suggestion that religion could be understood "within the limits of reason alone" is ridiculous. When one has been seized by the infinite and unconditional love of God, one responds in an excess of love, in an unreasonable, disproportionate, even scandalous self-offering. According to reasonable and sober reflection—like that of the disciples—this response can seem inappropriate or bizarre, but it is just this type of response that is praised and welcomed by Christ.

Celibacy is unreasonable, unnatural, excessive—and that is why it has been chosen, again transculturally and transhistorically, as one of the ways in which lovers of God have traditionally expressed their love. When one tries to "understand" this self-gift or to "explain" it, one misses the point. Its very strangeness and incomprehensibility is the point. It is not surprising that mystagogues, those who have been chosen by the Mystery to speak of the Mystery, see the appropriateness of this excessive stance and lifestyle. Called to stand on the horizon between heaven and earth, set on fire by the presence of God, the mystagogue rather naturally chooses this unnatural option of celibacy. People in love do strange things.

And it is this very strangeness is what gives celibacy its witness value. In the Incarnation, the ultimacy of the world was thrown radically into question. The presence of God in Christ shook and uprooted the "self-complacent finitude" of the sinner, turning him toward that power which is ever greater than he can think, feel, or imagine. The Christ reveals that the deepest love a human being can experience is the love for the infinite Being who grounds the universe and transcends time. Our destiny is not limited to the enjoyment of goods that we sense in this life; rather, the most basic and powerful orientation of our spirits is toward the undreamed of richness of God's life.

The celibate is someone who, in the strangeness of his choice of lifestyle, reminds the people of God of their most profound destiny, so easily lost sight of in a secularist and materialist culture. The celibate is that poet and prophet who, in his being, speaks of the uncanniness of the

Reality which has seized us, who reminds us that perhaps "something else might be the case."

What I offer in this brief reflection is not some "solution" to the crisis of confidence in the priesthood. What I offer is an image of the priest as mystagogue, an image that, I believe, comes close to the heart of what the priesthood, at its best, has always been. Were he conformed to Christ and confirmed in his role as mystagogue, it would be difficult, it seems to me, for the priest to be bored in his work and choice of lifestyle. The authentic bearer of the Mystery, the one living on the frontier between God and creation, the "hero" who journeys from earth to heaven and from heaven to earth, is not, I think, likely to find his life tedious or void of meaning.

I believe passionately in the centrality and indispensability of the mystagogue in the community gathered around Jesus Christ. What will kill us as a Church is a loss of the sense of Mystery, and what will contribute mightily to that loss is the weakening and dissipation of the priesthood. The time has come, not for dismantling and doubting, but for building up.

Chapter Nineteen

PRIEST AS DOCTOR OF THE SOUL

As many commentators have pointed out, there is a sort of crisis of confidence and identity among priests today. Many new ministries and roles of service have emerged in the Church, and lay people are assuming, legitimately, many of the tasks formerly performed exclusively by the clergy. This phenomenon has led some priests to wonder what their unique contribution might be, what they, distinctively, can offer to the people of God. In an earlier chapter, I presented the vision of priest as mystagogue, as the one who guides people into the grounding and sustaining mystery that is God. The mystagogue, I argued, is the artist and poet who fires hearts with the power of the Catholic imagination, the shaman who lures people into a confrontation with the Mystery which suffuses and transcends all our experience. The priest is not so much psychologist or social worker as he is spiritual leader, pastor of the soul, the one who leads people to a discovery of that deepest self which is in living contact with God.

DOCTOR OF THE SOUL

This description of the priest's "task" is, I think, correct but incomplete. Before someone can be conducted into the mystery that is God, he or she must be healed of whatever spiritual ill, whatever block, prevents that journey of self-surrender. Therefore, closely related to the role of mystagogue is that of "doctor of the soul."

The Gospels are filled with accounts of Jesus' healing encounters with those whose spiritual energies are unable to flow. Much of Jesus' ministry consisted in teaching people how to see (the Kingdom of God), how to hear (the voice of the Spirit), how to walk (thereby overcoming the paralysis of the heart), how to be free of themselves so as to discover God. It is interesting that Jesus was referred to in the early Church as the savior (*soter* in Greek and *salvator* in Latin). Both terms speak of the one who brings healing—indeed our word *salve* is closely related to the Latin *salus*, meaning health. Christ is the "bringer of the salve," the carrier of the healing balm. In imitation of Christ, the priest, I think, is the doctor of the soul, the healer of broken hearts and minds.

The "soul" is that still-point at the heart of every person, that deepest center, that point of encounter with the transcendent yet incarnate mystery of God. It is that level on which we are grasped by what Paul Tillich calls "ultimate concern." It corresponds to what the church fathers call the *imago Dei*, the image of God. It is the ground and source of all psychological and physical energy; it is the matrix and organizing power of the human person. When the soul is healthy, it is in a living relationship with God; it is firmly rooted in the soil of meaning and is the deepest center of the person. But when the soul is sick, the link to the energy and being of God is severed or at least rendered tenuous. When the soul is sick, the entire person becomes ill because all flows from and depends upon the dynamic encounter with the source of being and life who is God. It was this intimate link between the soul and the psyche that C. G. Jung was implicitly acknowledging when he remarked that, at bottom, all psychological problems are religious problems.

But what sort of "medicine" is prescribed by the priest as soul doctor? *How* does he unleash blocked spiritual energies and heal the wounds of the soul? The answer, it seems to me, is the energy, the power, the spirit, the new being, that appeared in and through Jesus Christ. We heal the soul by bringing to bear the *salvator*, the healer, the one who in his person reconciled God and us, who opened soul to the divine power. Where is this new being available? It is apparent in the Scripture, the liturgy, sacraments, Christian architecture, painting, and literature—and, in perhaps most rarified form, in Christian doctrines. These bearers of the new being—these prolongations, if you will, of the energy of Christ—are the "medicines" employed by the priest, the healing balms by which soul sickness is cured. They are "symbols of transformation" whose primary purpose is to change the lives of Christians by drawing them into the *imitatio Christi*. In various ways, the priest holds up the icon, the picture, of Jesus Christ in hopes that those who see it will be transfigured in its likeness.

Let me illustrate this point with a concrete example drawn from the spiritual tradition. When one prays before an icon of Jesus, one enters into a subtle process of consciousness transformation. The one who contemplates the icon is not simply diverted by a pious representation; on the contrary, he assumes the stance, adopts the vision, mimics the attitude, thinks the thoughts, and senses the emotions of the depicted figure. As a result, his mind and heart are reworked in a sort of alchemical process; his entire person is reconfigured through a spiritual osmosis. In the presence of the icon of the Lord, the pray-er experiences literal *metanoia* (to go beyond the mind), that is to say, he transcends the perspective that he has and finds a new one. The doctor of the soul, I would argue, creatively indicates the icon of the new being in Jesus Christ in order to effect this psycho-spiritual metamorphosis. To shift the image somewhat, he rubs in the salve of the Incarnation in order to heal the wounds of the soul.

I would like to demonstrate this process more concretely by drawing attention to one of the "medicines" mentioned above, namely, the dogmas and theological teachings of the tradition. On the face of it, these abstract and conceptual formulas seem unlikely candidates as mediators of soul transformation. However, I've become more and more convinced that theology, as practiced by the great masters of our tradition, is anything but a recondite and abstract discipline, a game of the mind. Instead, dogmas and theological formulations are meant to lure the believer onto healthy spiritual ground, to orient him or her to the God who is really God and not an idol. It is precisely because dogmatic statements are so spiritually charged that they have been at the heart of some of the greatest struggles in the history of the Church.

THE "MEDICINE" OF THE INCARNATION

The doctrine that stands at the heart of the Christian experience and that possesses the greatest transformative power is that of the Incarnation. What does it mean for someone to be grasped by this dogma, to be shaken and turned around by it? To live in the energy of the Incarnation is to know that real union with God, in the depth of our humanity, is, not simply a hope or a wild dream, but a concrete possibility. Jesus Christ, the Incarnate Word, shows to the world that the human being is made for God and finds rest only in God. More to the point, Jesus reveals that God wants nothing more than to come to life in us, to become incarnate in our words and actions, in our thoughts, fears, and insecurities. The Incarnation means that nothing of our humanity is alien to God or untouched by divine power: Birth, coming of age, rejection, triumph, friendship, betrayal, anxiety, bliss, the frightful darkness of death—all of it becomes, in principle, a route of access to the transcendent reality. Because of the coming-together of the divine and human in Jesus, we have the courage to explore a new and deeper identity, one rooted, not in the petty desires and fears of the ego, but in the eternal power and existence of God.

Obviously, my assumption here is that the language of the Incarnation is not meant simply to describe a strange and distant event, to speak a truth concerning Jesus alone. Rather, I echo the great medieval mystic, Meister Eckhart, in saying that if the Word does not come to birth in us today, it is no use reading about the incarnation of that Word in a person long ago. If, in short, we ourselves do not *participate* in who Jesus was, we miss the spiritual power that he meant to unleash. If John's Gospel is any indication, Jesus does not want worshippers but followers, or better, *participants:* "I am the vine and you are the branches; live on in me; my body is real food and my blood real drink. The one who feeds on my flesh and drinks my blood remains in me and I in him." The beautifully organic images that John presents are meant, it seems to me, to communicate the life-changing power of the Incarnation: The Logos became flesh, our flesh, so that we might allow the divine energy to come to birth in us. Much of this is summed up in the oft-repeated patristic adage that God became human that humans might become God. Many of our great theologians and spiritual masters speak unselfconsciously of "divinization," that is to say, a sharing in the symbiosis which is the Incarnation, as the proper goal of human life.

Having taken the doctrine of the Incarnation off of its dusty academic shelf, we can see how it functions as a healing balm at the disposal of the doctor of the soul. The Incarnation is the "salve" applied to someone who has lost his center, his existential bearings, his identity. Usually out of fear, we have the tendency to cling to ourselves, to root our lives in the desires and impulses of the ego rather than in the infinite reality that is God. In sin, we refuse to let go and surrender to the bearing power of the divine, convinced that we will find meaning and focus in reliance upon our own egos. In many ways, this sinful attitude is characteristic of our time and manifests itself in the terribly widespread feeling of rootlessness, meaninglessness, anxiety, and despair.

What the doctor of the soul can bring to this sickness is something which no psychologist or physician can bring: what the priest can offer is the good news and energy of the Incarnation. He can hold out to the sufferer the possibility of participating in the God who wants nothing more than to embrace the human condition; he can invite the one in anxiety or despair to root her life, not in herself, but in eternity, in the transcendent ground of meaning which is the creator God; he can offer her the body and blood, the life, of Jesus Christ. Again, this has not primarily to do with accepting doctrines intellectually; rather, it involves a sharing in a power of transformation.

THE HEALING POWER OF THE SIMPLE GOD

All Christian doctrines flow from the central teaching of the Incarnation, including and especially the doctrine of God. Something that one notes in almost all of the most significant Christian theologians is the insistence on dismantling the mythology of God as the supreme being. Augustine, Origen, Pseudo-Dionysius, Thomas Aquinas, Anselm, and, in modern times, Paul Tillich and Karl Rahner all hold that God is not *a* being, not the highest *being*, but rather Being itself, the infinite, all-grounding, all-enveloping power of existence. God can in no way be quantified or qualified or de-scribed in the categories that define the things of the world. Thomas Aquinas sums up his teaching by saying that God is altogether simple. By this he means that God is not a type of being, not an instance of being, not a thing in any sort of category, not one being among others, but rather that which simply *is*.

Now why have Christian theologians, from the earliest centuries of the Church, spoken this way of God? The answer, as I hinted above, is found in the shock and surprise of the Incarnation. The experience of the first Christians was that the divine and the human had come unspeakably close in the event of Jesus Christ and that Christ's humanity was not sup-pressed but rather preserved and enhanced through his union with God. This means that God cannot be a rival or competitor to human beings, not something standing over and against us, but rather something totally other, a power beyond and outside of the "normal" relations of finitude. The God who becomes incarnate in Jesus Christ cannot be one more "thing in the world," capable of being avoided, or worse, manipulated and controlled. Rather, the God of the Incarnation is that absolute, infinite, transcendent/immanent power of Being itself that continually lures us into greater life and more plentiful existence. In no sense a "competitor," the simple God is the one who, in his otherness, opens up the human heart.

Christian theologians have for so long stressed this strangeness of God precisely because they want to escape the danger of idolatry. It is at the very heart of the sinner's strategy to reduce God to the level of a be-ing, even the supreme being, since such a reality cannot be of decisive and transformative significance. Such a reality can be relegated to the distant past or placed at an infinite remove from us—"up there" or "out there" somewhere. Such a God is what the Old Testament calls an idol, a false god, a projection of the sinful human desire to be the absolute. The sim-ple God, the divine power that appears in Jesus Christ, is that which *can-not be controlled, cannot be set aside, cannot be ignored, cannot be turned into an idol.* "Thou mastering me God," is Gerard Manley Hopkins's magnificent address to this reality who will not be turned into a false god.

Once again, this clarification is not of merely academic interest and is not simply a more "correct" description of the nature of God; on the contrary, it is a matter of spiritual life or death. The paradigmatic sin of the Old Testament is idolatry, turning something that is not God into God, or better, reducing the absolute to the level of the contingent and finite. The Old Testament authors—and even more intensely, the Christian theological authors—were so concerned with this problem precisely because idolatry amounts to a shrinking of the soul. When the final reality of one's life is transformed into a "thing," the soul's access to the infinite has been denied, the proper destiny of the soul to transcend itself indefinitely has been suppressed. It is my conviction that, in one form or another, all spiritual problems are forms of this basic drying-up of the soul, modes of this "self-complacent finitude." Whether the absolute has assumed the form of sex, relationship, job, wealth, status, religion, the esteem of others, the spiritual sickness is the same: idolatry, a drying up of the soul's energies.

What does the priest as doctor of the soul bring to this sickness, which is perhaps manifesting itself as depression, loss of focus, anxiety, or compulsive behavior? He brings the healing balm of God's simplicity. In light of the power that flows from the Incarnation, he holds up to the sufferer the one reality that truly is absolute, the one power that truly can satisfy the longings of the heart, the God who is not any "thing" at all, but rather the ground and goal of Being itself. The soul doctor applies the salve of God's ungraspable, inescapable reality in order to quell the clinging tendencies of the ego and thereby to reorient the spiritual energies of the sufferer. One could say that the essence of sin is an absolutizing of the ego; and one could consequently argue that the essence of soul-healing is a questioning of that inflated ego in light of the simple God.

THE SALVE OF CREATION

A central Christian teaching that has flowed from the doctrine of the simple God is that of creation, or more precisely, creation ex nihilo, from nothing. According to this dogma, God continually creates and grounds the world, pouring being into it as a free gift. The things of the world do not stand over and against God as if they were fundamentally independent of him; rather, every moment they stand as sheer receptivity, literally as "nothing," accepting the grace which is their existence. In both classical and modern Christian theologies of creation, the creator God does not stand simply "at the beginning of time" as if he brought the world into being and then simply left it to its own devices. On the contrary, the God who is Being itself creates and renews the world unceasingly, pouring it out of himself in a great act of superabundant love.

Now what does this doctrine mean spiritually, how does it embody in some way the good news of Jesus Christ? The seemingly recondite, rather philosophical dogma of creation ex nihilo shows the believer how to root herself in the springs of life and meaning. To affirm that one is a creature is to feel, almost literally in one's bones, that one's entire being is a gift from a transcendent source. This doctrine teaches that at the center of who I am is a relationship of pure openness to the God who is giving himself in pure love. If I am a creature, then I am not a "thing" that confronts God; rather, I am a *relation* of joyful receptivity to the inrushing passion of the divine source. Everything that I am flows from this relation and is centered upon it.

Thomas Merton says that the heart of contemplative prayer is the discovery of that point at the root and core of my being where I am here and now *being created by God.* To pray, in short, is to realize profoundly that I am a creature, in every fiber of my existence and at every moment, a child of God. The doctrine of creation is meant to be a sort of icon of spiritual identity, a living reminder that I am called to find myself in an act of obedient surrender to the sustaining and self-offering ground of being. In short, creation is "soul" language, a description of what it means for my center to be linked in a living union with the center of all existence.

What happens when someone loses touch with his creatureliness? On the one hand, he might sink into despair since he has lost contact with the eternal wellspring of his being and identity. He might sense that his life has been drained of meaning, that he is cut off, adrift in a hostile world. On the other, he might experience ego inflation as he tries to turn his achievements and accomplishments into the ground of his life. This latter stance can lead to what Paul Tillich calls the concupiscent attitude. Caught in concupiscence, a person wants to "shove the whole world into his mouth," attempting to fill up the void within with money, fame, power, sex, and so forth. The whole addictive style can be an outgrowth or symptom of this fundamentally spiritual problem.

Faced with these sicknesses of the soul, the priest as healer can hold up the icon of creation ex nihilo. Under the influence of this "salve," one comes to see that he is essentially nothing, that his all-powerful ego is a sort of phantom or illusion, a creation of his desire. When he realizes that he is a creature, in every aspect of his being a gift from God, he can let go, relax his grip, stem his concupiscence. As a creature, he is centered and rooted in that power of being that is beyond space and time, beyond the vagaries and dangers of the world. Nothing but a relation to the creator God, he can say with Paul, "For I am certain that neither death nor life, neither angels nor principalities, neither height nor depth, nor any other creature could ever separate me from the love of God." Once more, this assurance of the soul is something that no psychologist or physician could bring. It is the healing balm offered by the doctor of the spirit.

CONCLUSION

What I have tried to show here is how the priest can recover and reclaim an ancient identity by accepting the responsibility of soul-doctoring. I have furthermore tried to indicate what sort of "tools" and "medicines" he might use in the process. Incarnation, the divine simplicity, and creation from nothing are not merely abstractions for the mind; on the contrary, in their original and most important form, they are, like all the other great doctrines, symbols of transformation, icons that illumine and open up the spirit. Like the other articles of the creed, they are bearers of the healing power that flows from the event of Jesus Christ.

It has struck me that Christian leaders and spiritual directors tragically fail to realize the treasure that is theirs, the wealth of wisdom that is stored on dusty shelves and buried in arid doctrinal formulas. The priest should drink deeply from the wells of that forgotten tradition and rediscover its enormous potential for opening up the hearts and spirits of those he serves. In soul-doctoring, he might also recover a richer sense of himself and his identity as a priest.

Chapter Twenty

Mystagogues, World Transformers, and Interpreters of Tongues: A Reflection on Collaborative Ministry in the Church

T HE TOPIC THAT I AM ADDRESSING—THE COLLABORATION OF the ordained and the nonordained—is difficult and complex. There are many reasons for this difficulty, but I would like to highlight one: the victory of Nietzsche. I am convinced that Nietzsche is the most influential of the great nineteenth-century philosophers, his impact outstripping that of either Hegel or Marx. He held, we recall, that the basic structure of reality is the "will to power," the bold assertion of self over and against nature and other selves. The universality of this striving leads, of course, to the struggle and tensiveness that characterizes being at all levels. Nietzsche's thought came into the twentieth century through a series of important disciples and commentators, including C. G. Jung, Martin Heidegger, Jacques Derrida, and Michel Foucault. And then through them it trickled into the popular culture, so that now it largely determines our political, cultural, social, and even ecclesial conversations. It is extraordinary how often and automatically we suspect games of power are at work behind the façade of human interactions: this is the effect of Nietzsche.

But when this Nietzscheanism—implicit or explicit—comes to shape our discussions of the relationship between ordained and nonordained, we are already lost. For what the Gospel holds out as the basic structure of the real is directly repugnant to the competitive and violent model proposed by Nietzsche. The message of Jesus is one of inclusion, forgiveness, and nonviolent cooperation; as such it is an organic teaching, one that emphasizes the play of complementarity, differentiation, and mutuality in a well-functioning body. A body whose organs are in competition with one another is, by definition, dying. It is, of course, not surprising that Nietzsche saw the ethic proposed by Jesus of Nazareth as the principal enemy.

If I may, I would like to witness to one face of the Nietzschean struggle seen from the perspective of my generation. I went to first grade in 1965, the year the Second Vatican Council ended, and therefore my entire formation as a Catholic was conditioned by the élan and style of the council. One of the dominant themes sounded in that immediate postconciliar period was that of the priesthood of all believers, the full involvement of the laity in the Church. Concomitantly, a huge emphasis was placed on the danger of clericalism. In fact, the "clerical" priest—clinging pathetically to his privileges, demanding special treatment, denying laity their proper role—became the chief bogeyman in the popular theater of the postconciliar imagination. Clergy and laity were seen as locked in a zero-sum Nietzschean struggle for domination. What followed from this was, to put it mildly, an underdeveloped and largely negative theology of the priesthood.

In an attempt to respond to this negativity, I have developed two images of priesthood: mystagogue and doctor of souls. In the first part of this chapter, I would like to present those images succinctly, since I have spelled them out in detail in the prior two chapters. But to avoid a reverse Nietzscheanism—newly dominant priests against lay people—I would like to show, in the second and third parts of this chapter, how the priest can and must cooperate both with the laity in general and with that community of lay people who are actively and explicitly involved in the ministry of the Church. Hence, I will explore the images of laity as transfigurers of the world and of lay ministers as "interpreters of tongues."

PRIEST AS MYSTAGOGUE AND DOCTOR OF SOULS

Mystagogue is an old term, one used in the early centuries of the Church in connection with the process of leading catechumens into the fullness of Christian faith. It refers, fundamentally, to one who leads others into the Mystery. In our tradition, God is not so much the supreme being as Being itself, the one whom Thomas Aquinas calls *ipsum esse substistens*, the sheer act of to-be. God is, accordingly, that energy of existence which surrounds, suffuses, grounds, and yet transcends all things; he is that Mystery which, though everywhere, cannot be seen and which, though unavoidable, cannot be grasped. Who is it that speaks for, from, and about this Mystery, who is formally chosen and ordained to lead others to it and guide their way into its fullness? In our Catholic tradition, it is, I submit, the priest.

In his masterful essay, *The Mass on the World*, Teilhard de Chardin speaks of the priest as a kind of border walker, mediating between heaven and earth, channeling upward the hopes, anxieties, and struggles of the human race and calling down the divine fire for the transformation of the world. Chesterton says that the only one who sees the world clearly is the one who stands on his head, for only that person perceives all things as hanging upside down, literally dependent. In Chestertonian language then, the priest is the one who willingly stands on his head in order to share his peculiarly accurate vision with the world. With Hans Urs von Balthasar, we may speak of the mystagogue as an interpreter of the patterns of grace. Though God is at work always and in all places, believers require someone with the requisite perceptiveness and spiritual intelligence to discern that work and bring it to light. In this sense, the priest/mystagogue is like the director of a drama or the conductor of an orchestra, creatively interpreting the "text" of God's activity that lies before him. Paul Tillich speaks of the homilist's art as "holding up the picture of Christ." Such display of the beauty and complexity of the "icon" of Christ is a mystagogic task.

Now what are the "tools" of the practicing mystagogue? What does he use in order to guide others into the Mystery? The fundamental power of the mystagogue is Christ himself, especially as he is present to his

Church in word and sacrament. The energy of the Incarnation is "stored" in those two places and the priest's responsibility is to open them, apply them, make them sing. But the power of Jesus crucified and risen is not restricted to the canonical Scriptures and the sacraments; rather, it is found, in derivative form, in all of the expressions of ecclesial life and culture: theology, spirituality, literature, architecture, art, poetry, sermons, the lives of the saints. These are all prolongations of the energy of the Incarnation, and thus they are all means of transformation. Teresa of Avila's *Interior Castle*, Juan de la Cruz's *Ascent of Mt. Carmel*, Augustine's *De trinitate*, Thomas's *Summa contra gentiles*, Dante's *Divine Comedy*, Michelangelo's frescoes on the ceiling of the Sistine Chapel, Newman's sermons, Rahner's prayers and metaphysics, Gregorian chant, and Chartres Cathedral—all are the "texts" opened up and applied by the practicing mystagogue.

In emphasizing this mystery-bearing quality, I am trying consciously to recover a more "rabbinic" dimension to the priesthood. The priest ought to be a sort of wisdom figure for his people, oriented to study, poetically inclined, theologically sophisticated, spiritually awake. He is not primarily a religious functionary; he is rather the poet of the depths.

The second image that I present is that of doctor of souls. Like mystagogue, *doctor animarum* is an ancient term. When the first Christians sought to name the significance of Jesus, one of the words they chose was *soter*, rendered in Latin as *salvator*, the bearer of the *salus* or health. This idea is wonderfully conveyed in the Johannine narrative of the man born blind. Born blind, this unfortunate is evocative of all of us born in the blindness of sin. Jesus spits on the earth and makes a mud paste (a sort of salve) and rubs it into the man's sightless eyes. Augustine's magnificent commentary is that the spittle represents divinity and the earth humanity, so that when the two come together in the Incarnation a healing balm is created that gives sight to the collective blindness of the race. Who is it that continues this literally "saving" or soul-healing work of Jesus? In the Catholic tradition it is, I would argue, the priest, the doctor of souls.

It would be helpful at this point to define a bit more precisely that slippery word *soul*. Obviously, this term, which we dropped thirty years ago due to its supposedly dualistic overtones, has become all the rage in the popular culture. *Chicken Soup for the Soul, The Soul's Code, Care of the Soul* are just a few of the titles that have appeared on bestseller lists the last several years. It has been revived, I think, because it names something of tremendous spiritual importance, something that cannot be adequately named otherwise. For most of our own great theologians, "soul" was never meant in a dualistic sense. Rather, it named what is central, grounding, elemental, that which undergirds and informs all of the energies of the human being—physical, psychological, spiritual. Thomas Aquinas, for example, comments that the soul is in the body, "not as contained by it, but as containing it." Soul is not inside or alongside of the body, but inclusive of it. The priest is the one who addresses this deepest dimension of the person, who speaks of it and directs it, who knows its workings and its dysfunctions, and who seeks to heal it when it is sick.

And what does he use in this work? He uses those very things employed in the mystagogic task: word and sacrament, art, architecture, literature, doctrine, poetry, and holy lives. These are not simply mystery bearing, they are also healing. Let me illustrate this principle with one example. As I've said elsewhere, one of the most visually arresting elements in a Gothic cathedral is the rose window. At the center of every great rose is, invariably, a depiction of Christ. Then, wheeling around this center in beautiful and harmonious patterns are the colored medallions that depict saints, patriarchs, kings, and so forth, and all of these images are connected to the central image by a series of spokes. The lesson of the rose, meant to be branded into the soul of the one who contemplates it, is simple: When one's life is centered on the divine power, the myriad energies of the soul—intellectual, voluntary, imaginative, bodily—fall into a harmonious pattern. Furthermore, this harmony is maintained precisely when all of the soul powers are properly linked to and grounded in the centering Christ. Thus, the rose is meant to have a soul-doctoring influence on the one who contemplates it, remaking her through a kind of psychological and spiritual osmosis. As one who spent many hours gazing at the north transept rose at Notre Dame in Paris, I can witness to the power of this spiritual alchemy.

In its transformative dynamic, the rose window is like the doctrine of the *imago Dei*. According to the spiritual masters, there exists in all of us a deepest center where we come into contact with the divine, where we are like unto God. John of the Cross called it the inner wine cellar, Teresa named it the interior castle, and Thomas Merton referred to it as the *point vièrge*. This is the inner Christ, the place of peace, where we can find security even in the midst of the greatest storms. When we are awakened to the power of this place, when the energies of our souls are centered there, we experience a rosewindow–like harmony. The *doctor animarum* is the one who understands such artistic and doctrinal "salves" and knows how to apply them in the appropriate pastoral situation.

Without moving into a full-fledged exegesis of relevant conciliar and postconciliar documents, let me simply indicate a correlation between the images I have developed here and the classical description of the priest as "priest, prophet, and king." The prophet is a teacher and proclaimer of the word, and the king is the shepherd or leader. The mystagogue, as I have described him, fulfills both of these functions inasmuch as he opens the word, as well as its doctrinal and artistic extensions, and as he shepherds others on the journey into God's mystery. And the priest is the sanctifier. What is sanctification but a healing and cultivating of the soul, the task of the *doctor animarum?*

LAY PEOPLE AS TRANSFIGURERS OF THE WORLD

As I have presented these images of mystagogue and soul doctor over the years, I have met with both a positive response and some lively criticism. One of the most common complaints is that these ideas represent a return to the preconciliar clericalism that we were happily rid of. One complainant said that I was putting priests back on a pedestal, elevating them above the laity, and another held that I was advocating the moral superiority of priests: "Why does Father Barron think that he is holier than my grandmother?" In response, I would remark, first, the somewhat knee-jerk quality of this reaction, the ghost of Nietzsche haunting us once again. Any attempt to name what is unique and distinctive about

priesthood is often met with this immediate and fearful counterargument. It is as though, in claiming something specialized for the priesthood, one is necessarily robbing the laity of something: the zero-sum
game rather than organic complementarity.

But what is most disturbing in this type of criticism is its implicit
but powerful clericalism. If, in naming the uniqueness of the priestly
charism, we are excluding laity from their participation in the life of the
Church, then we are implicitly assuming that full ecclesial involvement is
tantamount to living and acting as a cleric. If one holds that the view of
priesthood that I've put forward denies holiness to a lay person, then one
presumes that the only model of holiness is a clerical one. These assumptions are, I think, rampant, even predominant, in the ecclesial conversation today, and the sooner they are brought to light the better. In the
years after the council, we became, with regard to the question of lay-
empowerment, remarkably ecclesiocentric, inward-looking. Our goal
seemed to be to draw lay people as much as possible into clerical or explicitly pastoral roles. I once heard a pastor say to his people on a "ministry Sunday" that his hope was to enroll every single person into one of
the official ministries and activities of the parish. But his sort of clericalism is condescending to the laity *and it is directly repugnant to the stated intention of the Vatican II documents.* What emerges with great clarity in both
Lumen Gentium and *Apostolicam Actuositatem,* as well as in the postconciliar teachings on the laity, is that lay people have a unique, indispensable,
and distinctive role in the Church, one that is related but not reducible to
that of priests.

Lay people are called to be the agents for the transformation of the
world. They are salt and light, bringing the Gospel values of inclusion,
nonviolence, nondomination, and forgiving love to a society shaped by
decidedly non-Gospel ideals. If the mystagogue explores and articulates
the mysterious *communio* which is the trinitarian love, the lay person
brings the power of that *communio* to bear in the world. As such, she is a
world-transfigurer, a subversive force. In this context we can perhaps better understand Jesus' use of the image of salt. In the ancient world, salt for
the earth was hardly something positive or enhancing. When the Romans, for instance, conquered Carthage, they killed the people, tore down

the city, and then *salted the earth* in order to assure that nothing further would grow there. So the Christian transfigurer of the world is salt—annoying, destructive, stinging—to a culture predicated upon and oriented toward death and violence and hatred.

Now who is invited into this challenging role? In his letter on the task and ministry of lay people, *Christifideles laici*, John Paul II reflects on Jesus' parable of the workers in the vineyard. The owner comes out in the morning, at noon, in the afternoon, and in the early evening to hire workers, impatient lest *anyone* stand idle. This, says the Pope, expresses Christ's desire that all the baptized—all who share the divine life—be actively engaged in the mission, no one standing by. The mission of the lay person is to be a great Catholic lawyer, physician, journalist, business executive, truck driver, baker, manual laborer, parent—transforming all those occupations, and the worlds they form, from within. The Church needs people with the requisite skill, experience, and savvy to undermine and reshape the sinful society from within.

And what is the range of this lay mission? It is nothing less than the whole world. In the course of *Christifideles laici*, the Pope helpfully spells out the dimensions of this world mission. At the very center of all lay activity is respect for the rights, freedom, and dignity of the individual person. Created by God and redeemed by Christ, each human being is of infinite worth and can, accordingly, never be subordinated to economic or political forces. As he further articulates the mission of the laity, the Pope draws a series of concentric circles around this irreducible respect for the individual. Flowing immediately from the basic truth is the obligation to cultivate the family, which is the most fundamental expression of *communio*. Thus John Paul says that "the lay faithful's duty to society primarily begins in marriage and in the family." Next, the lay person must be concerned for the cultivation of the political and economic life, seeking to foster charity and justice. The baptized Catholic can never be satisfied with sociopolitical systems that rest on foundations of greed, violence, or lack of respect for the individual. And the circle is drawn even wider: The lay person must be concerned for the transfiguration of the culture. The Pope speaks of an "evangelizing of the culture," that is to say, a Gospel transformation of the arts, music, literature, popular entertainment, and sports. We Catholics send up sighs of despair regarding the depravity of the culture, but how many lay Catholics enter into the worlds of art and entertainment precisely for the purpose of changing them in light of revelation? And the Pope casts his net even wider: The baptized Catholic should work to cultivate the earth, caring for the planet. He calls on Catholic scientists, environmentalists, meteorologists, and biologists to protect and enhance that environment upon which all of life and culture depend.

Now I would like to know how anyone could think that this expansive mission of world transformation is less "spiritual" than the mission of the priest. And I would like to know how anyone could imagine that the work of mystagogia and soul doctoring is superior to, or somehow in competition with, this task. To me it seems clear that the two are powerful, indispensable, and complementary baptismal missions. Without the wisdom and guidance of the mystagogue, the world transfigurer would become discouraged, unfocused, and secularized; and without the practical work of the world transfigurer, the mystagogue would become abstracted, disconnected, and eccentric.

Lay Ministers as "Interpreters of the Tongues"

Having made these clarifications regarding the mission of the priest and the ordinary mission of the laity, we come to what is perhaps the most vexing question: What is the status and work of the lay minister in the Church? It has proven notoriously difficult to articulate a theology of lay ministry that does not turn the nonordained minister into either a quasi-priest or a less than worldly lay person. What I propose is a theological/spiritual identity that is unique to the lay minister and relates her creatively to both the mystagogue and the world transfigurer. The lay minister is the "interpreter of tongues."

We recall that in his first letter to the Corinthians, Paul spoke of a variety of charismata given for the benefit of the community as a whole. There is, for instance, the gift of speaking in tongues (a kind of ecstatic speech derivative from an intense experience of the Spirit), but this gift is useless unless accompanied by the charism of interpreting the tongues (a rational "translation" of ecstatic language into intelligible and practically applicable discourse). Though the comparison is far from perfect, the mystagogue/soul doctor, as I have described him, is a kind of speaker in tongues. In his lifestyle, his study, his prayerful way of being in the world, he stands in the presence of the Mystery and interprets the patterns of grace. He speaks of Incarnation, creation, redemption, transformation, salvation, in the hopes of inspiring the work of world transfiguration. Accordingly, his words are spirit filled and born of an intense and ecstatic closeness to God, but they remain less than effective unless they are translated into the practical language of the world transformers. It is this translation work that I see as an essential task of the lay minister.

Some time ago, I gave a Sunday homily on the importance of the lay mission to the world. After the Mass, a young man in his late twenties or early thirties approached me and told me how much this vision had affected him. But he had a pointed concern. He told me that he was a bond trader at the Chicago Board of Trade and that his daily decisions and moves had an influence on the world economy, determining, in some cases, whether businesses thrived or failed, whether people had jobs or not. The burden of this responsibility weighed heavily upon him, and he sincerely wondered how he could allow his Christian values to shape the important decisions that he made. "What exactly," he asked me, "should I do?" At this point, I was stumped, and I told him so. I just didn't know enough about the concrete workings of his world to give him precise and helpful advice. I didn't understand the questions, crises, opportunities, and pitfalls that occur in the financial–economic milieu that was his. He had been galvanized by the mystagogic language I had used, but neither he nor I could make the requisite connections to his world in order to unleash the power of transformation. We both needed an interpreter of tongues, someone who could move in both my realm and his and effect a conciliation.

I see the lay minister as this bridge, this reconciling figure. The mystagogue says, "be a great Catholic lawyer," and the lawyer responds, "how, exactly?" The soul doctor says, "be a great Catholic parent, on fire with the Gospel," and the parent counters, "what precisely does that look like?" The lay minister—perhaps a lawyer herself, perhaps a parent her-self—attempts to correlate those proclamations and those questions. There is, I admit, something of the old Catholic Action model behind these reflections: gather the faithful, break open the word in a serious way, and then, with intellectual and spiritual discipline, "see, judge, and act." Indeed, I think that the falling into desuetude of the Catholic Action approach has been a sad symptom of the clericalization I spoke of earlier.

What I envision is a gathering of, say, doctors, nurses, medical tech-nicians, led by a lay minister who has some connection to their world. Following the imperatives of Bernard Lonergan, they now analyze their milieu with Christian eyes and minds. First, they are *attentive* to their en-vironment, seeing clearly what is there, opening their eyes even to what they would prefer not to see; second, they are *intelligent*, sniffing out meaning, discerning the "forms" that undergird the surface; third, they are *reasonable*, judging which of their bright ideas is the right idea, which hypothesis best fits the facts and evidence; and finally they are *responsible*, resolving to act in accord with their judgment, making sure that their per-ception results in transformation of both themselves and their world. This same method could be followed by a lay minister and business ex-ecutives, young people, parents, lawyers, journalists, manual laborers, and others. I see the "interpreter of tongues" as someone who presides over this subtle process of intelligent, Gospel-based discernment, effectively translating the language of Christian mystagogia to and for a particular form of life—and all for the sake of changing the world into the *imago Christi*.

CONCLUSION

At the outset of this chapter, I cited the deleterious influence of Niet-zsche on the Christian community. And I proposed that an organic model must replace the competitive and violent one that has too often dominated our conversations. Allow me, by way of conclusion, simply to expand upon this image a bit. One of the elemental statements of the Christian spiritual life is this: Realize that your life is not about you! To be a Christian means—among other things—that one's desires, thoughts, body, imagination, relationships are seen as subordinated to a power beyond them. We do not dispose of ourselves—"whether we live or die, we are the Lord's"—we are part of a theodrama the contours and ends of which infinitely surpass our capacity to understand. It is only in the context of this theocentric and theodramatic world that our individual lives are rich and meaningful. To put this in straight Pauline language, we are all members of the body of Christ, all organs in a body to whose purposes we are subordinated and to whose health we are ordered. All of us in this body realize therefore that our lives are not about us.

It is, therefore, not for our aggrandizement or for the consolidation of our power that we exist; it is only for the sake of the body. And it is in this common subordination to a good beyond ourselves that all of us enjoy a legitimate equality: each of us having something indispensable to do and to be for the sake of the body of Christ. But this equality in service to the whole has nothing to do with uniformity. Otherwise one particular organic form would be elevated to the same level as—or even above—the body itself. It is this confusion of equality in service with uniformity that leads to the zero-sum struggles that unfortunately characterize ecclesial life. I want priests to be boldly and unapologetically priestly, not because I think priesthood is the best or most spiritual form of Christian life, but because I want the body of Christ to be well served. And I want lay people to be boldly and unabashedly world transformers, not because I think this "front-line service" is nobler than any other, but because I want the body of Christ to be well served. And I want the interpreters of tongues to embrace their task confidently and enthusiastically, not because I think they are the most special of Christians, but because I want the body of Christ to be well served.

It is precisely when we all realize that our lives are not about us that we, paradoxically enough, find ourselves most fully—and discover a way to live, not in competition, but in peace.

Chapter Twenty-One

EVANGELIZING THE
AMERICAN CULTURE

W HAT I SHOULD LIKE TO DO IN THIS CHAPTER IS EXPLORE THE
question of evangelizing in the American context. Before I reflect on this
challenge, however, it is imperative that I emphasize what must characterize any and all attempts to announce the Good News. To evangelize is to
proclaim Jesus Christ crucified and risen from the dead. When this
kerygma, this Paschal Mystery, is not at the heart of the project, Christian
evangelization effectively disappears, devolving into a summons to bland
religiosity or generic spirituality. When Jesus crucified and risen is not
proclaimed, a beige and unthreatening Catholicism emerges, a thought
system that is, at best, an echo of the environing culture. Peter Maurin, one
of the founders of the Catholic Worker movement, said that the Church
has taken its own dynamite and placed it in hermetically sealed containers
and sat on the lid. In a similar vein, Stanley Hauerwas commented that
the problem with Christianity is not that it is socially conservative or politically liberal, but that "it is just too damned dull"! For both Maurin and
Hauerwas, what leads to this attenuation is a refusal to preach the dangerous and unnerving news concerning Jesus risen from the dead.

But how do we accomplish this uncompromising evangelistic task
in an American culture marked by pluralism, secularism, and religious diversity? How do we manage to say, in a way that is not arrogant, violent,
or divisive, that Jesus Christ crucified and risen is of central importance?

256

How do we make persuasive this surprising and counterintuitive claim? I will try to answer these questions, first, by examining in some detail what is at stake in the central Christian affirmation, second, by assessing the American cultural situation in terms of its openness and resistance to the Gospel message, and third, by suggesting some concrete practices for effective evangelization.

THE COMMUNIO VISION

When a Christian speaks the good news about Jesus' resurrection, she is not simply talking about an extraordinary turn of events in the life of a particular individual. Rather, she is making a claim about the deepest structure of reality, about the way things, at their most basic level, are. According to the biblical witness, Jesus is not simply a great man, a prophet, a seer, or social reformer; he is the Word of God made flesh, which is to say, the intelligibility of being made present in visible, iconic form. A first consequence of this incarnational sensibility is that the death of Jesus must be construed as judgment on the world, *the* sign that all is not well with us. As Peter says in his kerygmatic discourse in Acts, "The Lord of life came and you put him to death." There must be something fundamentally askew in those who sought to eliminate, in the most brutally violent way, the bearer of the divine presence. It is important to note too, following Hans Urs von Balthasar, that the New Testament symbolically includes everyone in this judgment by showing how disciples, Romans, and Jews all contributed to his death.

If Jesus had simply remained in his grave, he would have been one of a thousand inspiring and failed religious figures that have emerged in the course of time, one more prophet, in Albert Schweitzer's words, "ground under by the wheel of history." But the evangelical claim is that he appeared alive to his disciples after his death, still bearing the marks of crucifixion and uttering a message of peace. Both of those details are significant. In most of the resurrection narratives, Jesus makes explicit reference to his wounds, inviting his disciples to see, or in the case of Thomas, to touch them. It is said that Teresa of Avila was able to see through a ruse of the devil appearing to her in the guise of the risen

Christ. "Begone," she said, "you have no wounds." The marks on the body of Jesus are signs of the violence that killed him and hence symbols of a perverted love of violence radically at odds with God's way of being. Seeing our own dysfunction in them is an essential aspect of the paschal experience.

But having shown his wounds, Jesus does something utterly surprising: he speaks a word of peace. In Luke's account of the appearance to the eleven, the disciples are terrified when the risen Christ comes upon them. This is not only because they are seeing something novel and unexpected; it is also because they sense that the murdered man, in accord with the structure of the classic ghost story, is back, undoubtedly to seek vengeance on those who denied, betrayed, and abandoned him. From ancient myths to contemporary crime stories, the rhythm remains the same: order destroyed through violence is restored through an answering violence. But the crucified and risen Christ—the most unjustly persecuted victim in history—does not respond with violence; instead, he says, "Shalom." The disorder of the cross, the killing of the Son of God, is restored, but through compassion and forgiving love. This is the novelty and revelation contained in the Paschal Mystery: The true God is not a practitioner or sanctioner of sacred violence; he is the one whose being and action have nothing to do with violence and vengeance. St. John would put it this way: "God is light; in him there is no darkness." Humanity killed the Lord of life, and God returned in compassion, which is why St. Paul could exclaim, "I am certain that neither death nor life, neither angels nor principalities, neither height nor depth, nor any other creature could ever separate us from the love of God that comes to us in Christ Jesus our Lord." Psychologists have said that a friend is someone who has seen you at your worst and still loves you. Thus, when the old spiritual says, "what a friend we have in Jesus," it is not trading in pious rhetoric; rather, it is getting to the heart of the matter. The death and resurrection of Jesus prove that God is our friend, because God has seen us at our worst and still loves us.

If God has disclosed himself as friendship and compassionate love, he must *be* friendship and compassionate love in his ownmost reality, and this entails that in God there must be a play of lover, beloved, and shared love. Accordingly, the idea that God is himself a *communio* of persons, a Trinity of Father, Son, and Spirit, flows from the surprise of the Paschal Mystery. It is, of course, in the Gospel of John that the connection between the drama of salvation and the trinitarian nature of God is first made unmistakably clear. The prologue to John articulates the distinctiveness of the divine being as co-inherence and co-implication: "In the beginning was the Word and the Word was with God and the Word was God." The true God is not a monolith, not a supreme substance, but a family, a conversation, a play of speaker, spoken, and speech. By insisting, furthermore, that the Word *is* God, John implies that the divine persons are not together as "ball bearings in a bucket" but rather as interacting and overlapping fields of force.

As the prologue unfolds, we see the implications of this understanding of God for a theology of creation: "All things came into being through him, and without him not one thing came into being" (John 1:3). So accustomed are we to the language and cadence of this verse that we might overlook its radicality. In both mythological and philosophical accounts of creation prior to Christianity, the being and order of the world emerge through a primal violence or manipulation. In the mythic framework, creation occurs through the battle of the gods, and in the philosophical matrix, as in Plato and Aristotle for example, cosmic order is established through the formation of matter. We glimpse in John something radically different, what theologians will later formulate as a doctrine of *creatio ex nihilo*, creation from nothing. When the true God creates, he doesn't manipulate, dominate, or wrestle into submission anything outside of himself, but rather through a sheerly generous and nonviolent act of love, he gives rise to the totality of finite reality. And because this act is ex nihilo, there is literally nothing that stands between God's causal presence and that which he makes. Therefore, even as he remains ontologically distinct from the world, God is, to paraphrase Augustine, closer to creation than creation is to itself. In short, the *communio* universe nests nonviolently in the primordial *communio* of the Trinity.

A further implication of the doctrine of creation from nothing is that all of God's creatures are intimately connected to one another in an echo of the primordial co-inherence of the trinitarian persons. Since all creation is centered in God, all finite things, despite their enormous differences in size, position, quality, or metaphysical status, are linked together as ontological siblings. All creatures are like islands in an archipelago, separate on the surface, but connected at the depths.

In the blazing light of the Paschal Mystery—Jesus crucified and risen from the dead—the first Christians saw the very structure of the divine being and the deepest truth about the world that God has made. In Jesus, the icon of the invisible God, they understood that Existence is co-inherence, compassion, nonviolent being-for-the-other. To proclaim this vision—with its political, social, economic, artistic, cultural, and indeed cosmic implications—is what evangelization means in the broadest sense.

I would like to close this section by attending to just a few expressions of the *communio* vision that have emerged in the course of the Catholic tradition. At the end of the *Divine Comedy*, gazing at the heart of the heavenly host, Dante sees the saints and angels clustered around the light of God and forming a harmonic display, much like a white rose. In his autobiography *Seven Storey Mountain*, Thomas Merton remembers the little French town of St. Antonin where he spent some of his childhood. The village was arranged in such a way that all of the streets led, like spokes, to the cathedral, so that wherever one walked, one was drawn, ineluctably, toward the spiritual center. Later in the *Seven Storey Mountain*, Merton saw the Abbey of Gethsemani in a similar light, describing it as the axis of the country, the secret center around which everything else turned. The most philosophically precise account of the *communio* view is Thomas Aquinas's theology of participation. For Aquinas, all finite things, from archangels to stones, participate in the to-be of God, who is the sheer act of existence. This in turn entails that all created things are interrelated, constituting an artistic work in progress, contributing to an overall design and purpose. All of these expressions—artistic, poetic, metaphysical—flow from and in their own manner articulate the good news of Jesus Christ crucified and risen from the dead.

The Compromising of the Communio Vision:
Protestantism and Secularism

Having spelled out in some detail the nature of the Catholic *communio* vision, I would like to examine the process by which that vision was, in both Protestantism and modern secularism, to varying degrees compromised, questioned, undermined. This examination is pertinent to our subject precisely in the measure that American culture has been so thoroughly shaped by these two great forces.

So many of the great Reformers were trained in the philosophical school of nominalism, with its roots in the speculations of the late medieval Franciscan William of Occam. Like his Franciscan predecessor Duns Scotus, Occam held to a univocal conception of being, according to which both the infinite existence of God and the finite existence of creatures are instances of a general, overarching category of being that contains them both. In sharp contrast to Aquinas's analogical understanding of being, this view effectively situates God and creatures side by side as discrete existents against a common ontological background. Though God is infinite and the creature finite, both are beings without an essential connection to one another. Thus the participation of creatures in God is denied and, as a consequence, the interconnection between creatures is attenuated. Indeed, William of Occam can say *praeter illas partes absolutas nulla res est* (outside of these absolute parts, there is nothing), signaling the triumph of the disassociated individual.

It is not difficult to discern certain nominalist themes in the writings and preaching of the Reformers. Martin Luther was throughout his career a great defender of the divine transcendence and hence remained suspicious of all appeals to mysticism and sacramentalism, anything that would collapse the radical distinction between God and the world or suggest that God was available in creation. This denial of participation metaphysics conduced, as in Scotus and Occam, to a stress on the isolated individual—which can be seen in the theologies of both Luther and John Calvin. In Luther's case, the spiritual drama centers around the justification of the individual discernible in the very private act of faith; and in Calvin's case, the focus is on the predestination of the individual, readable

261

through certain signs both interior and exterior. For both Reformers, the *communio* of the church, the co-inherent circle of believers, and the *communio* of creation, the co-inherent circle of things made ex nihilo, become secondary at best. Though essential elements of the Christian proclamation obviously remain in the Reformers, we do witness in their theology an attenuating of the *communio*/participation vision that held sway through the High Middle Ages.

This compromising of *communio* becomes, however, more dramatically apparent in the secular version of Protestantism which is philosophical modernity. The nonsacramental world of the Reformers becomes the disenchanted universe *tout court* in most of the moderns. Particularly instructive here is the thought of Thomas Hobbes. A thorough materialist, Hobbes held that reality is nothing but particles in motion, and his most famous application of this metaphysic was in the arena of politics and social theory. In the state of nature, human beings are isolated monads, motivated by the dominant passions to survive and to avoid violent death. The inevitable conflict of antagonistic egos (particles bouncing painfully off one another) produces a life that is, in Hobbes's famous phrase, "solitary, poor, nasty, brutish, and short," and this state of affairs, in turn, gives rise to the desire to enter into a social contract. Mind you, the forming of civil society has nothing to do with a classical conception of justice or the good life, and it is by no means the consequence of our essentially social nature, just the contrary. It is the attempt by a collectivity of self-interested individuals to mitigate the threat to life and limb that each presents to the other. The Hobbesian government (the Leviathan) is instituted precisely for the purpose of protection and not direction, any sense of social teleology precluded by Hobbes's metaphysics. A generation after Hobbes, John Locke produced a somewhat kinder and gentler version of this account. Though he retained strands of the medieval synthesis—the existence of a distant, rather Deist God and a truncated form of the natural law—Locke still saw government's purpose as protective of individual rights to life, liberty, and property.

Another extremely influential element in the modern secular conception of government was the insistence on the privatization of religion. In the wake of the wars between Catholics and Protestants that plagued

Europe in the century or so after the Reformation, most modern thinkers—Locke, Spinoza, Leibniz, Kant, and Hegel are examples—opted for a rational version of religion that could, on account of its reasonability, aspire to universality. Concomitantly, they encouraged a privatization of positive or revealed religion: Such expressions—and their attendant practices—could be tolerated as long as they did not extrude into the public realm of politics, economics, and social relations. Stanley Hauerwas has referred to this arrangement as "the modern peace treaty" with religion and has noticed how neatly it fit with the subjectivized versions of Christianity encouraged within Protestantism. The sequestration of faith within the confines of subjectivity, combined with the acceptance of a fundamentally antagonistic social ontology, spelled the dissolution of the *communio* vision during the early modern period.

PROTESTANTISM, MODERNITY, AND AMERICAN CULTURE

It is obviously a daunting task to name the elements that go into the shaping of a culture as rich and complex as America's. However, I think that it is not too wide of the mark to say that the two movements we have been describing—Protestantism and secular modernity—have played an especially powerful role in influencing American culture in both style and substance. Cardinal Francis George of Chicago expressed this dual influence with both humor and precision, saying that America was formed largely by "Calvin and Hobbes."

Let us look first at "Calvin." We have seen that the great Reformers stressed the inner experience of the individual believer, as the Holy Spirit, in either justification and predestination, made himself known. When Protestant theology became more rationalized through the speculations of seventeenth-century theologians, groups such as the Moravians, the Hutterites, the Anabaptists, the Quakers, and the Puritans reemphasized the role of inner experience or inner light. It is of no small importance that these groups were particularly well represented in the settling of the American colonies. Thus an already subjectivized Protestantism took on an even more radically interior and experiential form in this country. We can see it in the Wesleyan and Holiness traditions of tracking one's inner experience of God and giving expression to it in vivid and bodily ways, or of the Quaker insistence that no one speaks in church until convicted by the Spirit. Also, from the colonial period through the middle of the nineteenth century, American Protestantism has been fired regularly by revivals and tent meetings, forums where the keen sense of having been born again or converted were paramount. In more recent times, this tradition has been continued by evangelists from Billy Sunday to Billy Graham.

A more rarified and intellectual form of this subjectivism can be discerned in the liberal Protestantism flowing from Friedrich Schleiermacher and his disciples. Raised in a Moravian community, Schleiermacher never lost his keen awareness of the inner light, even as he transposed it into the feeling of absolute dependency. Schleiermacher's influence in our culture, mediated through the universities and the more sophisticated pulpits, can be seen in Yankee Unitarianism and eventually in Emerson's transcendentalism and Walt Whitman's pantheist mysticism. And these movements, in their turn, helped to feed, in more recent years, many forms of New Age spirituality, a movement that clearly emphasizes the inner states of the individual. I can't help but see, too, a purely secular expression of this tradition in the American cult of the talk show, that forum in which one is encouraged (even compelled) to manifest his inner states and experiences to an audience both fascinated and repelled.

Now lest this discussion become simplistic and unbalanced, it is most important to note certain features of American Protestantism that cannot be easily correlated to subjectivism and individualism. There has indeed been, perhaps despite itself, a politically and socially conscious form of Protestant religiosity in America. It can be seen in the Emancipation movement that shook the country profoundly in the middle of the nineteenth century, in the Social Gospel of Rauschenbusch and others at the beginning of the twentieth century, in the Civil Rights Movement of the 1950s and 1960s that came surging up out of black churches vividly aware of the implications for liberation in the biblical revelation, and in the radical nonviolence of the Mennonite tradition expressed by John

Howard Yoder and Stanley Hauerwas in very recent years. These I would read as remnants of the *communio* vision, still available despite the individualist revolution wrought by the Reformers. As we shall see later, the canny Catholic evangelist should be especially sensitive to these vestiges.

Now let us turn to "Hobbes." The fundamentally antagonistic social ontology of Hobbes, and its attendant agnosticism about ultimate ends, can be clearly seen in the founding political documents of our nation. According to Thomas Jefferson's Declaration of Independence, the purpose of government is the protection of one's threatened rights to life, liberty, and the pursuit of happiness. The last of this famous trio is perhaps the most interesting. Though the individual citizen's right to *seek* happiness is guaranteed, no indication whatsoever is given as to the telos of that quest. In accordance with the modern peace treaty, the determination of that goal remains a purely private matter, not subject to public adjudication. Thus, the society outlined by Jefferson and given formal structure in the Constitution is one that is protective and not directive. As Robert Kraynak has argued, this modern understanding of the self and its relation to government has conduced to a certain societal vapidity and loss of purpose: The Jeffersonian subject is well protected, but he has no idea where to go. Many commentators have seen the effects of this social philosophy in the shocking violence, litigiousness, and moral drift in our society. All of this obviously makes difficult the task of Christian evangelization, since the *communio* vision is at odds, not only with an antagonistic individualism, but also with a social space void of teleology. The dying and rising of Jesus *have* to affect politics, economics, social theory, business, entertainment—all of the public dimensions of human life.

As in the case of Protestantism, we can find a positive side to modern social theory, remnants of the *communio* mentality. I hinted earlier that the ferocity of Hobbes was mitigated by Locke. What softened things was Locke's conviction that God exists, that human beings are creatures, and that their rights are therefore not simply functions of desire but correlates of their dignity. This Lockean shift can be seen in Jefferson's insistence that the basic political rights of Americans are "endowed by their creator." In an evangelical framework, the dignity of the individual is grounded in the nonviolent and generous act of creation, and in the even more abundantly generous act of redemption. My suspicion is that these great Christian motifs appear, in admittedly obscured form, in Locke, Jefferson, and the best of the modern rights tradition. John Paul II confirms this in speech after speech, insisting that a culture of life must be predicated upon a respect for individual rights, especially the right of freedom of religion and conscience.

Another overtone of the *communio* harmony can be found in the American experiment in law-governed pluralism. From the earliest days, Americans knew that their society had to be formed from a wide, almost wild, diversity of religions, cultures, languages, and social styles. Accordingly, they appreciated the central importance of law, dialogue, tolerance, and civil conversation. Without these disciplining and unifying practices, diversity would devolve in very short order into violence. When he came to Chicago in 1979, John Paul II spoke to a typically American audience of tremendous diversity. Looking over the crowd, he reminded them of the beauty of the national motto *e pluribus unum* and suggested that there is a spirituality undergirding that sentiment. The Church of Christ is destined to gather into its fold all the peoples of the world, for the Lord commissioned his disciples to "preach the Good News to all nations." Therefore, the forging of unity out of diversity—*communio, e pluribus unum*—is an ecclesial as well as social mandate. Indeed, the Pope seemed to indicate that in the American experiment in liberal democracy an echo of the Church's *communio* can be heard. This insight is especially important given the fact that some evangelizers would want to romanticize the political arrangements in place during the Middle Ages or some other period of supposed Catholic ascendancy. While remaining detached from any and all particular social systems, the Church can find evangelical analogues and correspondences in classical, medieval, or modern political forms.

Thus, the one who would sow the seed of the kerygma in the context of the American culture confronts both stony and fertile ground. She faces a society that is, on the one hand, deeply marked by the unraveling of the social and intellectual fabric of *communio*. But on the other hand, she operates within a society that retains hints, overtones, colorings of the Paschal Mystery. What then, precisely, to do? I should like to propose a series of practices.

The Strangest Way

In the Acts of the Apostles, Christianity is referred to by the evocative phrase "the Way." What this signals is that Christianity is not simply a matter of articulate beliefs and organizational structure, but rather an entire pattern or form of life. As I've explained elsewhere, in the first chapter of the Gospel of John, we hear Jesus in conversation with two of the Baptist's disciples: "Where do you stay?" they ask him. "Come and see," he responds. Then the narrator tells us that they stayed with him the rest of that day. Only after that sojourn do they proclaim that he is the long-awaited Messiah. The message seems clear: Jesus wants not simply to communicate teachings and insights; he wants to share his life, his way of being; he wants to show them where and how he stays. Just as, in the Middle Ages or Renaissance, an apprentice would move in with a painter, watching his moves and imitating the rhythms of his life long before actually learning the techniques of the art, so the evangelist must move in with the Lord and learn his way before daring to speak of him. When the young Gregory Thaumaturgos came to Origen for instruction in the Christian faith, Origen told him that first he must share the life of the Christian community and only then endeavor to learn the truths of the creed.

I fear that this understanding of Christianity as a wholly integrated amalgam of thought, passion, movement, gesture, and practice has become largely attenuated in the modern period. In many of the modern philosophers, a sharp wedge was driven between body and soul or sensuousness and reason. When this dichotomy was applied to religion, it resulted, as we have seen, in a valorization of the subjective and interior dimension and a devalorization of the objective arena of ritual and practice. The very best example of this tendency is Kant's *Religion within the Limits of Reason Alone* wherein the philosopher argues for a completely subjective-ethical construal of the faith, and recommends the jettisoning of prayer, liturgy, ecclesial structure, and the particularities of revelation. We can hear echoes of the modern project in the dominant theologies of the twentieth century, including Tillich's and Rahner's, both of which commence with, and order themselves around, an inner sensibility. And in the popular preaching and theologizing of the past forty years in this country, the modern style has been in the ascendancy. Think of the myriad workshops, retreats, and sermons that have asked us to access a feeling or experience of God, without relating that experience to a concrete way of life or judging it in terms of a revealed tradition. It is my conviction that this mode of preaching and evangelizing has proven remarkably counterproductive, especially in an American context that is, as we have been arguing, so thoroughly and problematically shaped by the individualism and subjectivism of the modern period. In fact, it dovetails perfectly with the peace treaty we described earlier: religion is tolerable as long as it is privatized, sequestered in the arena of feeling or inner experience.

Accordingly, I propose an evangelistic style that is bold, public, embodied, and expressed in terms of concrete practices. I desire a Christianity that, in direct opposition to the terms of the modern peace treaty, shows up. Let us turn now to a consideration of just a few of these practices that constitute the distinctive Christian way.

One of the greatest works of medieval literature, *The Canterbury Tales*, centers around a group of people, in the rush of springtime enthusiasm, going on pilgrimage. For Europeans of the Middle Ages, there were few activities more important, dangerous, and exciting than pilgrimages. They crisscrossed the continent, from Cologne, to Paris, to Chartres, to Vezelay, to Rome, to Compastello—some even traversing the sea to Jerusalem—in order to look at the relics of saints. Many explanations—economic, political, social—have been forwarded to make sense of this enormous vitality, but at the heart of the matter is faith. Christian life is about movement, for it plays itself out around two basic poles: Jesus' call to conversion and his postresurrection commission to preach the Gospel. We move toward Christ away from sin, and we move toward the world for the sake of proclamation; the one thing we don't do is sit still. Thus, for the medieval mind, the pilgrimage to Compostela or Rome or Jerusalem—with all of its attendant dangers and excitement—was to mimic the demand and adventure of the spiritual path.

Can this practice still be part of the Christian way? Can it be a means to evangelization? In recent years, the Pope has revived the custom of the pilgrimage in remarkable style through the celebration of the various World Youth Days. So great a crowd assembled in Paris that young people, joining hands, were able to circle the entire city; the gathering at World Youth Day in Manila constituted, by most accounts, the largest single collection of human beings in history; so many young people gathered at Mile High Stadium in Denver that their cheers literally buffeted the Pope's helicopter as it came in for a landing. The attractiveness and spiritual power of this very public practice seem not to have faded. Why couldn't our churches encourage and organize pilgrimages to the National Shrine in Washington, or the tomb of Mother Cabrini in New York, or to Guadalupe in Mexico City, or to one of our great monasteries—St. Meinrad, or Gethsemani, or Snowmass? Or why couldn't we sponsor marches through our cities and neighborhoods, reclaiming them for Christ, or May crownings and Corpus Christi processions? That all of this strikes many of us as slightly embarrassing is undoubtedly a function of our formation in a privatized religiosity. But an evangelizing church is one that, like it or not, shows up.

During the past forty years or so, we have, in the Catholic world, built beige churches, that is to say, structures that are largely void of symbolism, imagery, iconography, and narrativity. In accord with the subjectivist prejudices of modernity, they are buildings where the pilgrim people of God gather, but they are not, themselves, narrators of the Christian story. The Gothic cathedrals of the Middle Ages, on the contrary, were not simply tents of meeting, but powerful repositories of Christian symbolism, places that, consequently, *formed* those who entered them and even those who passed by. The distinctiveness of the Christian *communio* metaphysics was on display in the rose windows, the glass, the façades, the orientation of the edifice, the decoration, and so forth. If our ecclesial buildings are to have an evangelical power, they must not simply blend in with the suburban environment around them or conform to the subjectivist and minimalist aesthetic of the time. Rather, they must be symbolic manifestations (both inside and out) of the understanding of being that flows from the dying and rising of Jesus.

Another central practice of the Christian community is the liturgy. According to the intellectual leaders of the liturgical movement of the last century—Romano Guardini, Odo Casel, Virgil Michel, Reynold Hillenbrand, and others—the liturgy is a sort of iconic display of God's justice or order, an aesthetic showing forth of *communio*. And this is why the Mass, for them, had such a powerful influence in the areas of politics and social organization. Dorothy Day saw this connection during the period of her conversion to the faith. Even with their baroque decoration and arcane liturgical language, the Catholic churches were the places where the common people, the immigrants, felt at home, even rubbing shoulders with members of the upper classes. The very way that we gather for the Eucharist, stubbornly compelling everyone to come together despite economic, racial, and cultural differences, constitutes in itself an embodiment of the *communio* form.

We find the same dynamic all throughout the liturgy. The commencement of the ritual proper under the sign of the cross signals the radical orientation of this community toward the trinitarian love. The readings and homily—in their symbolism and narrativity—open up the surprising world that appears when the true God is Lord. The prayer of the faithful is one of the behavioral implications of *communio*: Since we are bound to each other through Christ and in God, we bear each other's burdens, acknowledging that one person's need is everyone's need. Just before the eucharistic prayer, the song of the angels is invoked. This is designed to align our faltering communion here below with the fully cooperative and nonviolent communion gathered around the throne of God. At the heart of the matter, of course, is the making present of the Son sent by the Father in order to include the universe in the energy of the trinitarian compassion. After the eucharistic prayer, the Lord's Prayer is recited or sung: "Thy Kingdom come, thy will be done on earth as it is in heaven." Again, as when we joined our voices to those of the angels, we are engaging in an act and prayer of alignment, hoping that the *ordo* of heaven becomes the *ordo* of earth. The most ecstatic part of the liturgy is the eating and drinking of Christ's body and blood, for it is here that the co-inherence of God and creation becomes most intense. We are drawn out of ourselves in order to meet, with some adequacy, the ecstatic gift of self that Christ offers. Finally, it has been said that the most sacred words of the liturgy, after those of the consecration itself, are the words of dismissal: "The Mass is ended; go in peace to love and serve the Lord." Once eucharisticized through all of the ritual, symbolism, and narrativity of the

Mass, the community is sent in order to eucharisticize the world, to make densely real the *communio* that they experienced in the liturgy.

In a word, the liturgy at its best is the most intense expression of the *communio* vision and hence the most powerful tool for evangelization. The Mass is Maurin's "dynamite of the church," but too often we domesticate it or secularize it, turning it into a celebration of ourselves. This, above all, robs it of its power to transform the world.

A final practice, or better, set of practices that I would like to recommend are the corporal and spiritual works of mercy. Dorothy Day commented that everything a baptized Christian does should be directly or indirectly related to these concrete, active embodiments of the *communio* attitude: feeding the hungry, clothing the naked, giving drink to the thirsty, visiting those in prison, praying for the living and the dead, comforting the sorrowful, forgiving sinners, and so on. Many Christians would gladly claim that they are proponents of peace and justice, but without sufficiently specifying those abstractions. After all, every political philosopher from Plato to Karl Marx advocates some form of peace and justice. The corporal and spiritual works compel one to incarnate and instantiate those forms in a properly Christian manner and context. Because we are connected to one another as creatures and in Christ, because we participate in the primal *communio* of the divine persons, we must care for the needs of the brothers and sisters. Because we co-inhere in one another, we can never perceive one person's suffering as uniquely his own; rather, we must claim his hunger or thirst or loneliness as our own.

A few years ago, an article appeared in the *New York Times*, focusing on the difference between priests ordained in the 1960s and priests being ordained today. While the older generation of clergy were eager to be on the streets, working directly with the poor and disadvantaged, fighting for social justice, the younger clerics, it seemed, were content to remain in the sanctuary, concentrating their energy and attention on liturgy, prayer, and contemplation. The burden of the article was that this was an evolution much to be regretted. To my mind, what is to be regretted is the wedge that was driven between street and sanctuary in the years after the Vatican Council. For Dorothy Day—who attended daily Mass, recited the rosary, went on frequent retreats, prayed unceasingly—the link between contemplation of the divine mystery and the most radical work on behalf of the poor was perfectly obvious. Her practical mission grew organically out of her intense concentration upon the sacred *communio* —and this gave it, of course, its enormous evangelical power. She saw that the Church, giving visible witness to its belief in co-inherence, would have a transforming effect throughout the society.

CONCLUSION

I should like to close by returning to a key question that I raised at the outset: How can the evangelical message be proclaimed noncoercively in the context of a free and pluralistic society? What I hope has become clear in the course of this discussion is that the *communio* message is essentially a word of nonviolence. In the Paschal Mystery, the first Christians saw that the deepest meaning of the real is peace, compassion, forgiveness, connection. Therefore, to proclaim the Christian message in a coercive, manipulative, arrogant, or violent way is to fall into a sort of practical contradiction. But noncoerciveness by no means implies either reticence, indifference, or nonpublicness. Catholics eager to evangelize the American scene ought to know clearly who they are and ought to act visibly out of that identity. Richard Rorty has commented that at the heart of the enlightened liberal project is the conviction that cruelty is the primal moral problem, and from this he concludes that the essential public responsibility of the state is to foster inclusiveness and toleration. A Christian, it seems to me, might agree quite readily that cruelty is the sin of sins, but he ought not to conclude that something as bland as toleration is the solution. Instead, the Christian ought to propose that cruelty is best countered by love, *communio*, nonviolence—practices that flow from the Paschal Mystery of Jesus crucified and risen from the dead. These concrete gestures are, at the same time, deeply Christian and positively transformative in the context of a liberal, pluralist society. When the believer instantiates them boldly and unapologetically, he works, as the Gospel parable has it, like a leaven within a society compromised by the breakdown of *communio*.

INDEX

Cold War, 204, 210
Cologne, 268
Colson, Charles, 192
Columbine, 220
communio, 40, 45, 46, 48, 50; Dorothy
 Day, 272; examples of, 260; liberal
 democracy, 266; liturgy, 270, 271;
 as nonviolent, 272; pluralism, 266;
 remnants of, 265; undermining of,
 261, 262
Communism: modernity, as
 outgrowth of, 114
Company of Jesus. *See* Jesuits
concretissimus, 37, 49
confession: of sin, 175
Confessions (Augustine), 136, 175
Congar, Yves, xvi, 54, 73
Conjectures of a Guilty Bystander
 (Merton), 199, 204, 205
consequentialism, 36
Constitution, 265
Contra Celsum (Origen), 209
The Conversation (film), 192
conservatism, 4, 8, 11, 12, 21, 31
Coppola, Francis Ford, 192
Council of Chalcedon, 6, 7, 9, 10, 95;
 Incarnation, 109
Council of Trent, 215
Cousins, Ewert, 31, 79
creatio ex nihilo, 202, 212, 259; co-
 inherence, 260; as free gift, 241;
 Jesus, 242
creation, 46, 47, 202, 241;
 distinctiveness of, 215; as
 nonviolent act, 61, 135, 215, 218,
 259; peace, 211; as soul language,
 242; as violent act, 135, 259
creation metaphysics, 64

creation spirituality, 9
cruelty: as moral problem, 272
Crusades, 5
de la Cruz, Juan, 247

Daniel, 43, 194
Dante, 20, 128, 129, 147, 167, 177,
 230; *The Divine Comedy*, 26, 74,
 132, 176, 188, 201, 247, 260
Das Ganze im Fragment (The Whole
 in the Fragment) (Balthasar), 74
David, 195, 196
Day, Dorothy, 20, 26, 38, 45, 182, 207,
 270; *communio*, 272; mercy, works of,
 271; Roosevelt's New Deal, 29
Dean, John, 192
Declaration of Independence, 204;
 government, purpose of, 265
Dedalus, Stephen (character), 126,
 127, 128, 139, 152, 153, 154;
 absolution of, 157; epiphany of,
 158, 159, 160; hellfire sermon,
 156, 157; sin, 155
deification, 48, 171, 172, 180;
 Eucharist, 49
Deists, 113
Demiurge, 110, 129
De musica (Augustine), 136
Denver, 269
De potentia Dei, 88, 96, 100, 111
*Der Kultakt und die Gegenwärtige
 Aufgabe der Liturgischen Bildung*
 (The Cult Act and the Present
 Task of Liturgical Education)
 (Guardini), 53
Derrida, Jacques, 46, 244
Descartes, René, 15, 35, 55, 57, 58,
 63, 64, 77, 113, 134;